Extra                                                       who haven't

*I have read Hemphill's letters whe*                              *me. They are very funny, as is the US Senate* ...*uy. He needs to write more about Virginia, though.*

⌐US SENATOR MARK WARNER
FORMER GOVERNOR OF VIRGINIA

*I invited Hemphill to come to Geneva and give a speech to a venture capital forum being held at the embassy. It was the funniest business speech that I have ever heard! Unfortunately it's not in this book.*

⌐DONALD BEYER
FORMER LT. GOVERNOR OF VIRGINIA AND AMBASSADOR TO SWITZERLAND

*I hired Hemphill when he was a raw rookie GS-9 at the Department of HEW, and I taught him everything he knows. Where he learned to write like this, however, is a mystery. He was never this interesting when he was working in the government. And he's probably still a Democrat.*

⌐ FREDERIC MALEK
FOUNDER AND HEAD OF THAYER LODGING, REPUBLICAN FUND-RAISER,
MANAGER OF THE NOMINATING CONVENTION, AND
CAMPAIGN MANAGER FOR PRESIDENT GHW BUSH

*Hemphill's letters to his Dad are as funny as David Sedaris, but with more substance. I just wish he would write more about Virginia.*

⌐ U. S. SENATOR TIM KAINE
FORMER GOVERNOR OF VIRGINIA

*As a published author myself, I am glad to see my brother finally get something in print, even if he did have to pay for it. I just hope he got an editor like I told him to. Thank God he didn't try poetry like our parents.*

⌐ DAVID HEMPHILL
PROFESSOR AND CHAIR, GRADUATE SCHOOL OF EDUCATION
AT SAN FRANCISCO STATE UNIVERSITY

# dust tea, dingoes, & dragons

## Adventures in Culture, Cuisine, and Business from a Globe-Trekking Executive

## R. F. Hemphill

Published in the USA by

 Strelitzia Ventures

Published in the USA by

 Strelitzia
Ventures

# dedication

This book is dedicated to Roger Sant and Dennis Bakke, the Founders of AES, and to Tom Unterberg, the "Godfather" and key initial financer of the company. Without the vision, leadership and energy of these three men, the experiences herein would not have been possible and this book would not have been written.

# Contents

# foreword

I didn't come into the business world naturally; it was more of a breach birth. There was no one in my family, nuclear family, or extended family who was a business person. All my aunts, uncles, cousins, and grandparents were teachers or psychologists or dentists or doctors or soldiers or opera singers or academics of one stripe or another. My mom was a well-educated Air Force wife who supported all my Dad's twenty-five different postings and moves throughout his career and found time to write biographies of missionaries on the side. My brother and sister each made their way into careers in academia. My dad was a fighter pilot in World War II, and then a career officer in the Air Force for thirty years. He eventually retired in Hawaii and worked for a senior state Senator as his head staff person. He was a smart and organized professional, and I admired him as a kid. But about business he knew nothing, and so neither did I.

I cut out pictures of fighter planes and pasted them in scrapbooks as a kid. I built plastic models of airplanes, including my Dad's P-47 Thunderbolt. I could recite for you the details on every WW II US fighter plane, most of the German and Japanese ones, and the Italian one used successfully against spear-armed Ethiopians but nowhere else. However, if you said "balance sheet" or "profit and loss" or "sales and marketing," I was completely clueless. And none of my family or acquaintances knew this stuff, either.

Nonetheless, history is not necessarily destiny. I spent in my early years as first an Army lieutenant and then a low-level civil servant. It soon became clear to me that business had the potential to be more fun and more lucrative than writing government regulations. So I went to business school at night, and when two colleagues started a new company called

Applied Energy Services, a dumb name later shortened to AES, I happily signed on. After all, we had a million dollars of capital that had taken us a year to raise, a business plan that made little sense, and we were focusing on an industry—the independent electric power business—that really didn't exist yet. Moreover, we had a team, including me, which had never built or operated a power plant. How could we go wrong? Sometimes it's better not to know too much.

We were improbably successful. And as I kept being sent to strange places to attempt to do unreasonable things, I actually learned about business as it was really conducted. I had a wonderful time, and much of what I was doing was odd or funny or weird or all of the above. As I traveled and learned and had some success, I wanted to educate and amuse my Dad and convince him that I had made a good career choice. Since this was before e-mail, it seemed natural to write these experiences down and send them off as letters. And now these letters have become this book.

This book is about business done in the international arena, frequently in places where I would not recommend you take a vacation. I didn't know much about these places before I started being an "international business development expert," and so, as you'll see, the potential for misadventure was unlimited.

These stories are business adventures set in exotic climes. The stories are true and they certainly helped me to explain to my father what my life was all about. Over the years I have shared them with friends and they have been complimentary and encouraging. The letters are not didactic; this is not a how-to/where-to travel book. It's certainly not a typical business book. Nor is it really a memoir. Instead, it's a bit of all these. My goal is to be entertaining, and that's what my editor assures me this is.

Of course, I'm paying her to say that.

R. F. Hemphill
January 2014

# one

# it's ok to fool around with rich people's money

June 1991

Dear Dad,

So here we are in yet another airplane, slogging along in coach class at thirty-five thousand feet, scheduled to get in to Minneapolis at 10:00 tonight so we can check into the hotel and be ready for our 7:00 breakfast with potential investors ("PI's" for short, not to be confused with private investigators, especially since the potential investors seem to do relatively little investigating).

We are exactly halfway through an intriguing ritual called the "Road Show," which in turn is a piece of the larger economic ceremony called "Going Public." Alternatively, it's referred to as an "Initial Public Offering" or "IPO," the first time you try to/are allowed to sell your company's stock to unsuspecting and gullible members of the "public," as opposed to those smart people known as "Sophisticated Investors" who buy your stock when you are still a private company. Note if you will that none of these terms—"public," "private," or "sophisticated"—actually have the real-world meaning you would suspect. Hey, we're in Big Finance Land, so it's a whole new language. As I may have told you, in February we decided it was time to subject ourselves to the tender mercies of the SEC and the harsh impersonality of the stock market, and move from private to public. We had close to 470 shareholders, and at 500 you're forced to be public, like it or not. The SEC administers the laws that force you into this unique state of being, and once you are public, there are many rules to follow that you never had to worry about before. Mostly reporting and disclosure, but now if you goof them up, you get to go to jail, which seems like less fun than Cleveland. I guess it's OK to fool around with rich people's money, but not with the average guy's dough. Sort of an odd ethical break there, and if I ever get to be a rich guy, I guess I'll be glad that this distinction isn't used for such crimes as murder, just for stock fraud.

But back to our story. Having boldly decided to venture forth where none of us had ever gone before, we knew we needed a guide. Thus we called up our favorite investment banks, Donaldson, Lufkin and Jennerette (DLJ), and J. P. Morgan: big, famous institutions that "take you public," and Tommy Unterberg (whose firm, Unterberg Towbin, helped us raise our first million in 1981 and thus earned a place in our hearts as Investment Bank of the Universe), and we started down the path.

And it's an interesting and curious path indeed. One key part of it involves preparing something called the "S-1" or the "Prospectus." Two or three folks from AES get to sit down in a room loaded with lawyers and investment bankers and write a document that is supposed to be, all at once: 1) a confessional of past sins; 2) a cigarette package/Surgeon General-type warning that even if some good things have happened in the past, only a fool would expect them to continue—so watch it, buster, if you plan to buy this stock; and 3) a trumpeting puff piece that says how great the company has been and how much better it will be in the future. Do these sound like conflicting purposes? Does it make the people trying to write the thing act schizophrenic? Does a chicken have lips? I don't really know if a chicken has lips. I guess it depends on whether you count his beak. This has always confused me.

So you go through seven or eight drafts of this pretty long document, trying to think "Marketing!" on the one hand, "Full disclosure so somebody doesn't sue our bottoms off the first time the stock price drops" on the second hand, and "Let's not make this too explicit because all our competitors will surely read this, just like we read theirs" on the third hand—which has remarkably sprouted from the middle of your chest after your sixteenth catered lunch of excessively cute sandwiches. Or is it all the Diet Coke?

The darn thing finally gets done—or more accurately, everybody gets tired of arguing—and off it goes to the SEC as a "draft" on which they are required to comment in thirty days. And despite all the high-priced talent we "hired," guess who really did all the work? Right, us! Maybe I'm beginning to figure this finance stuff out. And I didn't even get to choose the sandwiches.

Then begins the real fun: organizing the slide presentation, because for some unknown reason (unknown to me until now, but don't skip ahead), PI's want you to come make a fancy presentation to them. You ask hesitatingly, "But what will we tell them that isn't already in the prospectus on which we all labored so hard and that has been distributed to all of them?" And the lawyers thunder in chorus, "Don't tell them anything that isn't in the prospectus!" And then you ask why they let people who can't read buy stock for other people, but since you're now being flippant or maybe querulous, you're ignored.

And so the slides are made, and the presentation rehearsed and critiqued again by all the investment bankers and lawyers, while at the same time the Schedule from Hell is being arranged. "Go out, hit a few cities, do a few presentations, have a few one-on-ones, then we'll have the SEC comments back and we can 'go effective'," say the bankers. This last term is Wall Street code for "finally sell the stupid stock and get the money." I wonder to myself about the one-on-ones. Why do we have to play basketball with Potential Investors? I sure hope Michael Jordan isn't interested in the stock.

"OK," we say, "we know about traveling, we're big, just tell us where and when."

"Oh," they say, "for a small issue like this we think only Los Angeles, San Francisco, San Diego, Denver, Kansas City, Houston, Minneapolis, Chicago, Philadelphia, Baltimore, Boston, New York, London, Paris,

Edinburgh, Glasgow, Frankfurt."

My, you wonder, if this were a big issue, could we add Beirut and Baghdad? How about Topeka and Santa Fe and Yorba Linda and Timbuktu, too? But it's too late, the prospectus has been sent out there to all these fund managers, the ones who actually buy the stock, and the schedulers are in control. So off we go.

Here's what they don't tell you:

» There isn't a free minute. Breakfast meetings starting at 6:45 AM, and then an endless chain of meetings (small ones with individual investors—these are the "one-on-ones" so it's not shooting hoops after all) or presentations (larger) where the three of us—Dennis Bakke, the President; Barry Sharp, our CFO; and me—present the same twenty-five slides and say the same things over and over and over.

» You get scheduled for a lot of breakfasts (with PI's) and lunches (with PI's) and dinners (with PI's), but since you're making the pitch and they're listening, they get to eat and you don't. However, since you don't have time to go to the bathroom, it all balances out.

» Almost none of the PI's has actually bothered to read the prospectus, and they seem, with few exceptions, a bloodless lot—"a buncha white guys in suits"—as one of our keepers put it. Maybe they're so busy, yeah, maybe the market's just full of new issues right now. ("We had five biotech companies in here at lunch," said one PI in Denver, "one of them doing something with bone fragments—thought I'd york.") Maybe they're all managing billion-dollar portfolios or maybe they actually can't read. As far as I can tell, we never actually really for sure talk to a person who, on his own for himself with his or her own real money, will buy and own our stock; we just talk to agents.

» The questions these guys ask are predictable but not key. "Why can't utilities do this?" "Who are your competitors?" "What are your future earnings projections?" I think the queries all come from a subscription service that circulates standardized questions to these guys. Mostly we answer politely, but after enough repetition and not enough sleep . . .

» In San Francisco a fat guy with a big walrus moustache and a goatee stands up and says with great detail and florid manner, "Pretend I'm your little old grandmother, who you love and adore, who has raised you since you were a wee baby, who worked two jobs to put you through college, etc., etc., and I, your cherished and saintly grandmother will depend on your stock for dividends to support me through the remainder of my pain-wracked life, etc., and I'm about to put all my life savings into it. (*Pause, dramatic flourish, drumroll if we could have had one.*) What do you say to me, your dear beloved grandmother, about your stock?"

» Dennis pauses thoughtfully, then answers, "Buy some shares, and get a shave."

» The obnoxious guys are just as likely to buy as the ones who tell you you're wonderful. It's totally unpredictable. For example, we had a dreadful meeting with Citicorp. We thought this would be swell, because they're our current corporate lender. They led the refinancing of one of our projects, so you'd think they would be at least receptive, but they were that finest possible Wall Street combination: arrogant ("We already know all about your business"); rude; and unprepared (they hadn't really read the Prospectus, and in fact they didn't know all about the business). They said things like, "Well, of course all this values crap will have to change once you're public." This was perhaps unwise as an introductory line, at least with us. At the end of the meeting Dennis politely suggested that they not buy the stock, at which point the two DLJ salesmen in the back of the room began sobbing. We left the meeting, and twenty minutes later they put in a big order. Go figure. Of course, they're probably the same ones who turn around and sell in a second. There is an awfully large amount of money in these here United States, and an awfully lot of less than wonderful people managing it.

» The salesmen don't do any selling. They set up the meetings with the fund managers, and they come with you to the meetings, presumably so you won't get lost. And I guess they advise someone on whether or not to have a meeting at all, although I didn't detect any particular fine screening going on. But you (we) do all the talking and answer all the questions. This is all fine, actually, as the salesmen haven't read the Prospectus, either.

» —These people don't seem to want to become our close personal friends. They don't even ask us for our business cards. We're spoiled, because most current shareholders are AES people or friends or relatives, not flinty-eyed fund managers trying to beat the S&P 500. What a shame, with us so charming and all.

» They don't ask about the two best things—the values of the company and the management practices—even though we highlight them. They're mesmerized by the numbers. For example, in Los Angeles at a breakfast meeting, Dennis was just about to start our presentation when he was interrupted in mid-sentence by a loud portly guy who said, "Wait a minute, wait a minute, what are the earnings projections?" I guess they can't read but they can count. The DLJ salesman gave him the numbers, because for some reason we're not allowed to. Of course, the DLJ people got them from us. If captured and tortured they'll probably rat us out. The fat guy looked them over and muttered, "Sounds like a growth stock to me," and ignored the rest of the presentation. And he placed a big order.

» Maybe some of them can't count, either. We spend thirty minutes with a guy from some fund. He asks how we decide to do a new project. Dennis gives our (by now) standard answer: 1) It has to be financeable, which means a coverage ratio of 1.25 to 1.35, on an all-debt basis; 2) It has to have an internal rate of return of 9% real, regardless of financing; 3) It has to provide a net present value of $50 million to the company, discounted at 15%. The guy is awestruck for some reason. He ends the meeting by saying, "I've never met a management as quantitative as you guys are!" I desperately hope that this is not true and make a mental note not to invest the pension fund with this person, since this is Finance 101 stuff. It was probably a good thing the meeting room had a name on the door and not a number.

» The investment bankers fly in First Class while we fly in coach. This seems odd. One wonders idly if they're being paid too much.

Tomorrow I finish up in Minneapolis (well, OK, I didn't know it was a big center for capital, but at least it's not January) and Roger Sant, the CEO, takes over my piece to finish the tour. Dennis, hardy soul that he is, will have done all the meetings; Roger and I will each have done half. Thank goodness that boy has so much energy.

One last funny thing: we were very clear in the Prospectus that the four AES values (fun, fairness, integrity, and social responsibility) govern how we try to act in our business dealings, and not "maximizing shareholder wealth" or other similar economic goals. The SEC lawyer did read the Prospectus during his thirty-day comment period and actually had a comment. He now wants us to move this discussion of values from where it is right now, in "Management of the Company," to another part of the Prospectus called "Risk Factors." "Boy, that's pretty funny," said one of the salesmen with us. "Our government's saying it's risky to try and do business in this country by relying on fairness and integrity." We agreed.

Love,
Bob

# two

# hot, wet, and dirty

November 1992

Dear Dad,

When you heard about the AES program that puts each corporate officer to work in one of our power plants for a week each year, you asked me what it was like. What it's like, in general, is that you do stuff that gets you hot and wet and dirty. Not that all the jobs are like that, but you have to remember that none of us officers, despite our high salaries, have any real skills. So we do what we're told, and the jobs we can do tend to be hot, wet, etc. I've worked a week at a plant every year for at least six years now: three times at Beaver Valley and once each at our Deepwater, Placerita, and Thames power plants. In fact, I just got back from Thames, our 180 MW coal-burning plant in Connecticut. Let me give you an idea of how it went.

I flew up to New London on Sunday evening, checked in to the Radisson Hotel, and bright and early Monday, I showed up to find that there had been a tube leak in the external heat exchanger (EHE) of the boiler on Saturday. Lest you be confused, this is a BAD THING. The steam inside the boiler tubes, which is under high pressure, goes squirting into the inside of the boiler and causes enormous havoc. We're not talking about a little dribble here. For one thing, the ash inside the boiler hardens into cement when mixed with water (unless, of course, you're doing it on purpose to make pellets out of the ash, in which case it doesn't, but more on that later.) We have had tube leaks before, and after chipping out the cement from inside the boiler or the EHE, we got smarter. We (and of course by this I mean the men and women of Thames, not your number one son) now shut down faster and start pulling the ash out immediately so we don't get inadvertent concrete, and the unit cools down quicker so some fortunate soul can crawl inside, find the leak, and fix it.

By the time I got there, it was allegedly cool enough to go inside the boiler. I was placed in the care of Dave Burley, my boss for the day; he is a very good guy, but he probably eats Sugar Pops for breakfast because he has way too much energy this early in the a.m. or maybe any time. He says we're going into the back end of the boiler.

Let us now pause for a brief technical explanation. Boilers are big. When we first got into this business I had a vague mental picture of something like a large teakettle sitting on top of a fire, water boiling merrily away, and steam coming out of the spout. Well, no. Boilers are large, square, metal things, sort of like eight-story milk cartons. The walls are made of tubes all welded together, one beside the other, and called "tube walls," which seems reasonable. This is where the water circulates. The coal is ground finely in accurately named pulverizers and is injected into the middle of this thing, at the bottom, along with a bunch of air. It then burns fiercely in a swirling mass, heating up the tube walls and the water inside them. Water turns to steam, steam goes to the turbine, big wheel keeps on turnin', Proud Mary keeps on churnin', etc. End of lesson, which is good, because we're about to the end of my technical education. I don't run' em, I just finance' em.

———

Back to our story: our job will be to find the big pieces of refractory that have fallen off or eroded from the walls. The refractory is a brick-like material sprayed, glued, or otherwise attached to the inside surfaces to protect the tube walls in areas where these surfaces aren't involved in heat transfer. This is important, because the essence of these boilers when they're working is a lot of very hot, gritty, abrasive material whirling around inside—ground up burning coal, bits of limestone for pollution control, ash from the burned coal, etc. Think about the space shuttle reentering the atmosphere with all its heat-shield tiles glowing, but in a giant red-hot sandstorm.

Anyhow, Burley finds me some coveralls, a mask, helmet, goggles, and earplugs, takes me to the manhole (a very small, square door in the side of the boiler), and I wriggle through. I find myself in a smallish room with about a foot of brown sand (the bed ash) in the bottom and an ambient temperature of probably 115°F. Lights had been rigged inside so you could see. Burley sticks his head through the manhole and says, "OK, Bob, now find the chunks of refractory and then find where in the walls they came from and put 'em back in their holes." He then disappears.

OK, I'm a good trooper, so I start combing through the sand, sorting out big chunks of refractory. Some are the size of your hand, many range between that and a half dollar, and I decide to classify anything smaller than a quarter as "sand," not "chunk." I also notice, gazing through the rivers of sweat that have clogged my goggles, that some chunks are brown and some bright blue. Aha, I deduce, a clue to figuring out where each chunk came from. See how useful an MBA's analytical ability can be in almost any situation? So I make a blue pile and a brown pile and start to look around to see if I can figure out what came from where and, since the area where the refractory covers the tubes goes up a bit, probably twenty feet, I wonder where I can get a ladder. And I assume that Dave must have gone somewhere to get the adhesive to glue these chunks back in. I'm pleased to be doing such an important job, but I begin to worry about just how perfect a fit I have to get on these chunks, and how long this will take, and whether they'll make fun of me if I'm not fast enough—and besides I hate jigsaw puzzles and this one is three-dimensional. And there's no puzzle box top with clues.

Burley returns, comes into the boiler, notices my carefully sized and color-coded piles of chunks, laughs fiendishly, and says, "You didn't really think we were going to try and fit all those chunks back in, did you?" He hands me a shovel and says, "Just shovel the bigger chunks out the manhole and I'll clean 'em up outside." He disappears back through the manhole.

*OK*, I think, *I should have been smarter than that*. I know refractory needs to be applied with great skill and precision, not stuck on with Duco Cement. I'm sure not going to be fooled a second time. I may be a rookie inside the boiler, but I'm sure no dope. So I pick up a big shovel full of chunks and sand.

Now I must pause to note, with reference to the earlier technical note on what a boiler is and why you would want one, anyway, and remember the part about air. One way we cool down the boiler is to run the induced draft fan, a very large fan located at the end of the path the combustion air takes as it moves through the boiler. This baby sucks a big draft of air through the boiler, with the air coming into the boiler through all the available openings at essentially gale force. Disregarding or ignoring these facts, I take my big shovel load and-- *swoosh*— throw it out the manhole. I immediately hark back to my agricultural forebears in Nebraska who no doubt used the wind to separate the proverbial wheat from the chaff, because I notice that the big chunks of fallen refractory indeed go out through the manhole, but all the sand, grit, and smaller stuff comes right back at me at 90 mph, covering me entirely. I begin to suspect this is not a good system, especially when I try a second shovelful with the same effect.

"Hey, Dave," I yell, sticking my head out the manhole, "in accordance with the Japanese concept of 'kaizen,' also known as continuous improvement, how about you get me a bucket? I don't think this shoveling's going to do it." He does, and I spend the next hour or so picking up chunks, putting them in the bucket, and handing it out to Burley. This is a high-skill task I can do.

Eventually Dave drags me out of the boiler. "We've got to unplug some coal feeders," he says. Away we go to the coal chutes. These are large pipes, about two feet in diameter, where the ground-up coal slides down into the boiler. We start to chisel out the areas where the coal particles have built up inside these pipes. This involves working largely by feel, perching uncomfortably over a bunch of valves and such. No, it was never envisioned that coal deposits would build up on the insides of the chutes, so you can't really get all the way into the chutes through the small openings that are provided, because they're more like observation ports. And you can't see. Either your head or your arm fits inside, but not both. It's a bit like chipping paint on a boat, I guess, although I've never done that either, but wonderfully more dirty. However, after being sandblasted all morning, hygiene is not a concern that's high on my list.

I am rescued (I mistakenly believe) by Mitch Reynolds, the head of the turbine area, who stops by and says, "How'd you like to help us shoot the condenser water box tubes?"

Ever the good sport, I reply, "Sure. My goals here are to get hot, and dirty, and wet, and so far I've only accomplished the first two, because sweating doesn't count."

Mitch only grins mysteriously and says, "Follow me."

Another manhole and I'm inside a dim, wet, hot, confined space, which is the inside of the condenser water box. This particular infernal device is about the size of a Volkswagen van and takes the used steam that has already been through the turbine and cools it down further. I am staring at 3,500 open ends of the tubes through which the water we take from the Thames River runs to cool the steam before we put it back in the river. Our task is to place small, blue plastic things, kind of like darts for a blowgun, into the end of each tube, and then use a gun thing to "shoot" the darts through the six-foot length of the tube, using water and compressed air. Since the darts fit tightly into each tube, their passage cleans the inside of the tube of any gunk therein residing. And gunk there be—slime and stuff—and especially black mussels, small but noxious animals that come in with the river water, eluding the filters and screens, and then happily grow. The most wonderful part of this is that the bottom of the vessel has a bunch of dead and stinky mussels in it whose time for funeral rites has long since passed. This job is not only hot, and wet, and slimy, but you get to smell bad! I catalogue this as a new peak in my record of fun power plant jobs. Also, you can't stand up straight, and you can't really sit on anything; it reminds me of Korean War prisoners being placed in "the box" for discipline. So Mitch and I squat there for four hours, loading each tube with a dart. This process gives one a whole new level of respect for what a large number 3,500 is.

Just when the real fun starts—the shooting—I have to leave to go to Boston, because I have foolishly agreed, since I am "in town," to give an after-dinner speech to the Parsons Main strategic planning meeting. They are one of the firms we engage to build our plants. Even though I take a very thorough shower before I leave, no one at the dinner seems to want to stand too close to me during cocktail hour. And they don't understand why I turn slightly green when the first course turns out to be moules and frites. Thus endeth day one.

Tuesday morning I show up at the maintenance shop at the plant as requested. I am assigned to Joe Oddo, a maintenance technician. Our job is to clean one of the two coal crushers and change the grease in the bearings. This is essentially preventative maintenance, and the task is dictated by our computer system, reassuring that we have such systems and that we pay attention to them.

We walk over to the crusher building, Joe carrying a bucket of fresh grease. This seems to me perhaps some sort of macho overkill—a whole bucket? But wait. First, what's a "crusher building"? When folks dig coal out of the ground, it comes in relatively big lumps. When we blow it into the boilers, it has to be in very small particles both for complete combustion, and because it's burning in suspension, not sitting on some fireplace grate sort of thing. So you want to make it into smaller and smaller pieces as you go along—but not too small too quickly. For moving the coal from place to place, big lumps are great, small dust-size pieces are no good. Coal, sadly, has a mind of its own and refuses to go quietly into that good night, and doesn't break into the size pieces you need when you need it. It either breaks up too soon or not soon enough. The black coal dust that bedevils power plants is from the "too soon" problem. The crusher building is the first step in how we correct the "not soon enough" aspect of coal's character deficiencies. I now know more about coal than is really interesting, as you can tell.

Coal is conveyed in at the top of the crusher building, falls through a crusher—a big grinding machine with rotating flails or hammers inside a cage-like structure—then falls into a conveyer at the bottom of the building, and goes by conveyor up to the power building. Dirty work, but the building is essentially spotless. I know that's hard to believe, but there are brooms, and brushes, and dust pans, and trash cans everywhere, and the people at Thames have even rigged up an internal vacuum system. We have other crusher buildings at other plants that are clean, but this one is immaculate.

Joe opens the access doors, and we begin to chip away the encrusted coal on the various surfaces, edges, crannies, etc. One does wonder why the equipment designers didn't think more about what the inside of their machine would be subjected to. But at least this is a job I can do. After all, I've practiced on the coal chutes. After an hour or so of this Joe hands me an air hose and says, "OK, now blow it out."

Well, Mr. Cooperative, not noticing Joe rapidly backing off to a far distant corner of the room, sticks the air hose in and, yes, great billowing clouds of coal dust immediately engulf our hero, thus completely satisfying his Day Two need to get dirty. When I tell someone else at the plant about this later, he remarks that they don't usually do that because it's not necessary, and the guy holding the hose gets filthy.

We then get to work on the bearing casings. We pull the top half of the cover off of both bearings. The rotating shaft for the crusher flails is supported by bearings at either end, and I begin to see why all the grease may be needed. There is a ton of blackish heavy grease, sort of like solidified bacon fat but more viscous, packed around the bearing. "We got to take that out," says Joe, so I look around for the automated grease remover. After all, we spent a dodecajillion dollars on this highly automated, state-of-the-art, low pollution, high efficiency power plant showplace of the Northeast, and we even got a computer to tell us to do the job.

"What equipment do we need?" I ask politely. Joe looks at me as though I am retarded. "Well, our hands," he says. So we dig in using fingers, rags, screwdrivers, and human energy. This is one yucko-squisho job, but perhaps good for the cuticles. It's amazing how much grease there is, and we have to get it all out, because it gets coal dust in it over time, thus eroding its lubricatory powers, turning it into an abrasive of sorts, and assuredly turning it black.

Finally we finish, then slather in a bunch of new grease, again largely by hand. The new grease, strangely, is a pleasing dark green color. The last task is to clean up the area, so I am manipulating the vacuum hose and immediately get too enthusiastic and suck up a couple of too big lumps of coal which jam the system. Joe good-humoredly says, "Happens all the time," which I suspect to be an overstatement, and he unplugs it while we finish sweeping and cleaning up. Remarkable how big a mess we made and how much coal dust and grease I have managed to distribute about my person.

As Wednesday begins, I resolve to rectify a serious fuel shortage I have noticed at the plant. Power plant experts will all agree that plants theoretically run on coal and oil, or gas, but actually they run on coal, oil, gas, pizza, and doughnuts. I've been at Thames for two days and had pizza three times, but NO DOUGHNUTS. This karmic imbalance must be corrected for the long-term welfare of all involved.

So I stop at Dunkin' Donuts on the way in and pick up sixty doughnut holes (five kinds, but no chocolate; it's not a good concept) and bring them in. I am assigned to work with the materials handlers that day, the group in charge of moving the large amounts of coal and limestone that the plant consumes each day into the plant and then the combustion by-products, of which more later, back out and off to somewhere. I immediately notice a difference between them and the maintenance techs. A typical maintenance person looks into the box, says, "Well, no really, well, OK, maybe one, aren't there any chocolate?" then carefully selects a particular variety. He later returns and picks out another, kind of like a guy picking out just the right tool for a difficult job. The material handler, on the other hand, cruises by the doughnut box, dips a hand in, grabs as much as he can of whatever's there, and moves it all up to his mouth in one continuous motion. Analogies abound.

I am sent out to the barge with Jeff Davis and Dave Thomas, two of our coal handling specialists, to work on unloading coal using the monster Star Wars unloader we have. This fascinating piece of capital equipment is a big continuous chain of buckets, each about as big as half an executive's desk, mounted on a vertical arm which in turn swings out over the barge from its base on the dock. The buckets on the digging arm scoop into the coal on the barge and then rise, filled, to the top of this arm. They dump out onto a conveyer built into the support arm, which runs the coal back to the dock. And the height of the digging arm, its speed and its angle forward or back, as well as the position of the base of the machine (mounted on rails so it can move back and forth along the dock) is controlled by a radio gizmo about the size of a car battery. You walk out onto the barge and watch the coal and direct the monster that way. It's like managing a mechanical dinosaur with a Nintendo joystick.

After a little bit of instruction, Jeff turns the controls over to me. "Wait a minute," I say, "I'm the guy that broke the vacuum in the crusher building. You sure about this?" But they were, so I strapped the transmitter on and started digging coal out of the barge. What fun, and much better because it was a sunny fall day in New England and Jeff and Dave were great to talk to.

At 11:00 a.m. we stopped because it was time for the plant manager's monthly meeting. Held in a conference/lunch room next to the control room, Dave McMillen, the head guy, goes over all the operating results from the last month and all the income and cost figures. Everybody's invited and lunch is served, and lots of people come. It's a very good way to share information with everyone in the plant on how we're doing. And it's information that's essential for everyone to have, or at least awfully useful.

Jeff, Dave, and I spend the afternoon unloading the barge, except for a break of about an hour when I am sent up to water down the coal pile while others run bulldozers and front-end loaders around on it. This is a low-skill, dirty, and wet task well suited to my abilities, especially as it requires only the use of a hose. No transmitter. When I finish up working the coal unloader, I am assured that I have done a much better job than Dennis Bakke, the last officer to try his hand at this. I was only sorry that we hadn't yet gotten down to the bottom of the load so I could try and dig through the steel bottom of the barge. I attempted this once at Beaver Valley, our coal plant in Pennsylvania, and everyone was quite impressed.

On Thursday, after again helping to end the doughnut drought at Thames, I was sent off to work with Mickey Reavis, Dave Fisher, and

Nelson Briggs on changing the bearings on one of the primary air fans. We were having problems with one of the boilers, and this fan showed a temperature spike at the bearing. It was hard to tell whether it was a faulty thermocouple, the device that measures the temperature, or actually a bad bearing. It could also have been a problem with the transmitter that sends the data to the control room. There are daily problems here, much like this one, which are essentially Kantian in nature: are we observing the "thing-as-itself" or merely the sensory (or electronic) transmission and interpretation of the thing. Reality is often hard to sort out. In this case, it turned out to be both the thermocouple and the bearing that needed to be replaced. I mostly handed or fetched tools and cleaned up oil spills since the space was very cramped, as well as hot and noisy.

One interesting thing about everybody at Thames: there's never any question about hard hats, safety glasses, or hearing protection. Everybody puts them on automatically.

After lunch, the pelletizing people took me over and toured me through all the hardware that has been put in place to try and turn our ash—the powdery gray residue that's left after the coal is burned—into cute little hard pellets that look like they're related to rabbits. We wish to do this so it can be more easily shipped back to the mines it came from. It has turned out to be a far more costly and complex process than we first thought, and it doesn't work right yet. After giving me a thorough orientation, Mark Bargnesi, the technician in charge of me, indicated that it was now time to clean up the third floor of the hydration building.

Now these may not sound to you like words of much portent. But I had noticed that one of the places Mark had walked me through had seemed a bit dusty. Mark pulled up the vacuum truck, hooked up a big hose, and off we went. It turns out the third floor was covered several inches deep in fly ash. This is different than the brown sandy stuff I'd covered myself with on Monday. This is gray and extremely fine, finer than talcum powder. It flows like water, and at the least disturbance floats in the air. You really can't even sweep it. You have to run a squeegee across the floor to pile it up. It is major-league nasty and unpleasant, and therefore just the job for me. We spent several hours working the room and all the equipment because the stuff had settled everywhere. My hot/wet/dirty criteria were met easily and exceeded. It didn't smell as bad as the condenser and the dead mussels, but that was about all that was missing.

On Friday I spent the day making the "Balance of Plant" rounds with Bob Piscitello. This fairly utilitarian term means "everything not directly connected to burning coal." This consisted principally of water treating. We collect and treat all sorts of water at the plant, not only normal water used in the steam-making processes, but rainwater that falls on the coal pile, for example. It all has to have the solids settled out and the acidity/alkalinity adjusted before we can send it on to the local sewage treatment plant. Much of our day was spent running up and down steps and ladders and peering into tanks, or taking samples and doing the chemistry ourselves, all to make sure the instruments were reading accurately—another take on reality vs. what's being reported. Bob was a great teacher.

Just as important, we finally stopped a trend I'd inadvertently started. Since I don't have any coveralls, every day someone would loan me a set, always with a nice little name embroidered on it. On Monday I was "Dawg," on Tuesday "Joe," on Wednesday "Pete," and so on. By Thursday I noticed this had caught on and people were wearing someone else's coveralls. I had no intent of organizing or promoting a cross-dressing chapter at Thames, so I was relieved to finally be "Bob" on Friday.

To sum it up, I had a great time at Thames. I discovered that it isn't just the people at Beaver Valley, our really old coal plant where I have also done a work week, who have to do real physical labor. I got to better know some remarkable people, I didn't mess up the plant safety record, and I assuredly did get hot, wet, and dirty. And smelly.

Love and kisses,
Bob

## three

# how's a guy get a drink around here?

September 1993

Dear Dad,

I recently got back from a two-and-a-half week trip to Pakistan, India, and China, checking on business prospects in those countries for AES (great!) and the general nature of the countries (weird). Since the last time I was in these places was with you when I was twelve, and the family was traveling home from Tokyo on that big ocean liner, the MV *Asia*, I thought maybe you'd be interested in some of my observations on the trip. I'll skip the business stuff and focus on what could probably be called Miscellaneous Travel Notes.

1) DON'T DO THIS: When flying to Pakistan from Washington, D.C., do not fly overnight to the UK (losing one night's sleep because of the six-hour time difference); land at Gathrow/Heathwick (or whatever silly names those UK airports are called); hang around in a crabby daze for ten hours, by which time even the best airline lounge has lost its shaky allure; get on another big crowded airplane; then fly overnight—again—to

Islamabad, losing another six hours (time change) and another night's sleep. I repeat: do not do this.

2) The Brits, who have a noble tradition of bad food to maintain, have decided that it is OK to put fresh corn in (on? what's the correct syntax?) pizza. At least in the pizza they serve to sleepy crabby Americans at Hedgerow or Gasthouse, or maybe at all of their airports. They are wrong. It is not all right to do this.

3) When you arrive at 7:00 in the bright hot morning in Islamabad—a relatively new "planned capital" like Canberra and Brasilia—after two consecutive nights of not much sleep on two different airplanes, you are surprised to note that there is no traffic on any of the roads. Not just "not much traffic," not just "a little traffic," but essentially no traffic. Initially you think, *Well, the airport's pretty far out of town.* But then you get into town, so you think, *Well, it's early,* but by then it's 7:30, which ain't so early. So you think, *Well there's been a coup* or *Well, I got off at the wrong stop and I'm in the Maldive Islands,* but there are, respectively, no soldiers and no water around. *Well, there'll be more traffic during the evening rush hour,* you think. At 5:00 p.m., on the main street of Islamabad, the street running between the Presidential Palace and the legislature—both big hotels are also on this street—the amount of traffic is: two cars, two donkeys, and three guys walking, all on a four-lane divided roadway. You could shoot a cannon down the street and not hit anybody. It was almost spooky, or maybe like Brasilia when it was still in Niemeyer's head. Maybe they finished the city but nobody announced it was open.

4) Advice You Shouldn't Have to Be Given: Never order the chocolate doughnuts in a hotel where you can't even get a beer. Boy, were they ever bad. Maybe Asia and doughnuts don't mix. Where's Krispy Kreme when you need them?

5) I forgot that in an Islamic country you can't order alcohol. Traveler's hint: Is Pakistan an Islamic country? Remember, the name of the capital city is Islamabad. In the Marriott in Islamabad, you can get room service to bring you a drink, to be consumed in your room. You must, however, fill out a document acknowledging that you are a nonbeliever and thus destined for unpleasant treatment in the afterlife. One of our people staying there

did fill out the form, so we went to his room to drink. He, of course, became known as the Designated Infidel. This all raises certain complex theological questions: If you fill out the form, but then don't order a drink, are you still doomed? What if you use a fictitious name on the form? What if you cross your fingers?

6) On my second day in I-bad (I'm sure that's not what it's called by the Pakistanis, but we liked the hip American sound of it—if only we'd brought our black high-tops and baseball caps to wear backwards) we had a meeting set up with the Minister of Water and Power. It's pretty eerie to be getting out of an elevator to meet with the equivalent of the Secretary of Energy and find a whole entryway of people kneeling on rugs, praying. You have to carefully pick your way around them to get down the hall, trying not to step on the rugs. Can't say, however, that this isn't just as effective a way as we used in the US to come up with a national energy policy.

7) The Rose and Jasmine Garden of Islamabad, which is touted as one of the major tourist attractions of a city which has precious few of same and which I duly visited, doesn't in fact have any jasmine, and the roses could use more than a little work. This could be a metaphor for Pakistan, the country.

8) If it only costs $25 to fly first class on Pakistan International Airlines vs. $15 for tourist, then go first class. This is probably where the phrase "false economy" originated. Believe me.

9) After three days in Pakistan, I flew to New Delhi. There really are cows in the streets here, no kidding! Also on the sidewalks, usually eating garbage. There really are a lot of people here, no kidding! Usually walking in the streets to avoid the cows on the sidewalks.

10) We plan to consider a significant increase in insurance level for people who work/live/travel in Asia—both death and disability. I didn't see a car anywhere with a seat belt. Or a cow with a seat belt.

11) There is something slightly odd about eating dinner on the top floor of the Taj Mahal Hotel in Delhi, at an Italian restaurant called Casa Medici, looking out at India Gate, a monument built by the British in honor of British and Indian casualties of WW I, while the band plays "I Left My Heart in San Francisco." When "global" goes bad . . .

12) During our big dinner in Pakistan where we entertained all the government energy officials we could find, the Pakistani delegation had no sooner arrived and been introduced all around than the lights went out. Tony Colman is our country manager in India. At his house in Delhi on my first day there, the lights went out both in the morning and in the afternoon. What great places for new electricity business!

13) On my fourth day in India, Tony and Glen Davis, our number two person in India, and I took off from New Delhi on Air India for Bhubaneswar. This is the capital of the east coast state of Orissa where we're going to build our plant. We had an interim stop at Varanasi, and the pilot announced that we had to sit in the plane on the runway for a while, without air conditioning, because the weather in Bhubaneswar was too bad for him to land. Very warm. Very, very warm. After about an hour they decided to go back to Delhi. This is, one supposes, not a terribly productive way to spend a Saturday. On returning we tried to schedule a trip to Bhubaneswar on Tuesday. Nope, no planes that day. Glen and I began to suspect that Paul Hanrahan, our head guy for Asia, has just made up Bhubaneswar and it doesn't really exist, so he is having a good laugh at all of our expense. I can spell it, I can pronounce it, but I don't seem to be able to visit it. I mean, have you ever heard of it? Or has anyone in Olympia, your damp current city of residence? Well, maybe that's not a fair test— nobody in India has ever heard of Puyallup, Washington, either.

14) Rigdon Boykin, our counsel here, has not only increased the life and disability insurance for his people in Asia, his firm has also purchased Medevac insurance. He says it's cheap and quite reassuring. Rhetorical question: Would you like to be sick/treated in a hospital in India or China? Easy answer. If you fail this, go back to "Is Pakistan an Islamic country?" and start over.

15) In Bangalore in southern India, I kept asking everybody where they made the torpedoes. All I got were blank stares. In all candor, I mentioned this same interesting tidbit to my wife and received exactly the same blank stare. I am aghast that no one seems to know that, in infantry circles, a "Bangalore torpedo" is a long metal tube or pipe, filled with explosives,

which some foolhardy soldier carries. He runs up to the enemy barbed wire, scoots this thing underneath, detonates it, and voila!—or perhaps *Boom!*—a path is blown through the wire. It is said that this piece of military hardware was invented by the Indian infantry who fought for Great Britain in WWI. One presumes they were from you-know-where. No, not Islamabad. After this fascinating explanation, my wife suggested that I stop asking Indians about the torpedoes and stop telling this story.

16) On this trip I was visiting some potential local partners from a company called BPL. They served me a local "cola soft drink" at the BPL offices. Sure enough, it tasted like Coke with just a hint of curry.

17) In the Bangalore airport waiting room, the trash cans—all of them—are almost four-feet-tall plastic or resin statues of large monkeys clothed in black-tie formal dress, and also wearing black cowboy hats. Their arms are wrapped around the trash cans, which they clutch in front of them. I checked, and these are in fact made locally—but what alien space being gave them the design?

18) Almost nobody in India wears T-shirts. Hard to believe that somehow this universal clothing item hasn't made it, but you just don't see any T-shirts, except on Westerners. Usually fat Westerners who are also wearing Bermuda shorts. You see lots of short-sleeve open-collar shirts, occasional suits, sometimes just shirts and ties, some knit shirts with collars, but no T-shirts. And no baseball caps, either. What a backward country. They've probably never even heard of the Oakland Raiders.

19) "Weren't you worried about getting sick?" you may ask. After all, everyone who goes to India gets sick. Worried? I was petrified. I took along three different kinds of diarrhea medicine. I religiously drank no water, limiting myself to beer, although this in itself didn't seem so much of a hardship. Paul pointed out to me the motto of Kingfisher, one of the local Indian beers: "Most thrilling chilled." I was especially careful about ice, specifying "no ice" every time I ordered a drink, even beer. In fact, I even got to the point that when I introduced myself, I'd say, "Hi, I'm Bob Hemphill from the AES Corporation. No ice." This confused several potential business associates. And despite this hypochondria, I got mildly sick, but I'm pleased to report that the pills worked fine.

20) The food in India can make you sick, but at least it tastes good. In China, it's another story. During a dinner in Harbin, a plate of cold, smoked meats was served—the dreaded "regional specialty." Most of the AES people declined, claiming a sudden and miraculous conversion to vegetarianism. But one guy took one helping, then another, explaining later that it at least seemed to be something vaguely recognizable. He found out afterward that it was slices of smoked cow penis.

21) I quickly decided that the most important words to learn with regard to Chinese cuisine are: "No reptiles and no insects, please." I had our people in Hong Kong teach me how to say this in Mandarin. They were very amused. I was serious.

Your loving son,
Bob

# four

# it's cabbage season in the beijing of my heart

March 1994

Dear Dad,

Well, I've made several more trips to India and China recently while you've been sitting in Olympia contemplating the rain and becoming a real estate magnate. Congratulations on buying the house—actually a duplex! Do you know Donald Trump yet? Some of this travel has involved delving even further into areas of the countryside where our projects are likely to be located. It makes me feel something like a cross between *Apocalypse Now* and *Raiders of the Lost Ark*. You remember the old joke your dad used to tell about the guys on the hunting trip who agreed that the one who complained about the cooking would have to become the cook for the others, until the next person complained? Everybody quickly figured out that complaining had consequences, so one guy got stuck with the job. Frustrated, he went out and collected a bunch of moose droppings, which he served as pancakes the next morning. The first person to take a big bite exclaimed, "Ugh, this tastes like moose poop—but it's good, I like it!" Somehow that story kept playing through my mind on these trips. A healthy positive mind-set is very important to have when doing business in foreign countries. Consider the following:

*Impressions of India*

A) How not to have meetings in India, long version: In Delhi we had been careful to set up, in advance, a number of meetings for me (a.k.a. the really important Mr. Big Cheese, President and CEO of AES Transpower, the Asia subsidiaty of the leading independent power company in the US and elsewhere in the galaxy, etc.) with three officials of the Federal government ("the Centre" as it is called by the Indians):

1) Mr. Verma, the Chief Cabinet Secretary

2) Mr. Salve, the Minister of Energy

3) Mr. Aluwalia, the Finance Secretary

We also had arranged a meeting with

4) ISEC, our advisers.

In addition, I was invited to a special dinner in my honor to be given by Mr. Patniak, the Chief Minister of Orissa, the Indian state where our project was to be built. In Indian states, the Chief Minister is the equivalent of a U.S. Governor, but more powerful. Of these prearranged meetings, numbers 1, 2, and 3 canceled; Mr. Patniak became ill (although his Energy Minister presided in his stead); and I was fifteen minutes late for number 4, and they already had another meeting going on, even though we were paying them. I did have a brief audience with the Chief Minister of Orissa earlier in Delhi. He yelled at us to hurry up and get the project done. What fun.

B) How to not have meetings in India, short version: Set them up ahead of time. Maybe we haven't quite gotten this "global" stuff down yet. Part 1:

Recently when we needed some help on a project in the Philippines, Paul Hanrahan, our leader for Asia, called one of the guys at Barbers Point, the Hawaii coal plant, who had earlier professed an interest in helping. During the conversation, Paul reminded him that the Philippines is one of those backward places where you still have to have a visa to get in. "Oh," he said. "Does that mean you need a passport, too?"

Maybe we haven't quite gotten this "global" stuff down yet. Part 2:

At a special dinner we were hosting in Bhubaneswar, the capital city of Orissa, we realized we hadn't brought any gifts or anything. Fortunately we had some T-shirts left over from the AES India group's picnic, which had written across the front "AES-Transpower" in three languages—English, Hindi, and Oriya, the local language in Orissa. With great fanfare at the end of dinner we presented one to our guest of honor, the Orissa Energy Minister, a quiet man and former University professor of the Oriyan language. He looked at it bemusedly, seemed pleased but not overwhelmed, and then pointed out softly that the Oriya portion was printed upside down. We apologized but promised we wouldn't build the power plant upside down.

On my last trip to India I couldn't get to Bhubaneswar (or even spell it); this trip I couldn't leave. The Air India flight the day I was to leave was several hours late, causing me to miss connections to Manila. So I decided it was my karma to hang around, and I stayed for the all-day meetings with the Indian bankers and for a site visit. When God gives you mangoes, make mango chutney.

The trip to the Ib Valley plant site was really fascinating. Major eye-openers:

This plant is really truly out in the middle of farooshing nowhere. To get there you can drive twelve hours on narrow, winding, dusty, traffic-laden (walking folks, bicycles, motor scooters, motorcycles, peddled pedicabs, motorized pedicabs, cars, big buses, small trucks, small buses, big trucks) roads, or you can land at the WWII air strip at Sambalpur and drive an hour plus on the same roads. It's interesting, but it ain't Houston or even Poteau. Forget local support for anything when building or operating the plant; it will all have to come out of Bhubaneswar (there's not that much there, either) or Calcutta/Bombay/Delhi. It's not desolate; actually it's flat green farm or rice paddy land and dozens and dozens of small villages, but nothing else. You can probably get a motor scooter fixed, but that's about it. There will be a big need for substantial spare parts inventory at the plant, an airplane, and a nice compound for the people who will work there.

Construction by hand. We will build and operate units 3 and 4, and units 1 and 2 at the plant site are already in construction by the Orissa government. One of the things I wanted to see was these first two units. At one point there had to have been heavy equipment on-site, but now there is nothing but trucks; no dozers, no cranes, no cherry pickers, no front-end loaders, etc. All the cement is carried in baskets on the heads of women. There are, all told, 7,000 (yes seven thousand, that's not a typo) people on-site. No safety hard hats—well maybe one out of a hundred—no safety glasses, no safety shoes, in fact it's mostly bare feet or sandals. It does look exactly like a power plant in construction, only one covered with people. For reference, building the same size plant in the US would employ maybe 700 people at its peak.

If you need coal, it's nice to have the coal mine nearby. And on a dedicated rail line connecting directly to your plant. OK, that's a trick; the coal is why the plant was built here. On our way by road from the plant to the mine we were stopped, as were the six trucks ahead of us, by a homemade roadblock of large rocks put up by the villagers nearby. It had been erected, or rather rolled into place, because that morning a villager had been hit on that road by a truck or a motorcycle. It didn't seem advisable to interfere, as a large group of angry truck drivers was already discussing the pros and cons of this matter with the equally agitated assembled villagers. Procedures of the American Arbitration Association did not appear to be in force.

At the coal mine we visited, we saw a number of curiously miscellaneous hortatory signs: "Work is worship," "Religion by another name is duty," "Work safely," "Eternal vigilance is the price of liberty," and "Always stop for red lights." The last one was a stumper because, between all of us, we couldn't come up with the location of a traffic light anywhere in the entire state of Orissa.

On the way to the airplane (which had to take off before dusk because Sambalpur is not a lighted field; in fact, come to think of it, there's not a control tower, either), Janette Kessler, the AES person in charge of the plant's financing, summed it up: "You know, we might be crazy to even try and do this . . ."

On long trips you invent conversation topics. The most recent is derived from the Indian practice of discussing numbers with the help of two Hindi words: *lakh*, which means 100,000; and *crore*, which means 10 million. Since there are currently 30 rupees to the dollar, this makes big-number discussions simpler, as in, "This power plant will cost 945 crore rupees." The game: lakh and crore riddles. To wit:

» What do you call a country with 100,000 citizens? Lakhistan

» What do you call a country with 10 million citizens? Croratia

» What term describes a person with 100,000 excuses for putting tasks off? Lakhadasical

» What do 10 million Indians put on their Christmas trees? Decrorations

» What is the sound made by the 10 million frogs in the Hirakud Reservoir next to the Ib Valley plant? Crork

» What are the 10 million reptiles trying to eat these frogs called? Crorcodiles

Our last night in town five of us went to dinner at the Suryea, one of the hotels in Delhi (known as the "Surreal" to expatriates for reasons that will become clear), and found ourselves in a room with live entertainment and, on each table, small "band request" slips. We immediately asked for "American Pie," "Take Me Home, Country Roads," "Blowin' In The Wind," and "Homeward Bound." The band responded with "All That She Wants [Is To Have Another Baby]," the Ace of Base song. Yes, there you are.

### Impressions of Beijing

» Lots of taxis, lots of bicycles, but few motor scooters or motorcycles; not bad traffic; and very busy and serious people. There is nobody standing around; everyone is moving here and there in quite a determined fashion.

» Wide streets, even boulevards, and almost everyone in Western dress, but lots of sweaters and long underwear, because it's already nippy and the heat in the government buildings doesn't come on, by policy decree, until November 15. I suspect the buildings won't even be all that warm then.

» Lots more consumer goods and more choices than in India, and lots of "foreign" stuff like Coke, and Snickers, and even several McDonald's. Everyone we talked to spoke at least once of the transition "from a planning economy to a market economy with socialist tendencies." We weren't quite sure what that was, and I think they weren't, either. I figured they might be talking about California.

» The fearsome banquets weren't so fearsome, at least in Beijing. There were no snakes, no grasshoppers, and there were some very exceptional dishes. Mao-tai, the 120 proof "brandy" that you drink lots of shots of, is as bad as advertised (Ned Hall, our number two person in China, claims that it tastes like diesel oil smells) and the language is a huge barrier.

» There is some evidence that they haven't gotten this "free market with socialist tendencies" stuff perfect yet. It was cabbage season in the autumn of my heart. There were innumerable trucks rolling down the streets, piled six feet high with "Chinese cabbage." Well, OK, it is China, but they were bigger heads than we see in the US, and they were absolutely everywhere. Big piles of cabbage lined the edges of the sidewalks and spilled out into the streets, even blocking traffic at some points. There were cabbages laid out in orderly stacks everywhere—to dry? To cure? for decoration?—on the railings of apartment balconies, on rooftops, on windowsills. Somebody is going to be eating a *pile* of cabbage in Beijing.

Maybe we haven't quite gotten this "global" stuff down yet. Part 3:

» As the last dish of the special banquet in my honor one evening, hosted by the Governor of Shanxi Province, we were served a small plate with an orange tart, a dumpling shaped like a bunny, and, in the center, three small exquisite replicas of leeks, a big fall favorite in China—second only to the cabbage—that looked like they were made out of marzipan. It is reasonable to assume that a certain amount of alcohol had been consumed, and toasts extolling friendship and appreciation made back and forth, and warm relations built, so we plunged right in and ate one of the leeks. Big mistake: it was basically rice flour and water, uncooked, and yucky, but beautiful. The Governor, sitting next to me, watched this performance carefully, then leaned across me and said something to Li-Ming, our Beijing person. She giggled, the Governor laughed, and then she said to me in a low tone, "Bob, the Governor says it's OK. They all like AES, so you don't have to eat the decorations."

Hong Kong, 2 January 1994. You've never seen a city with so many Christmas decorations! Giant buildings wrapped up like presents and snowflakes, "Merry Christmas and Happy New Year" written out eight stories high, and Santa on his sleigh driving across the two-story cavernous entrance of the Bank of China, key bastion of PRC's economic control of China. I thought that the Confucian/Buddhist/Taoist tradition was not that high on Christmas, and I had no idea that Santa had entered the pantheon. Actually when you go to Toys "R" Us, or Circuit City, or Gap and find that *everything* therein was made in China and exported, you begin to understand. I decided that all the decorations were just a Chinese way of saying, "Thank you."

### Rural China

» Paul and I, at one point, were sitting on a small drive-on/drive-off ferry, crossing a narrow tributary of the Perfume River, on our way to visit a power plant in southern China. There were no other "gwailo" (Westerners) for miles and miles. I remarked to Paul, "Boy, this business certainly lets you visit some interesting places, doesn't it?"

"Yes," he said, "but the bad part is that nothing seems strange anymore."

» The slogan for the Blue Sky Hotel in Weihai: "A splendid building like a fairy pavilion falls onto the world."

» You could sure become a fat alcoholic very easily in China. In northern China we had a dinner one evening with much mao-tai toasting and pledges of eternal friendship, sincere cooperation, and goodwill. Then at lunch the next day, the same thing, maybe with even a bit more drinking because the Mayor wasn't there. It was the local version of mao-tai, the serious liquor with the really dismal aftertaste.

Paul said that Ned Hall, our number two guy in China, came by his house after work one evening in Hong Kong. Paul asked him if he'd like a beer. "No, thanks," said Ned, "I only drink on the job."

### Favorite Chinese English

» Sign in Wuhan: "DON'T SMOKING IN BUSINESS CENTER"

» Amusement Park Equipment Co., Ltd.: "New products we are now developing include: alarming house, shooting range, boating facilities, park tour bus, and terrible city."

» "Our company is in the process of researching world-class superlarge facilities such as universal space exploring and joyful world equipment."

At a banquet in central China—actually a luncheon, but still replete with toasts, lots of hard liquor, and so forth—one of the first dishes to arrive was a plate of small brown things that looked kind of like buttons with humps, but which turned out upon unfortunate closer inspection to be silkworms. Not silkworms with ginger sauce, not silkworms with broccoli and cashews, just silkworms. I asked my interpreter, hoping against hope, just what these things were. "Silkworms, local specialty," she said. "Bugs," she added helpfully.

As a guest of honor I got the first helping. I thought suddenly of former President George Bush and one of the truly defining moments of his presidency when he laid out his vision on broccoli: "I'm the President and I'm not going to eat broccoli anymore." Since I was the President of our China subsidiary, I decided to apply the same rule, but not to broccoli. I faced down the silkworms. Several other members of our party ate theirs, and Paul noted (gratuitously, I thought) that these silkworms weren't as good as the last ones he'd had.

Then out came a dish of brown, lengthy, thin things, which looked like slightly wrinkled French fries. "What's that?" I asked my interpreter. "Chicken fingers," she whispered. *Wow, great!* I thought. *At last, something familiar.* I took a bunch and eagerly bit into the first one. Crunch, crunch—almost broke my teeth. They really were chicken fingers, chopped off of each little chicken claw. They do not serve these at KFC. And I can tell you why.

At the hotel in northern China I was allocated the room, a suite really, where no less than the President of the Republic of Singapore had stayed, as I was told five or six times to emphasize the honor being accorded to me. The quarters were furnished with heavy, ornately carved Chinese furniture, and both a lovely sitting room and a study; there was also a large bedroom and a large and elaborate marble bathroom. There was, however, no hot water. At first I thought I just hadn't hit the right switch, and that there must be some sort of point-of-source heating or something, surely. So I ran around cold and naked and ready for my shower, pushing every damn button or switch or lever I could find, anywhere in the bathroom, and there were a lot of them. Then I would run back to the shower and stick my hand in it to see if it was getting warmer, find that it wasn't, curse, then try another switch or button, and so on. Eventually I gave up and took a cold shower, which is quite possibly my least favorite form of activity in the world. As I stood there shivering and washing, I asked myself if the President of the Republic of Singapore was as peeved as I was when he took *his* cold shower.

Later that morning I asked each of the three other folks in our party if they'd had hot water. Both the Westerners said no, but our one Chinese member, Guo Liming, said, "Of course." *Darn*, I thought, *none of the stupid Americans could figure this out; it must be cultural*. I knew there was a secret button.

"How did you get it?" I asked her. "Where'd you find the switch?" She looked puzzled, then responded. "Well, it was just where it always is in Chinese hotel, in the thermos outside your door, for your tea."

### Tokyo Survival Manual

Have friends take you to dinner. Despite Japan's much-noted economic difficulties, I assure you things have only gotten more and more and more expensive there. I was in Tokyo for four days, visiting the banks we've borrowed money from, saying, "Thank you, thank you, thank you," and visiting suppliers who we're encouraging to bid to us in India and Pakistan, saying, "Please, please, please, please." On one of my four nights in town I didn't arrange for dinner, so I looked over the room service menu. When I revived from fainting at the shock of the prices, I ordered fried shrimp for 3,200 yen, which is $28. Soon they arrived on a nice little tray with a small rose in a vase, white linen, and a round metal plate cover to keep the shrimp warm. The room service waiter removed the cover with a flourish, and there they were: two shrimp, and not very big ones, either. *Gosh*, I thought, *$14 a shrimp. My, my . . ..*

Hope this finds you well and happy. Once we finish selling the Chigen stock, we'll all get back to work in China.

Love,
Bob

# five

# who took our boats?

June 1994

Dear Dad,

I thought I should report on several more trips around the globe. If I'm going to go to these places, the least you can do is read about them. Not content with battling the vagaries of China, ("Hah!" you say. "World's largest country cannot contain your interest? How fickle.") I have also recently returned from a trip to Swaziland. If you're on *Jeopardy!* and they ask you where it is, it's not:

> » A recently autonomous republic of the former Soviet Union;
> » One of those small countries carved out of Borneo (whose new name, of course, is Kalimantan, but that's probably for Final Jeopardy); or
> » A country perched on the top of South America where a bunch of disgruntled Californians killed themselves.

Those were my first guesses, but then I found out that it's a pretty neat independent country sitting almost entirely inside of South Africa. But first, more China escapades:

On Sunday during my most recent trip to China, I was in Hong Kong with nothing much to do, so I decided to visit Lantau Island, a big island that's part of Hong Kong but poorly (well that's a relative term, only 20,000 people) settled. It does, however, have, according to the hotel's guidebook, the "World's Largest Outdoor Buddha" at the Po Lin Monastery. I'm immediately suspicious. Why is this description qualified? Is there a bigger "Indoor" Buddha? Is there a larger outdoor something else? Youth wants to know, even if I'm not that young any more.

Energized and undeterred, I catch the ferry over to Lantau and note a whole bunch of families, all with baskets, kids, umbrellas, backpacks, etc., on the same boat, no doubt going, I speculate, to one of the three or four beaches for which the island is also known. Once on the ferry I am a bit perturbed about how I will find the World's Largest etc., once I get there. Well. When you get off the ferry at Mo Pi (which allegedly translates to "Silvermine Bay" but who knows): a) there are dozens of big, huge signs, in English, with arrows saying "Bus to World's Largest Outdoor Buddha— This Way," and "Buy Tickets Here—$45.00 for Air-Conditioned Bus, $22.00 for Regular Bus" for WLOB, and "Form Line Here" for WLOB; and b) all the folks on the ferry are going there anyway so if you wanted to go elsewhere it would be a struggle. Quickly evaluating the situation I decided that I would be able to find the Po Lin Monastery after all.

After a moderate uphill and down dale bus ride (reason for small population: this is a rugged, hilly, and steep island) we get to the top of the second highest hill on the island, us and twenty-five other buses. The World's Largest Outdoor Buddha is at the top of about ten thousand steps up another hill, and at the base of the hill is a very large queue, but collapsed into recurrent "S's" like Disneyland crowd management. Also in front of the steps is a gatekeeper who periodically lets a new slug of folks onto the steps.

*Well, I'm here*, I think, which seems irrefutable, so I get in line. I pull my trusty Swiss Army knife from my knapsack and cut up an apple I've been clever enough to bring along. The queue moves as people poke me with their umbrellas, and soon I plod up to the top of the steps and see the WLOB up close. Yes. It is a Buddha, and it is large, and it is outdoors, and I am sweaty. Around its base are six female deity images, each seated but holding up a different item—bowl of stuff, torch, plate of stuff, dish of stuff, bunch of stuff, roll of stuff. Because, after all, this is still Hong Kong, people have decided to toss money at these statues and try to land coins on/in the bowl/dish/platter, etc. Obviously it's good luck if your money sticks in the stuff. Monks (no fools but see later) have put little fences around each image to make the game more competitive. Many coins are flying. I try my luck, but my fond wish for a job as starting point guard for the Celtics continues to elude me.

I walk back down the stairs and see the sign: "Po Lin Monastery Tea House, Horseback Riding, and Roller-Skating Rink" with an arrow. The guidebook had mentioned the teahouse, but what's the rest of this? Seized with disbelief I set off down the path as indicated. Indeed, here are some tired old horses and various young Chinese riding on them around a small rink, with pictures being taken. Then comes the teahouse, but no sign of that big building you need for a roller rink. I follow more signs and find a corrugated roof over a round concrete floor patch about twice the size of a standard dining room. No one is there but me. "Roller Rink" says the faded sign, and I begin to deduce a reason for commercial nonsuccess of this endeavor. You'd screw yourself into the ground skating in there—not quite clear on the concept.

I wander on to the monastery where fortunes are for sale. Great! A sign sitting above the heads of two severe little Chinese ladies who hand out your fortune slip explains how this works. It says:

$1/Fortune slip
For Big Buddha Fund
Change Not Available
Say the Number
Not Text Explanation

I am charmed beyond words and decide that this is a mantra that describes the entire process of doing business in China. I buy two fortunes (having only a $2 coin and "Change Not Available"). When translated later by my Chinese associates ("Not Text Explanation") both say, in essence,

"Be patient." Terrific.

During the entire trip to the WLOB and back I am:

a) the only person wearing an Arkansas Razorbacks hat,

b) one of two Westerners, and

c) constantly surrounded by people with Chicago Bulls and Georgetown hats, T-shirts, jackets, etc.

Nolan Richardson, the Arkansas basketball coach, would be surprised to find how little an NCAA championship is worth.

Prior to one of our numerous Chinese banquets and associated toasts with fiery but unpalatable mao-tai, an associate reminds me of Don Chandler, former Consul General to China, and his Three Rules on Chinese Toasts:

Rule 1: Belabor the obvious;

Rule 2: Use every cliché known to man; and

Rule 3: It is impossible to overdo Rules 1 and 2.

At the meeting which precedes a banquet in Shanxi, we are sitting with all the Queso Grandes of the Province, from the Party Secretary down through all the Governors, Vice Governors, Executive Vice Governors, etc., five or six of them, all in Western garb. After a fashion. When the meeting is over, Ned Hall says to me, "I've finally figured out the official Chinese fashion guideline: have your socks match your shirt." He's right.

Current winner in the "best excuse at dinner" contest: "I'm sorry, but my doctor has put me on a low insect diet."

At a restaurant in Beijing I have something called "Green Peony Tea," which is—sure enough, tea—except all the tea leaves have been exquisitely sewn together to resemble a peony flower. It's really wonderful, especially as it gracefully opens in the hot water, so I decide to try to find some. Later, during the inevitable one-and-a-half-hour flight delay at some provincial airport, I ask my smart, young Chinese associate, Flora Zhao, about this wonderful tea, describing it in rapturous detail. She says, somewhat dismissively I feel, "Oh, that's just something Chinese do to cheat Americans; no Chinese people buy that."

On our first morning in Tianjin, capital of Shanxi Province, I get up early, leave the hotel, and go jogging down the street. Soon I come to a large building with "National Coal Museum" blazoned in big letters across its roofline. It has a fenced front courtyard, and a small crowd is gathered outside the fence looking in. Peering intently inside as I run past, I see that in the courtyard are probably sixty otherwise normal-looking couples—boys with boys, boys with girls, girls with girls—in business attire doing a very sedate and serious jitterbug to the broadcast strains of loud rock and roll (I think) music in Chinese (I'm sure). At 6:30 a.m. Nobody had any coal, and Dick Clark was nowhere to be found.

Shanxi does have a great black vinegar, of which the locals believe you should take a tablespoon a day for your health. I remark on how much I like it, so they give me four beer bottle-sized bottles to take home. So they won't break, I put them in my rucksack that I carry on the plane. But one bottle leaks. I get to Hawaii and start through customs. It's been a long trip. I'm tired. I'm not home yet. The young woman in the uniform of the Customs Service starts poking through my bag, puckers her nose, and says, "Eeeuw, what's that?"

"Well, either the black vinegar leaked or it's my dirty underwear," I remark, unwisely it turns out, as she then decides to inspect every shred of my luggage. One more reason not to have a smart mouth.

When I get home, China still follows me.

Toward the end of a banquet we are having in New York City for a visiting delegation from Fujian, conversation lags a bit, as has been known to happen; so your son, ever the cheerful host, asks each of the three Chinese officials there to name the best book each has read this year. There is much animated conversation among the three of them, and a bit of laughter. Then one responds that for all three it's the same book: *Selected Works of Deng Xiaoping, Volume Two*, but actually they haven't read it yet. Each one has a mandatory two-week training period already scheduled to go off to a class and read it, and they're all positive it will be the best book they've read this year. I decided not to ask about movies.

A delegation of Chinese officials visits us in Washington, so we take them to a restaurant called the Sichuan Pavilion on K Street for the obligatory banquet/toasting/picture taking. We start to order, but the waiter says something like, "You were here last night. I know what you'll like, trust me." Well, we weren't, but anyway we do. The third dish: sea slugs. Damn, I didn't even know you could get them here and now I'm paying for them. Paul says supportively, "Gee, in China we're always *glad* to see sea slugs, because then at least you know what you're eating."

**Swaziland. Huh?**

I flew here because Roger Sant, our ever-accommodating Chairman of AES, has a friend who has a friend at U.S. Agency for International Development. One or the other of these friends said to Roger, "They really need a big coal plant in Swaziland. They are currently dependent on the South Africans for all their electricity. You should send somebody there to check it out."

Well, guess who is the official AES "checker-outer"? Yeah, me. So I get on an airplane, or several airplanes serially, and with about as much prep time as it has taken you to read this paragraph, I head off.

What an interesting surprise. This is not an "elephants at the watering hole, cheetah resting in the branches of the thorn tree" kind of place. Boy, do I ever know squat about Africa. The geography resembles a cross between Northern California and northern New Mexico, rocky and hilly but not mountainous. It's definitely not quaint or picturesque; native garb appears to be dark suits, white shirts, and ties. The native pastime is shopping in one of two major shopping malls in downtown Mbabane, said malls being complete with a video rental, a jeans store, and a Kentucky Fried Chicken. Native cuisine, as far as I can figure, is either steak Diane, corn on the cob, or curry (yes curry, go figure). You can drink the water, their roads are paved and busy with cars and trucks, motorcycles and bicycles, and there's hot water for the showers. Government works fine and is run by a king. It surely doesn't fit any mental picture of Africa I've ever had. They also play golf and take credit cards.

My favorite three Swaziland businesses (observed as one drives along the road but unfortunately not visited):

» Cuddle Puddle Hot Springs
» Swaziland Tattersalls (maybe the Brits stayed here too long)
» Swaziland Gearbox and Diet Centre

For the first couple of days, people kept referring to so-and-so as "from RSA." I couldn't get it—Royal Swazi Archives? Royal Swazi Architects? Royal Swazi Assassins? But there was no thread of connection between the references. On the third day I finally tumbled to the fact that it meant Republic of South Africa. And just so you'll be able to avoid another embarrassing gaffe, Johannesburg is always referred to as Jo-burg. So there. Of course that one is easier.

Even the scandals seem charming. While I was there it came to light (somehow) that ten years ago a unit of the Swazi government had invested in three commercial vessels, duly named *Swazi Queen*, *Swazi Princess*, and *Swazi* something else, at the behest of a firm (American) called Boulder Shipping Company from that well-known US nautical center of the same name in Colorado. They had set up a separate government corporation to control this venture: "Swazi Mer." The venture got in trouble, was provided a loan guaranteed by the Swazi government, and then the ships disappeared and the $2 million guarantee was called. Understandably embarrassing and funny, at least to us visitors. Remember, this is a totally landlocked country, although a good deal closer to the sea than Boulder, Colorado (see above). I suggested that one way to recoup the losses was to print up and sell T-shirts with the legend: "Royal Swazi Navy—Who Took Our Boats?" Several officials to whom I broached this suggestion seemed distinctly chilly to the idea, however, so I went back to power plants. This military stuff will only take you so far. As both of us have found out in our careers.

Love and kisses,
Bob

# six

# watermelon and rolled pants

August 1994

Dear Dad,

I keep wondering if these places that I go to are really as odd and interesting as they seem. I try not to think about the fact that it just may be me that's odd. Of course, then I look at the fact that Michael Jackson is married to an heir of the King—surely they aren't going to live in Graceland!—and I think that it could just be humanity in general. To wit, here is a summary of experiences from my latest two-week sojourn into the middle of the Middle Kingdom.

We started with a two-day business meeting with all our Asia folks in Beijing to discuss strategies in various countries, tell stories, complain, etc. On one of the nights of our conference, we all went to dinner at a Chinese restaurant, of course, which had a big TV/karaoke setup—the music videos, the words on the screen, the microphones, the whole works. This actually turns out to be a pretty good way to integrate folks who don't work together, and who don't come from the same countries. For example, when "Take Me Home, Country Roads" is played, we've all trained ourselves to say "Bhubaneswar," the location of our proposed project in India, instead of "West Virginia." Works fine. But the video portion of these—I think the laser discs are actually a Chinese production as there's no way these babies could have been pirated from Hollywood—is particularly fetching. For example:

&raquo;   The video of "Jambalaya," the classic Hank Williams tune celebrating Cajun life in Louisiana, has some interesting transcriptions from the song; it refers to "fillet gumbo" when as we all know it's "file gumbo," a reference to the file powder made from the sassafras root and used as a thickener. But this is almost a technical mistake, compared to spelling "pirogue" as "piro" and, even worse, confusing "bayou" with "bay-o." (Perhaps the pernicious influence of Harry Belafonte—no, that was "day-o." Never mind.) But the oddest part of all is that the whole thing is shot in the middle of a big courtyard with a bunch of young Chinese men and women playing around in heavy snow. Now the last time I checked heavy snow wasn't a characteristic of much of Louisiana, let alone the Cajun portion. Ah, me.

&raquo;   The "Country Roads" video, previously mentioned, features the Sydney Harbour Bridge and the Opera House prominently in the background.

&raquo;   My favorite of all was the one of a classic Chinese song featuring solely and exclusively an attractive young Chinese woman, at the beach, wearing a relatively skimpy bikini and sort of writhing about while the camera shot her closely from various, somewhat personal, angles. I was for some reason more interested than average in the excellence of the camera work (probably my guy training) so about halfway through the song I asked one of the only Chinese persons there who wasn't singing what the song was about. He said, "It is traditional song about missing your country when you are far away from home; when you die you want to be buried at home and have your blood water the ground of your homeland."

Of course, when one thinks of one's homeland, the image of a girl in a bikini always appears. Or at least it will for me in the future.

Here are some incidents from a four-day trip through northwest Hunan Province, accompanied by my fearless Chinese associate, Flora

Zhao, looking at hydro sites:

Rural Hunan is actually picture-book pretty: terraced green rice fields, farmers in straw hats, misty rugged hills in the background, squash climbing all over everything and highlighting the greenness with its bright yellow blossoms. But, ugh, the roads. Every day we drove about 240 kilometers on dusty, twisting, mountainous back roads, some paved, some oiled, some dirt, all up and down and zigzag. All the roads cluttered with people on bikes, motorcycles, small tractors, trucks, pulling water buffalo, buses with stuff on top, people carrying stuff, all with the assumption that the exact center of the road is the only place to be. And these all serve our driver as targets to honk at, swerve around, and swerve back into his "lane" (the middle) after passing. Rewards are given for highest acceleration, sharpest deceleration, and most near misses. Our driver won all the awards and is moving on to the Provincial finals, where it is expected he'll go to the Nationals. Our kidneys and lower backs in general go with him, since they no longer function for us.

Watermelons. Watermelons. Watermelons are everywhere in Hunan. For sale at *every* roadside stand. Usually with nothing else. Getting served pitchers of watermelon juice (mostly without seeds) to go with your Chinese banquet is a new and not bad experience. Sort of offsets the nasty liquor mao-tai, although nothing really can. Watermelon for breakfast, lunch, and dinner does not grow on one. At some point on our journey someone asked us if there was watermelon in the US. I thought, *Not anymore; they've all emigrated to Hunan.*

Specialties of the province are peppers (good), lotus root (actually quite good), bloated chicken feet (not so good), pig stomach (so-so), and rice lees from making rice wine (like a slightly alcoholic, loosely constructed rice pudding; not bad). No insects so far, but there is a drink made from birds' nests called, beguilingly, "Bird's Nest." Did I mention watermelon?

Every citizen of Hunan Province appears to have been recently issued a large load of building material, mostly red bricks, but also occasionally cement blocks, paving stones, gravel, sand, roof tile (curved), roof tile (flattish), and less often wood, usually in small strips. Fleets of trucks have deposited these materials in the road in front of every house, sometimes in neat stacks, but more usually, especially for the red bricks, in jumbled piles. These industrious citizens, confronted with this windfall, are busy putting it to use. About every third building you see is under construction. Probably need more room to store the watermelons.

It is very hot in Hunan, reportedly 40° centigrade. Yes, I've even learned to convert that one. It's 104°F, although converting steam pressure in kilograms/square centimeters into lbs/square inch still eludes me.

Because there is no or precious little air-conditioning, it is an interesting time to be clambering around dam sites, sweating like a Westerner. The Chinese complain about the heat, but then they don't seem to sweat much. One intriguing and somewhat disconcerting tactic used by the men: when you sit down to have a meeting, most of them take their long pants and nonchalantly pull them up over their knees, creating ersatz shorts. These then usually reveal with more clarity than is really necessary thin nylon socks and clunky business shoes. Ah well, development first, fashion second.

Useful observations: several of the Chinese I met in Cili County (my associates informed me) had a long discussion about whether I was really an American or not. They were concerned that my nose wasn't big enough. "Big noses" is probably one of the more polite terms applied to Americans. I don't know if cosmetic surgery is indicated or if I should just wave my passport around convincingly and ask how the Yankees are doing.

The strangest conversation of the trip took place in Lixian, at 7:30 in the morning, sitting in the lobby of the hotel, which was hot and dark as the electricity and water were both out. A young man in a red silk shirt comes up to me and says in what I take to be very good, unaccented Chinese (altho how would I know, really?), "*Ni-hao.*" (Hello.)

Me: "*Ni-hao.*" (One of the few Chinese words I know.)

Red Shirt: (In English) "Where are you from?"

Me: (In English) "Washington, D.C."

Red Shirt: (In English) "Oh, you speak Chinese."

Then he walks off.

Old Mosquito Teeth (Who? Read on.) and I stay at the Lixian Grande: After dinner at Cili our second evening (more warm beer, more toasts with herb wine), we took off for Li county and another jolting, bumpy, rocky, dusty three-hour ride. We got there about 9:30 and were informed that the original hotel picked out for us wasn't so good, so they were putting us in the best one and had even bumped several people to get us in. Some parts of the command economy still work. But first we had to meet with, and be formally welcomed by, the County Chief. OK, another rectangular meeting room with plush armchairs (of a sort) lining the walls, nothing in the center of the room, little tables in front of each set of chairs, bedecked as usual with tea cups, an ash tray, some fruit, etc. Guess what kind of fruit. And speeches, frequently videotaped for God-knows-what reason, along the lines of "We welcome you to X location, we want to sincerely cooperate with you on this project, we hope this cooperation will be very successful," to which one responds, "We're very happy to be here, we're very sincerely interested in this project, we look forward to discussions about it and to successful sincere cooperation." Very formulaic. Key differences this particular evening:

» Someone had taken all the seating cushions out of the armchairs so you sat down about three inches lower than normal and on the hard wooden inside bottom of the chair on which the cushion used to sit. I asked Flora if this was some exotic regional design for armchairs, but she said, "No, they take the cushions away when it's hot." And hot it was with no air-conditioning, just an ineffectual fan.

» The ever-present ceremonial watermelon, about ten pieces per person, was all over the little tables along with hot tea, yep, hot tea. Now there's what you need on a warm August evening. A parenthetical foot-note: tea is not the best thing they make in northwest Hunan. Actually, it is made from the middle and top leaves of the dust bush seen growing along much of the roadside. Picked by hand, these succulent young leaves are not further treated (no harsh chemicals, no man-made additives) before being put in your cup along with hot water. The result, a cup of tea with a pleasing sheen of dust on top, muddy brown leaves at the bottom, and a clearish liquid the color of the insoles of your shoes whose taste has the sluggish tang of mud. I say this with regret, because I thought I'd never meet a Chinese tea I couldn't drink, but the famous "Dust Tea from Hunan" is not very swell. Even Flora didn't like it. End of parenthetical note.

After everybody is introduced we all sit down, but instead of the speeches, everybody—at least all of the men—immediately reaches down and pulls their pants up over their knees, including even the County Chief. Then everybody grabs a piece of watermelon and starts chomping away, spitting the seeds on the floor between their now mostly bare legs. I begin to wonder if I'm not making a serious cultural faux pas by not pulling my pants up over my knees and spitting watermelon seeds on the floor. Then I notice with relief that Flora is spitting her seeds into her hand, then daintily transferring them to an ashtray. However, she's wearing shorts, so she's no help with the pants question.

After enough watermelon is consumed we exchange ritual speeches and are escorted off to our rooms in the hotel. This is an experience. The room does have an air conditioner, a "through the window" type. Only in this case it really is. A rectangular hole has been somewhat jaggedly cut in the window and an air conditioner installed. This isn't a precise piece of work, so the excess space has been filled with chunks of Styrofoam. At least on the top and one side. The other side just has a two-inch gap. A moth blunders through the gap and I chase it round the room. I guess I was afraid someone would catch it and try to feed it to me. The bed has no sheets, just very hard box springs. No, that's not right, it was so hard I doubt there were any springs, no mattress, and a yellow bedspread all folded up to use as a cover. In the bathroom there was a sink/toilet/tub but only one small hand towel-sized towel the thickness of a dishcloth. I began to wonder about taking a shower in the morning. The other key feature of the room was its windows. They extended in an unbroken set of panels all across the front of the building, and the individual walls separating the room of one guest from the next stopped about two inches short of the window. This provided one an unparalleled opportunity to eavesdrop on the television tastes of the guy to your left and the spirited conversation of the man and woman in the room to your right. Eavesdropping when you don't know the language turns out not to be so interesting, however.

After some time I went to sleep, but at 5:30 the air conditioner sticking through the window cut off and it rapidly got hot in the room. I got up to see if I could fix it, found the light switch, turned on the light, but no light came on. Because I'm an Electricity Professional (Do Not Try This In Your Home) I began to suspect we had a larger problem. I waited to see if the electricity was going to come back on (this is Step One in the Electricity Professional's Handbook), but after a while this got boring and it wasn't. Then I thought I'd go out and run, so I went to the bathroom, flushed, and then listened with dismay as the toilet began imitating a person gagging, coughing, hacking, and choking to death. I briefly wondered if I was confronting an electric toilet, but then I tried the tap and I found: no water.

*Well*, I thought, *this solves the riddle of the small towel*; you don't need to provide much of a towel when there's no water to wash with. I did contrive to use the thermos of hot water provided for tea to shave with instead. And then, otherwise unwashed but in clean clothes (one must keep up appearances, mustn't one) I went down into the dark, hot lobby to meet the county hydro people. Flora came down a few minutes later looking disconcerted and out of sorts. I asked her what was wrong (other than the obvious), and she said that in the limited light in her bathroom she had confused her toothpaste with her mosquito repellent—also a paste in a tube—and started to brush her teeth with the latter. "It didn't taste good," she said, which I took to be an understatement, "but no water." I told her that she should look on the bright side: no mosquitoes were likely to bite her teeth for the next several days. She seemed not so amused, but then the county officials showed up. They gave each of us a gift of our own package of Dust Tea, and took us next door for a breakfast of watermelon.

At one of the dinners in Cili, feeling expansive (perhaps too much warm beer?), I decided to deviate from my usual policy on Chinese toasts and compliment my hosts on the food, saying something like, "Boy it's great, lots of hot peppers and no insects." Just as I was ready to stand up, another dish came to the table (a bunch of chopped-up stuff), and Flora said to me matter-of-factly, "Steak."

"Why would they cut up a steak into such small pieces?" I asked, reaching for some.

"Not steak," she said, "snake." I decided to stick with the noodles. And the traditional form of a toast.

More unfathomable conversations (this one reported): Roger Sant (our Chairman) was meeting in Beijing with a senior official in the State Planning Commission or some such body, and noticed that the official had one of those fancy/trendy ties on with tennis racquets and tennis players on it. "Oh," Roger said, "you must be a tennis player." After suitable translation, the response was both a blank look and a verbal, "Oh?"

"Your tie has tennis racquets on it," Roger explained warmly.

"I never noticed before," said the official.

At a dinner in Beijing we found that someone had ordered the fried scorpions, which were served scattered all over a mound of rice noodles. They looked eerily like they were crawling all over the plate. Everybody ate one or two, including me; they don't taste like anything except fried crispy stuff, and they're small, about the size of the last joint of your little finger. Besides, it was a test. Someone at the table pointed out that I had said I didn't eat insects, so I had to respond that scorpions are in fact arthropods, not insects: eight legs, two segment bodies, etc. I also said a quick prayer that no one would find spiders on the next menu.

And finally—

Places I Would Have Liked To Visit In Beijing But Only Saw Advertised: Mr. Beef Seafood Restaurant, Ltd.

Commercial Products in China That May Not Be Ready for the Mass Western Market Yet: In Changsha, I saw a vending machine dispensing a Gatorade equivalent to drink after working out, named "Pocari Sweat." Probably technically accurate, but drinking sweat?? I think I'll stick to drinking birds' nests, although it's a close call.

Love,
Bob

## seven

# smiling french fries at bimbo's hamburger stand

December 1994

Dear Dad,

I've made a number of foreign trips lately, most all of them related to work but not all to China for a change. In many cases the most interesting things that arise relate to language. I'm eternally grateful to the Air Force Academy for the year of Spanish they taught me; that was maybe the only useful thing about that whole experience. Of course, I'm discounting the fun I had throwing up twice in one day during the two orientation flights in the jet trainers that the Academy organized my first summer there. This was set up as a big motivator for all us cadets and was probably better (in concept) than doing five hundred push-ups. Naturally, no airsick bags were provided because, of course, manly and gung ho Air Force Cadets love to fly and never get airsick. Except one.

To keep from making a real mess—they were very clear that if you ralphed in the cockpit you had to clean it up, and those cockpits were, as you remember, full of an infinite number of nooks, crannies, crevasses, etc.—it seemed important to be creative, and thus I ended up throwing up in my flight gloves. I suspect I presented a very strange picture: a slightly green young cadet, gingerly climbing out of the backseat of a T-33, carefully holding by their tops two gloves that had a clear resemblance to balloons. But they were not filled with air. As the only cadet of all the six hundred to barf on both the morning and the afternoon flights, I did begin to suspect that I was not to be the next Chuck Yeager—but I digress.

I made a particularly interesting trip to South America last month. The first stop was our plant in Argentina, located near a place called San Nicolás. San Nicolás is a town of about 100,000—small, Spanish, and very pleasant. And you can read the words on the signs! Wow! It's different from China! Of course the words are in Spanish, but you at least have a fighting chance. All our folks there got together Sunday evening at the house of the plant manager, Kerry Varkonda, for an Argentine barbecue called an *asado*.

Kerry was the plant manager at our Jacksonville, Florida plant before heading south, or more south, and is a very good guy. He explained to me that the ceremony really served the purpose of letting the men, who naturally are always in charge of this part—the roasting or grilling of the cow, complete with special recipes, secret marinades, particular types of wood, maybe special incantations, who can tell—stand around and tell stories and drink beer and red wine all afternoon. Made sense to me, and I was reluctantly willing to participate in this charming native ceremony. Eventually us guys have enough to drink, so the grilling gets declared as done, and everybody sits down and eats a lot of roasted red meat and a little salad made by the women. But, I noted gleefully, no snakes, no turtles, no insects. They did forget to tell me about a few of the details, like they really do cook the whole entire cow—the good parts first, the more exotic parts later—to wit, stomach, intestine, brains, and perhaps even less charming portions. I didn't inquire that closely.

As the sort of guest of honor, I naturally had to try all these things. Mmm, the brains and intestines and stomach and pancreas are not so good as the T-bones. Not as bad as camel hooves, maybe. Then I had a vision. There's an old Gary Larson cartoon showing little businessmen with briefcases being pooped out of the back end of a cow, and it's titled "The Birth of Advertising." I speculated about somebody in the late courses of an asado saying to himself, "Maybe this stuff would be better all ground up together . . . the Birth of Hamburger!" Having had this vision, I couldn't decide if I now liked hamburger less or more.

The next day I spent with Kerry at the plant, then in the late afternoon flew to Porto Alegre in Brazil. One of our AES guys met me and said that some coal suppliers wanted to take us out for a typical Brazilian meal. I said fine, and so we ended up eating lots of roasted red meat and drinking red wine, but this time there was no identifiable esophagus or bladder involved, at least not of the animal being grilled. The next morning we toured coal mines and power plants, then went to a ranch for a lovely Brazilian lunch of—yes—meat in the form, this time, of baby goat roasted on wood sticks over an outdoor fire by a bunch of guys standing around drinking a Brazilian beer called "Antarctica" and telling stories. I began to sense a pattern.

I flew on to São Paulo, commercial capital of Brazil and a huge city of thirty million residents that, as one of the people with me said, looked like "midtown New York City, but forever." We immediately went out for a typical meal at "the best restaurant in São Paulo," which featured, you'd be surprised to know, roasted red meat! Que sorpresa indeed-- I did begin to have an errant thought or two about chicken with peanuts.

At the asado in San Nicolás I ended up sitting at the end of the table with most of the women. "How could this be?" you ask. "Just luck," I reply. After all, I'd already stood around all afternoon getting smoke in my eyes with the men. Toward the latter part of the dinner, maybe around when they served the pituitary glands, we were all getting pretty chummy, so I started to ask about how, in Spanish, you spoke to your husband or boyfriend when you wished to use endearing words. Were there special individualized pet names you used or was there some generally recognized standard. Some suggestions followed: "Mi carita," "My dear one;" "Mi amorada," "My loved one;" "Mi cielo," "My heaven;" "Mi bombon," " My piece of candy." Then they got more interesting (or maybe more honest): "Mi bichita," not what you think it means, but instead "My little woman," or how about "Mi gordita" or "Mi flaca," which mean respectively, "My little fat one" and "My thin one." I couldn't get it clear if in the case where your true love was fat, you were supposed to call her thin, or whether being called fat (plump? rotund? Reubenesque? The translation is key) was OK. It seemed awfully risky to me.

But my real favorite was "Mi enano negro," "My black dwarf." I had to ask five or six times to make sure I was getting this right, since it didn't seem too politically correct to start with, but everybody swore it was the height of loveliness. Enchanted by these assurances, I have tried this endearment several times in my personal life and it works great—in Spanish. However, the results when translated are far less satisfactory, so I am giving real thought to going back to "My thin person," until and unless I start actually dating a midget. Then maybe.

---

From Brazil I went on to Peru. Lima was the big surprise hit of the trip. It's a warm, pleasant city on the ocean and reminded me of a combination of the best parts of LA and Tijuana. The people were very friendly, forthright, and happy to be Peruvian. I was sort of afraid there would still be evil terrorist guerrillas from the Sendero Luminoso ("Shining Path") running around blowing me up, even though their leader, Abimael Guzmán, had been captured about a year previous and put in six varieties of chains in a deep dungeon on an isolated island off the coast, but no such thing. At dinner the last night we were there we ate at a beachfront restaurant, the moon reflecting on the water, the Pacific Coast Highway equivalent behind us, running along some big bluffs fronting the beach. You could have been in Santa Monica if you blinked. I was finally able to try out my bilingual joke that I'd been saving (when you read it you may well ask, "Why?") on the Peruvians who were with us. It goes like this:

Q: Up until the remarkable capture of the Peruvian guerrilla chief, *que es la cancion mas popular de la fuerzas armadas Peruviano?* (What was the favorite song of the Peruvian army?)

A: "A Guzmán Is Hard to Find."

The Peruvians we were with thought it quite funny or at least they were polite. Ron Lumbra, the AES person with me who was in charge of Peru for us, wasn't as impressed. It's good to have honest associates. I suppose.

In Lima one of my purposes was to visit the group of hydro and thermal power plants we were considering purchasing, since: 1) bids were due soon, 2) it was a not small amount of money ($300 million or greater, all equity), and 3) we had two interesting (some would say curious) choices for partners. One of these was Houston Industries, the parent of Houston Lighting and Power, our very first customer but not an especially enlightened utility. In fact, during the most recent political/congressional debates on the issue of further opening the US electrical system to more competition, they led the self-characterized "Just Say No" group and with no apologies to Nancy Reagan.

The other potential partner was Electricité de France, the gigantic, seriously nuclear national French utility that probably would adopt the same motto ("*Seulement Dit Non*") in debates within the European Union about the same subject. We, of course, consider ourselves quick, non-bureaucratic, and very adaptable and so sort of look up our noses at these big guys. However, they do have plenty of money and people. And better language skills. Anyhow, you can see why I at least was nervous, although the thought of joint venture board meetings in Paris did have some attractiveness. "Another croissant, monsieur?"

On the morning in question I piled into the backseat of a car from ElectroLima (the company selling the assets) along with Ron and a smart interpreter named Tania Diaz. In front were a driver and our tour guide, a talkative but engaging engineer named Carlos Marchand. We fought our way through the downtown Lima traffic to the outskirts and then into the stark brown mountains outside of Lima to see our first hydro plant named Moyopampa. Along the way we carried on voluble discussions, bilingually and with much hand waving, and gesturing, and some diagramming. Fortunately Carlos had had the presence of mind to bring along a pad and a pencil. We talked about such neat stuff as system load factor, load duration curve, summer vs. winter peak, and availability vs. capacity factor. All of this may sound like electro-babble, and to some extent it is, but it's also how utility people make sure they're really dealing with other utility folk, not some horrible intruder like an environmentalist or regulator. It's sort of like dogs sniffing each other—no, that's too graphic—but it's a ritual we all practice and enjoy. A bit harder in Spanish, especially since Tania had great colloquial English having lived in LA but did not have the technical jargon to keep up.

Pretty soon we were all getting pretty comfortable with each other; we all knew the secret handshake, we were all in the same fraternity, just different chapters, and I was getting increasingly sure of my Spanish. So I said, "Que es el problema technical mas grande de los plantas?" which almost anyone can tell means, "What is the largest technical problem with the plants?" The engineer looked at me and then burst off with something about *cojinete* and *eje* and so forth. I looked blank, and Tania looked cross-eyed, and Ron, ever cool, looked diplomatic.

Carlos repeated the same thing, more forcefully and with more animation. This is the same strategy we all use with foreigners: just say the English louder, maybe they'll get it. Tania confessed to us that she hadn't a clue as to how to translate all this. Finally the engineer looked at us, clearly piqued. Gee, we were doing so well up to this point. Then he made a circle with the thumb and forefinger of his left hand and stuck his forefinger of his right hand into the circle, while again saying something about *cojinete* and *eje* but adding *lubricado forzado*, which even I could see was "forced lubrication." It seemed to me that we were talking universal symbols here and I couldn't figure out why he was so mad as to start making nasty signs at us. I restrained my natural impulse to reply in kind, and instead we resorted to digging out the Spanish dictionary and found—hooray!—that *cojinete* means "bearing" and *eje* means "shaft" and that the *turbinas* have bearing problems because the forced lubrication system is poorly designed. I was quite relieved, I must say, and truly delighted to add these useful words to my vocabulary, as well as the illustrative hand symbols for them.

Coming back in the afternoon from seeing the various plants, Ron and I get Tania to take us to her favorite fast food place for the best *hamburguesas* (obvious what that means) in Lima. This turns out to be a place oddly named Bimbo's, but not populated with any well-built blondes with vacant looks and short skirts that I can see. It is full of young junior high school girls all eating hamburgers the size of cantaloupes and smoking ferociously so they can look cool. Maybe they all aspire to be bimbos. We go to order, and they have two kinds of French fries: one normal—*"papas fritas"*—and one stamped out in the shape of a round "happy face." I am intrigued by this so I step up boldly to order same and, using my best pronunciation say, *"Papas smee-ley,"* since that's what they're called, except it's spelled "papas smile." I get a blank stare from the nice young counter girl.

*"Papas smee-ley,"* I intone again, trying for a non-gringo accent, except there aren't any "r's" to trill. More of same blank look.

Tania giggles and then overrides my order, saying, *"Papas smile."* (Pronounced "smile" just like in English).

"Oh, phooey," I say. "That's cheating; besides, *cojinete* to you, too." And the potatoes aren't that terrific, but the hamburger truly does live up to its billing.

I was puzzled in Lima about one thing, and I asked a lot of people but got no good answers. I couldn't find the beans anywhere or get anybody even to admit that those nasty frozen green things you and Mom used to serve us at every other meal actually came from around there. I was expecting a big bronze statue of one somewhere in "Bean Square."

My favorite (but most puzzling) news item was in the newspaper in Lima the first evening we were there. It was a picture showing Nelson Mandela receiving an award from the former Secretary General of the UN, Pérez de Cuéllar, who is a Peruvian (hint as to the picture placement and why it was even in the paper). Bill Clinton is in the middle of the picture applauding. The award is called "Premio Africa" (First Africa? Premier Africa? I couldn't quite get it) and, most interesting, the President is referred to not as a really big deal, but *"el mandatorio nortreamericano."* What can this mean? You had to have a gringo at the ceremony? Clinton couldn't be anything else and thus was forced to be North American? I'm baffled. At least they didn't call him a dwarf.

———

OK, now quickly back to the US and yet another interesting Chinese incident, just so you won't think I'm no longer paying attention. About a month and half ago there was a big delegation of big cheeses (I am sad that I have not learned to say this in Chinese) from Beijing—the regional government, not the central government—who wanted to sign an agreement for (surprise!) a power plant with us. As we slowly get smarter about this stuff we realize that a trip to the US is an expensive perk for any Chinese official, so they feel better or maybe get more credit if they come home with agreements for Westerners to come and invest money in China, even nonbinding ones (the agreements, not the Westerners). In fact, one group insisted that we sign the same agreement again that we'd signed in China a month earlier. But hey, we're easy, we signed it. At least we think it was the same agreement.

Anyway we got a sudden call saying, "You must come to San Francisco and sign this on Sunday instead of going to New York next week as previously planned." And the call came on Friday. So me and my faithful companion Flora Zhao, teeth now free of bugs, agreed and flew out Sunday morning for the ceremony and the inevitable accompanying banquet, for which Jennifer [my lovely sister-in-law] helped us pick out the restaurant. We went to the same one she and David [my brother] had the wedding dinner in, if you recall. Of course, we were sponsoring the banquet and thus paying for everything, but the good news is we got to set the menu.

We get to the cheap motel near the San Francisco airport and check in, and Flora gets on the phone to finalize stuff. She talks a long time, gets more and more agitated, and then says to me, "Problem."

"What problem?" I ask idly.

"Big guys can't sign today," she says.

"What!" I stomp around the Days Inn, muttering imprecations like, "I fly my tail out here for five hours on a perfectly good Sunday," and so on and so on. I calm down and say, "Well, it must be a political emergency; maybe Deng Xiaoping died and we weren't told. Maybe someone's kid was in a car accident and he had to fly home suddenly." I'm being too harsh; these are responsible professional and civic officials. I'm sure there's a good reason, etc.

"So," I say to Flora, "Why can't they sign? Where did the big guys have to go?"

"Oh," she says, "Shopping. But they still want to eat dinner with you if we can give them a ride to San Francisco."

We salvaged things by calling Mark Woodruff, the very capable guy running our San Francisco project, and importuning him to show up on Monday at the signing ceremony and sign for us. He was initially nervous, of course, but I assured him:

1) We all look the same so substituting one of us for another won't matter much;

2) Whatever we're signing isn't legally binding;

3) Since he can't read Chinese he won't know what he's signing, but this is usually the case with us anyhow. And even sometimes when the documents are in English.

So on Monday he does go to the trade fair and even finds the right group of folks plus an interpreter (a nice young Chinese woman still working earnestly on her English). The Chinese keep him hanging around for more than two hours, hoping he'll buy something, but I guess he didn't need any ceramic ashtrays shaped like Santa Claus. Or at least he didn't need a gross of them, as this was the minimum order. Then they got ready for the actual signing. They are all standing in front of the inevitable big red banner, but first they couldn't find the right agreement to sign, then everybody had to rearrange places, etc.—you get the picture. Finally the young interpreter leans over to Mark and the AES people and utters an emphatic remark that has rapidly become an internal company classic: "Is very mess." Sort of summed it up for me, yes sir.

Love and kisses,
Bob

## eight

# scorpions from the kingdom of womanhood

April 1995

Dear Dad,

I just got back from a trip to both China and Singapore, where we have a recently established an office covering all of Asia except China. The visits were productive (except when a longtime Chinese partner told us to jump in the lake) and the rest of it continually fascinating, even to a desensitized traveler such as I.

I hadn't been to Singapore for five years, and I'd just like to confirm that it's still a LONG WAY from San Francisco. You get in the plane about midnight California time and then you fly and fly. And fly. And fly. I guess you get my point. And it stays dark because you're going with the sun. Wait, that sentence didn't make sense. Eventually I couldn't sleep anymore so I wandered back to the galley and was promptly offered a "snack" by one of the Singapore Airlines stewards. It turned out to be a package of three finger sandwiches: one with cream cheese and chives; one with ham; and one, surprisingly, filled with thick slices of carrot and celery, hold the mayo. As I ate it anyway—there's not much to do on a *really long* airplane flight—I thought groggily that they shouldn't be called "finger sandwiches" because how else would you eat them other than with your fingers? So it's redundant, or alternatively, they're never made with fingers for filling so the name is misleading. Oops, I correct myself; maybe they would be in China.

Singapore is a lovely, clean, and orderly city, but it also has some of the characteristics of a giant shopping mall run by the Nazis. And boy, they're very serious about the rules in Singapore, and there are lots of them.

Examples:

» Chewing gum, as a pastime or as an article of commerce, is NOT ALLOWED. You can't buy it anywhere, and you can't chew it, either. Our folks there said that they went to a concert recently—Phil Collins was in town—and all the Westerners were sitting around together, but unlike the old days when they would be sharing a marijuana cigarette, instead they were passing around sticks of gum and, and . . . even chewing it! Talk about risky behavior! I remembered the small package of Dentyne in my luggage when I heard this story and wondered if I were about to become a GUM FELON and whether this would elicit as much media interest as a caning. Then I wondered if they caned you for being a gum felon.

» If your driver's license has been issued within the last year, you are obviously a new driver and you have to put big Day-Glo orange triangles prominently on the front and back of your car to warn other people of your novice status. Of course if you're from overseas where licenses are reissued from time to time as they expire, you can show up in Singapore with a recently issued license. The wife of one of our people did just that. She's a Yale Law School graduate who has been driving for rather a while. She argued that she really wasn't a novice and in fact had been safely piloting cars about for fifteen years. Rules are rules in Singapore, however. Eventually she gave up, put the stupid triangles on the family car, and then just to show them, promptly went out and banged into a set of guardrails. Now it seems that other Singapore drivers give this car especially cautious treatment.

» The television is carefully censored. *Baywatch* was considered far too stimulative for the average Singaporean to watch. In case you haven't seen it, as I for some reason haven't, although now that I know it's banned in Singapore I plan to watch it religiously. Well, maybe "religiously" isn't the right word. I don't think it has Heather Locklear in it or Pamela Anderson, though I'm still trying to find out who they are. The show consists largely of beautiful lifeguards with remarkable bodies, female and male, running up and down a beach in bathing suits in California. Sure sounds seditious to me. My associates point out, however, that as a substitute one can watch a TV program called *Models Inc.*, which has six beautiful and well-endowed young men and women sharing a house on the California beach and frequently finding it necessary (it's probably in the "Model's Handbook") to . . . yes, run up and down the beach in bathing suits. Plot and characterization are equivalent to *Baywatch* and Heather and Pam maybe aren't in this one, either.

WHEN YOU'RE AWAY FROM HOME, DON'T ACT LIKE IT: According to the *Straits Times*, the Singapore newspaper, the Sultan of Johor, a Malay ruler in southern Malaysia, owns six Harley-Davidsons (and an eleven-seater airplane with lambskin seats). It's good to be the Sultan. His favorite bike is a turquoise-colored, chrome, customized Electra Glide 1340, which he rides while wearing a gold helmet and a gold vest. He entertained the Singapore chapter of HOG (Harley Owners Group) who rode north from Singapore to his palace at Batu Pahat. This largely expat group, all mounted on big Harleys, first took a ride through the Malaysian countryside, which was described by a less than enthusiastic reporter as one of "crushing monotony and stupefying boredom." I interpreted this to mean she didn't like it. She also pointed out that Muslims such as the Sultan are offended by the idea of pork, but the Sultan didn't notice the symbolism, and for some reason neither did any of the HOGs. A good time was said to have been had by all, except the reporter.

THE EMPIRE STRIKES BACK: Guess what this is a list of? Marina Bay, Lavender, Novena, Braddell Heights, Newton, Orchard, Somerset, Lakeside, Buona Vista (spelled that way), Commonwealth, Redhill, City Hall, Raffles Place, Chinese Garden, Queenstown, Outram Park. Give up?

These are the names of some of the stations on the Singapore subway. Pretty neat and anglophilic, I'd say. There are also Chinese and Malay names, but not nearly so many.

---

THE TIGER BALM GARDENS LIVE! On Sunday my plane didn't leave Singapore until early afternoon so I took the opportunity in the morning to revisit a scene from my childhood. I don't know if you remember, but in 1958 you took all us unsuspecting kids to Tiger Balm Gardens, maybe the one in Hong Kong (there are two). Both were built in the 1930s by the Singaporean millionaire Aw Boon Haw, who earned his fortune from Tiger Balm ointment, a cinnamon-smelling paste or lotion said to cure anything (headache, stinky feet, the heartache of psoriasis) if you just rub it on the afflicted portion of your anatomy. I've been back to the one in Hong Kong, and it's fallen on rather hard times. The paint is fading, and it is surrounded, in typical Hong Kong fashion, by high-rise buildings that surely weren't there the first time we visited it.

But the one in Singapore, now that's another story: it's been turned into an amusement park. Let me quote to you from the promotional material: "Haw Par Villa [for some unknown reason they've changed the name, but they freely acknowledge that it used to be Tiger Balm Gardens. I don't get it—Haw Par Villa doesn't seem to me an improvement] stands as the only Chinese mythological theme park in the world. A theme park where the theme happens to be salvation and damnation." Or as another ad puts it: "See Chinese legendary characters and heroes come alive. Sail into the belly of the Dragon and witness exquisite tortures in the Chinese underworld." That is true. The whole place is a bunch of life-size (and bigger) plaster statues painted in very bright colors and arranged in tableau, wherein there is no sparing representations of blood, cutting off arms and legs, shooting folks with arrows, ripping them open, stabbing, burning, and disemboweling them, and other pieces of similar exquisiteness and wholesome family entertainment. It's really folk art to a wild Chinese degree. There are English signs for most of the tableau, so you wander around from set to set, initially trying to make sense of it but finally—because so many of the references are to Chinese legends that as a Westerner I've never heard of—just gawking at the color and the carnage. It's a wonderful and wacky antidote to the rather tightly controlled society outside the gates. For example, I learned:

» Of the "Eight Immortals," a famous group of semi-deities you can call on for help in tough situations, only one is a woman (no surprise there) and each has a special gift or characteristic. Most are predictable: "The Beautiful," "The Strong," "The Wise." But two of them I liked especially: "The Witty" and "The Entertaining." I tried to think of a special situation where these two guys would be helpful and came up with lots of situations, like a bad dinner party, for example.

» Old Aw Boon didn't care too much for women, or maybe it's just Chinese stories. Two exemplary captions from the park, in front of scenes with bare-breasted women behaving seductively toward a warrior:

"Spider demons, under the pretense of innocent women, invited Tang Seng and his disciples to stay as guests. Actually they intended to eat Tang Seng's flesh so that they could turn into immortals."

"These ladies were originally scorpions but after years of training and meditation were able to change and disguise as women. They collectively form the Kingdom of Womanhood."

» There does seem to be a nod or two toward updating the garden so it conforms to current Singapore "political correctness." As you ride in the rather tame boat ride inside the dragon tunnel ("sailing into the belly of the dragon"), on both sides of you are carefully labeled scenes of various eternal punishments for specific classes of offenders. You've got your murderers, thieves, and corrupt officials all having this or that part of their anatomy carved out, lacerated, or otherwise rudely treated, but you also now have "drug dealers" and "journalists who write slanderous or deceptive things," and both get about equally ugly processing. Got to have your priorities straight.

As I was leaving the park I saw my favorite sign, which I wanted somehow to take home and display prominently on stately occasions like testifying before Congress: Legends and Heroes Theatre Closed Due to Technical Failure.

But on to China. You probably read that the US and China have resolved, at least on paper, their intellectual property rights issues. US companies were legitimately concerned with Chinese pirating of trade-marked or copyrighted material—CDs, videos, etc.—and it was a serious problem. But enforcement of the agreement is another issue. On the flight from Guangzhou to Wuhan, I was given a foil-wrapped package of the ubiquitous peanuts (Query: What would the peanut growers of the world do without the airlines? We'd probably all be drowning in peanuts) to eat with my mysterious can of red juice. Emblazoned across the front of the package, in both Chinese (I checked) and English was the legend: "Air Nuts." Does Michael Jordan know?

Paul Hanrahan, the guy who heads up our efforts in China, is moving to Beijing, at least that's the plan as soon as his house gets built. There have, however, been certain delays. The Chinese have discovered force majeure, the elegant Western legal concept that excuses contractual performance when unpredictable Acts of God (floods, hurricanes, etc.) make timely performance impossible. The Chinese interpretation is, as one might suspect, different than the traditional Western approach. Paul's contractor told him the house would be late in completion because of force majeure.

"What exactly happened," asked Paul, who hadn't seen any tornadoes in Beijing recently.

"Oh," came the reply, "Chinese holidays."

Yes sir, you just can never tell when God will reach down and stick a few holidays on the calendar you didn't expect.

———

Maybe it's just the language. We're still trying to understand this one. One of our people was negotiating with the Guangdong Province Power Bureau, and they were complaining that electric demand had fallen off, in some cases by 30%. In electricity land where I live and work, this is an unheard-of decrease. When pressed—our first thought was they meant 3%—they confirmed the number and then explained that there was a new decree from Beijing that had caused a crackdown on vice, and they thought that was the problem. "Vice?" our guy asked. "I had no idea massage parlors used that much electricity." This apparently was untranslatable.

---

Naturally there were chicken fingers at most of the Chinese meals I ate, including one where the whole claw was presented, boiled but cold and yellowish white. Kind of looked like some dead person's hand. One of the irreverent expats at the table and I got into a discussion about what happened to all those chickens who had their feet cut off—did they have to go around in little chicken wheelchairs? Did they get the benefit of handicapped chicken parking? Why didn't the signs inside the subway cars say: "Please surrender this seat to a handicapped chicken should he or she request it."? We were amused, which only goes to show you at least one of us has been to too many of these dinners.

Love,
Bob

# nine

# the coriolanus effect is alive and well? oh, coriolis.

November 1995

Dear Dad,

You may think that these letters seem fixated for some reason on food, and that we don't do much else on these trips except eat. "When do you actually do any business? Or is this just one big boondoggle?" you may ask. Well, the business stuff isn't always all that interesting. Or maybe not interesting to anybody but us. Take Australia for example.

I first went there a couple of years ago, long before we ventured into more alien venues. At least I thought it wasn't alien. Someone assured me before we left that they speak English, the money works, and you don't get sick. This seemed sufficient for us to decide it was worth the trip. We have low standards.

So I got on an airplane and flew six hours to California, and then got on an airplane and flew six hours to Hawaii and took a day to visit our plant there. Then I got on an airplane and settled in for what I figured would be another six hours or so and I would be there. What time it would be and what day were not knowable to human beings since I was crossing the date line and that always changes things, and besides I was also crossing the equator and who knows what that could mean.

Well, Mr. Sophisticated World Traveler and Big Business Executive finally staggered off the airplane in Sydney seventeen hours later, which included for some reason a stopover in Bangkok.

"Goodness," I said to myself, "that was a long time to spend in a middle seat in coach. Good thing I had a magazine." One of our consultants in Perth (another five hours by plane from Sydney) informed me that as a matter of geography, if one stuck a needle into a globe at Perth and passed it directly through the center of the earth, it would emerge in Washington, D.C. This explains everything but Bangkok.

We were responding to an invitation to bid on the construction and operation of a new 300 MW coal plant to be built in Western Australia, one of the six states of Australia located, as luck would have it, in the western part of Australia. The State Electricity Commission of Western Australia, known not very euphonically as SECWA, had decided to try some of this "privatization" stuff. They hadn't actually heard of us, but they had sent an invitation to bid to Marubeni, the mammoth Japanese trading company who has sold us lots of Japanese power equipment, and Marubeni had in turn invited us in to the lead the team. We were pretty flattered by this.

The plant was to be in a small town south of Perth called Collie. It turned out to have no relation to a certain breed of dog known for rescuing little Timmy out of the abandoned mineshaft. Rather, it was the site of an extremely big, large, and maybe even gigantic open pit (Australians say "open cast" for no reason I could ever figure) coal mine, coupled with an existing 800 MW coal plant with no emission controls on it whatsoever, thank you very much. Not even the most rudimentary particulate controls—just burn the coal, whoosh the exhaust up the stack, and there you go. I do not think there are such plants in existence today in the US. It's pretty surprising. The new plant is to be much cleaner. Won't be hard.

The town is named for the coal, as that is about all that's there. How it got misspelled into "Collie" I cannot tell, nor again could anyone explain. Best explanation, late one evening at a bar: "It sounds a bit like coal, so it's close enough. This is Australia, mate. Another round?"

The business part consisted of:

» A several-hour presentation of our credentials to the SECWA senior folks in charge of this project and discussion thereof. What we had submitted so far was a detailed response of our qualifications—us, Marubeni, and Black & Veatch, the general contractor who Marubeni had also invited to participate. This had been good enough to get us invited to meet, which was good because they had received eighty-three responses to their initial proposal and invited in only eight of us. They used the oral interviews to limit the list to four groups, who would then actually be allowed to bid on the project. Given that (as it turns out) even just flying to Western Australia is challenging, and preparing a full bid is an expensive and complex task, this was a thoughtful process.

» Many meetings with potential local banks to try and figure out who we could get to help finance this project, mostly taking place in Sydney and Melbourne. We didn't have the dough and neither did SECWA. But that's what banks are for.

» More meetings with local contractors to get some idea of local costs, availability of skilled labor, materials, heavy equipment, etc.

» A meeting with the local labor union for power plants, because one of the requirements was to be that the plant was to use union labor. One notable peculiarity of Australia is that the work force is still about 54% unionized, probably the highest percentage in any capitalist economy. The US comparable number is less that 15% and going down.

» Meetings with the local and federal environmental regulators to get some idea of the rules and requirements and the process for obtaining the necessary permits.

OK, OK, OK, I told you it wasn't really that interesting. Here are the surprising parts for a dumb American:

1) Mistah Kurtz, he dead. Australia, he big. Maybe you knew that but I hadn't ever really registered it. Six times the size of Texas, world's biggest island, the seventh continent, etc. Flying back and forth between Perth in the west and Sydney (the commercial center) in the east was a long flight.

2) Australia, a tiny bit boring from a geologic point of view. As one Aussie said to me, "What can you say about a country where a bleeding nine hundred-foot rock is the biggest tourist attraction?" He had a point.

3) "Mate" is a very useful word, and it is really easy to pronounce, although most Americans have trouble with this. It is pronounced "might." When you pronounce it correctly the Australians love you and buy you another beer. Of course, when you say you're from the US they love you and buy you another beer. And sometimes when you don't say anything at all.

4) No rivers to speak of; the whole country is pretty flat, and pretty dry. The reason no one much lives in the outback, which probably includes 95% of the entire place, except for sheep and such, is due to the above dryness, sameness, and perhaps sheep-ness. Outback also includes kangaroos (many) and dingoes, which may be out-of-sorts large dogs or perhaps hyena wannabes; it's not possible to get a clear answer. They do not appear to eat kangaroos, preferring sheep. Ugh on both, say I. I couldn't find the platypuses. Platypusi? Platypusae?

5) Demographic peculiarities: there are six big cities dotted around the edge of the country; then the next largest cities tend to be ten or twenty thousand people. It's really odd. No Chattanoogas or Louisvilles or Albanys or Tacomas. And the small towns also are along the coast, unless centered on an economic activity, usually mining, in which case they are— you guessed it—next door to the mine.

6) They drive on the left-hand side of the street. Well, let's deconstruct that. They drive on both sides of the street, as do all people in cars in all countries. What this means, of course, is they drive forward on the left-hand side of the street. Well, no that's not right. Does that mean they drive backward on the   right-hand side of the street? And besides, which side of the street exactly is the left-hand side? I give up. You've been to the UK; it's the same. Also same as Japan but the Aussies have bigger cars. But what is more interesting is that the Coriolis effect has peculiar applications here. One of the first days I was in Perth I was going to a meeting with our lawyers in a big office building. I forgot to include this in the previous list of Boring Business Activities, but even in Australia they have

lawyers. Sad. Took a cab from our cheap hotel, found the place, started to walk through the revolving doors into the foyer, and just about broke my darn nose. Wow! I ran right into the glass door, because it was rotating the wrong way! Or at least the wrong way for me, and not the way they rotate here and in Europe. Who would have thunk? I knew about the water going down the drain in reverse whirlpool direction, but the revolving doors? Probably works on tornadoes, too, but fortunately I didn't see any. Don't know about Maypole dances. Or merry-go-rounds.

Here is some neat stuff. One of the first days I was there I didn't have much scheduled so I got our rental car and decided I would at least go look at the proposed site for this new power plant. Sometimes this tells you Important Business Secrets like: "Oh look, it's the location of a sacred native shrine and ancestral burial ground," but usually not. On the other hand, it was a nice day. This meant that I had to drive south of Perth about an hour and a half to the Collie area. Given that there are basically only a few places to go in Australia, and they're all on the coast, and they're all connected by the same one road (world's largest beltway), it wasn't hard to find. What I didn't count on was the wildflowers. It was spring in Australia, and there were fields and fields of wildflowers. Remember that Australia is mostly open ranch-type terrain, not even much cultivated. So you can have this. It was truly unbelievable. Not just some nice wildflowers growing beside the road, but acres and acres and acres of brightly colored flowers, like those pictures of Holland at tulip time but not tulips—freesia, bluebells, something like Indian paintbrush, etc. It turns out Australians know about this (how could they not?) and it is a feature only of the west. Tour buses make three and four day trips of it. But in the guidebooks I checked it gets at best one sentence. Goodness. Come see this sometime if at all possible.

The beaches are wonderful. And the whole country seems to have beaches, which again isn't surprising. See island notation earlier. There is a bit of concern about sharks, but I say don't go that far out into the water if bleeding heavily or carrying large chunks of raw tuna.

The people really are nice. The SECWA guys, in recognition that we have come a long way to present our credentials to them, take us out for dinner several times and even invite us one of the weekends we are there to play tennis with them at their club. They are smart and very good guys. I worry about whether I should beat them at tennis or let them win. It turns out this is not a problem as they clean my clock. Also there is decent beer, brewed in Australia, which we sit around drinking after the matches. As it should be.

They have terrific names for their beer, not tongue-in-cheek names like the American microbreweries— no "Old Overshoe" or "Pale Yale Ale." My two favorites were Redback Beer, named after a poisonous spider, and Dogbolter, named after I don't know what, but whose trademark was a big-headed chow-type dog.

The climate is so benign in Western Australia that you can grow both roses and hibiscus here. This may be my definition of horticultural heaven. You cannot, however, get the Sunday *New York Times* on Sunday morning, nor have I ever been able to find any doughnuts. Or Doritos. I suspect these latter two problems could be fixed, and maybe I don't care that much about the *New York Times* after all.

They don't have football either, but since I have never much liked football, I guess that isn't such a problem. They have a professional league that plays rugby, a sport that I have never understood. They also have something that has some of the characteristics of rugby, in that the players wear rugby shirts, have cauliflower ears, and don't wear helmets or padding. It seems to be played by a different set of rules, it is popular enough to have a separate pro league of its own, and it is perversely call "football," or more precisely "Australian rules football." I know this; it says so in the papers. Now the rest of the world says "football," but it really means "soccer" in American terms. When they say "rugby," they mean "rugby." To further confuse matters, the Australians also play "soccer," which they call Herman. Actually I don't know what they call it. All I can tell you for certain is that there is a lot of all three of these games on television and precious little basketball.

But I have seen more interesting things on television:

1) Dwarf tossing. This started in bars. It requires a dwarf (or possibly a midget, terminology is unclear) who is grabbed on each of his legs and arms by a larger person, four in total assuming a dwarf with the normal

number of appendages, and then in a coordinated motion the four throwers slide the dwarf along a table tilted upward at an angle. The laws of physics prevail; the dwarf goes airborne and then is caught by some more people once he comes down. Goal is distance, not altitude, thus in artillery terms angle of table elevation is pretty critical. There has been some bleeding heart liberal press criticism, which in turn has been answered by the spokesman for the League of Little Persons, who suggests the protectors of dwarf abuse butt out, since the dwarves in question are actually paid nicely for being tossed, and this beats working for Snow White in some diamond mine somewhere and will do fine until the remake of *The Wizard of Oz* comes along.

2) Female mud rugby. A bunch of people stand around a big square of dirt, while several of them use fire hoses to soak the whole area down. The two teams line up, generally consisting of big women wearing rugby shirts, as one would suspect. Someone kicks off. There is much running around and falling down. Soon everyone is covered, literally covered, head to toe, in mud. Coated in mud, actually. You might think from the title that this was some sort of sexy idea, see it in a seedy nightclub type of thing, which is, I believe, where female mud wrestling began. I of course have only read about the latter in the newspapers, never actually seen it, but I understand that the wrestlers wear bikinis, not rugby shirts and corduroys. Well, now I have seen female mud rugby in the flesh, and sexy is about the last thing that it is. After about one minute every player is totally brown—their pants, their shirts, their hair and faces. And they weren't exactly Playmate of the Month to start with. You can't tell one team from the other, and it also appears that the players can't tell who is on their team and who's the opponent. It all starts to look like one big muddy game of "Kill the Man (Woman) with the Ball." After a bit one begins to wonder what the point of it all is. It isn't titillating, it isn't a sport likely to qualify for the Olympics any time soon unless synchronized diving gets thrown out, and it isn't really much of a game. "It's Australia, mate, have another round."

Even though Australia doesn't superficially look like Mars, except for the peculiar sports, nonetheless as we go about our business we are very careful to try to fit in. Us Americans who have gone to business school and taken classes in international business have had it drummed into our heads over and over about how bad Americans are at international stuff. We don't speak the language, we aren't culturally sensitive, we assume everybody will do business the way we do, we assume everyone not like us is inferior, we dress funny, and we chew with our mouths open. You remember, the Air Force told you all the same things before you went to Japan. And we are counseled repeatedly to be more careful, more sensitive; to try and fit in; not to assume you know the right way to do things; to not be a clod, etc. Kind of makes you paranoid. Sometimes makes you act funny.

One of the first mornings we are in Australia, on our second trip there, Paul Hanrahan is with me. We have made the cut on the power plant competition and are one of the four groups to be allowed to bid. Paul will actually do the work on all this. He's an extremely capable Naval Academy and Harvard Business School product. We are staying at the Orchard Hotel, an average cheap commercial hotel in Perth. It's the first day there of our second visit. As you can understand, sleep is completely screwed up when you fly that far across that many time zones. We have agreed to meet for breakfast, but Paul comes down a bit ahead of us as he's up already.

He's about the only person in the dining room because it's so early. The young waitress comes over and says, "G'day," just like they all really do (it's not just Paul Hogan in *Crocodile Dundee*, they really talk that way). Paul orders cereal, and she duly notes this on her pad. He then asks the waitress if they have any fruit, because he'd like some fruit on his cereal. She says, hesitantly, "Yes, I think so, I'll have to check." She comes back out of the kitchen, says, "Yes, we have watermelon." OK, thinks Paul, I'm an American, I'm a guest in this country, we are culturally sensitive, we are eager to fit in and not be noisy or unattractive, I have been careful to wear a conservative business suit, not mismatching plaid shorts and a T-shirt saying "I'm with Stupid." So he says, "OK, that will be fine; thank you."

We come down a bit later, and Paul is sitting there eating a bowl of cornflakes with big pink chunks of watermelon on top of it. With me is another AES guy named Dennis Spencer, who now works at our Deepwater plant but used to work in Australia, actually in Western Australia where he ran a chemical plant for four years. His daughter still lives in Perth and is married to an Australian. He can actually say, "G'day" without feeling embarrassed. We sit down with Paul and get some coffee. I look at Paul, notice something (I am nothing if not Mr. Observant) and say, "I didn't know you liked watermelon on your cornflakes, Paul."

Paul regards us with a look of sincere superiority. "In Australia they eat watermelon on their cereal," he informs us. Sounds OK to me. In a place with "Watch Out for Kangaroos" as one of its principal road signs, anything could happen. And it's so important to fit in.

Dennis looks at him incredulously. "No they don't!" he says.

"Oh," says Paul, pausing to spit out a watermelon seed. "Well, actually it isn't very good on cereal."

I have this vision of the little nineteen-year-old waitress going back into the kitchen, saying, "I don't know, we have some Yank out here, wants watermelon on his cereal; he doesn't look dangerous. I think he's actually staying here; should we let him have some?"

Another recent trip with Paul: a big German construction company named Fichtner had come to visit us in Arlington, saying that they wanted to get into the business of building power plants. As we are always looking for such folks, since we really don't want Bechtel to take over the world, we were encouraging, although we did note helpfully that their current experience, which was in building ports and bridges, was probably not 100% transferable. They were not put off and encouraged us to come spend a day with them in their headquarters so we could get to know them better and be willing to include them in our next project.

Eventually we were in Europe so we arranged to go visit the company. They told us they were located in a small town called Pragsattel best reached by taking the local train from Mannheim. We asked sensibly, *How do we find it once we get off the train?* but were only told vaguely that we could find it. Didn't seem like great directions, but away we went. Actually I was a little crabby and anxious about the whole thing. We got on the train in Mannheim, rode for an hour, and got off at the small train station in Pragsattel. I had been quizzing Paul on the train about how we would locate the doggone offices, and he said reassuringly that we'd take a cab from the station, and if that didn't work we'd call them and ask them where they were. If we were really important, I groused, they'd offer to pick us up at the station in a limo. Paul remained unflappable.

We exited the station—no cabs. Pragsattel is a small clean German town. Also cold. However, about one half block away in this small village was the only building taller than two stories, the only building not looking cute and Germanic, and certainly the only building with the word "FICHTNER" emblazoned in two-story-high letters across its black glass fifteen-story presence. "OK, I guess we'll be able to find it," I allowed.

Skip the business stuff—we meet with a bunch of the Fichtner guys, in their very modern aluminum/ chrome/rubber/black leather offices. We discuss what they do, what we do, what we want from them, what would they be willing to do, etc. etc.—standard getting-to-know-you business stuff. Then it's time for lunch, so I have visions of going to some darling little German beerhouse-type restaurant and getting sausages and sauer- kraut or some other light meal. Instead they take us to their in-house dining room. It really does look like a restaurant. We sit down in an elegant black leather booth. The waiter comes over. He is an older gentleman, dressed in a tuxedo. He gives us menus, takes our drink orders (iced tea for the Americans, coffee for the Germans) and departs. He returns shortly and says in decent but pretty German-accented English that we have "der spezials" for the day and that one of them is "der medallions uf vild boar mit der frezh entrailz."

Well I don't have much experience with Germans, as you well know, and it's all your fault anyway, keeping us kids all tied up in the Far East and stuff like that. So my internal picture is uneducated by any real data. I am, I must say, put off by der spezial und der frezh entrailz. *Hah,* I think, *it's still alive, the Nuremberg trials didn't work, this is the Germany with the skinheads about to take over, it's just like them to have wild boar with entrails.* I order the sauerbraten with noodles. Paul, for reasons I truly cannot fathom, orders the entrails. Even the two Germans with us don't order it. I believe this is a clue.

Our plates come, and everything is food-like in appearance. Paul's pork has little crumpled-up brown things on top of it. At least they don't give you a *lot* of entrails, thank God. Soon I can't resist. At a break in the conversation I lean over and say, "Paul, what do the entrails taste like?"

"Not bad, kind of like mushrooms," he replies.

The light comes on. The dish is wild boar with fresh *chanterelles*. Actually, I am relieved. But I don't ask for a taste.

OK, final food story, from my last trip to China. We are at yet another Chinese banquet, this one in northern China. There generally they give you better food, as in somewhat more identifiable and less weird. And because they grow grain in the north and rice in the south, you get the noodle dishes in the north. These are among the best things I have been served in China. Hard to goof up noodles, really.

One of the dishes they presented to us was a bowl of noodles, big round ones with a small hole in the middle, each noodle about the size of the palm of your hand. They were served in some kind of broth that was pretty tasty, with shoots of green garlic. The noodles didn't seem to be fully cooked. In Chinese food, as you know, it's OK to use your chopsticks to pick up a big piece of whatever you've been served, if it's too big to eat all in one bite, and bite off a bit. So I did this with one of the noodles, but it was pretty hard to even chew off a smaller piece. Then I chewed it for a while, and finally got it masticated enough to swallow. I tried another bite off another noodle. It wasn't just that the pasta was al dente, it was actually pretty darn rubbery.

Finally I turned to my interpreter, handily sitting next to me. "What is this?" I asked.

"Camel hoof," she said.

"Come on, really, what is it?" I asked, even though it has been my experience that Chinese aren't big on making jokes, preferring the sort of "Westerner falls in mud puddle" type of humor. "It can't be a camel hoof; it's thin, it's some kind of noodle. It's not some peculiar take on osso buco, as found on the western steppes." She assured me it was in fact camel hoof, prepared by taking the hoof and slicing it horizontally in nice little slices. Viewed that way, it did seem credible.

"You know," I said to the interpreter, "don't say any of this to all these fine official Chinese-type persons who have been so gracious as to arrange this lovely banquet and whose good offices we need to do the project we have been discussing, but I have been around for a few years, and I've been eating for most of those years, so I know what food is, and *this is not food*. And I believe I can go even further and declare, without fear of rational contradiction, that the hooves of no animal I know of count as *food*, either. Not horses, not pigs, goat, sheep, llamas, cloven hooves or uncloven hooves or whatever the opposite is, just forget it. So there."

Made me feel better. Probably didn't change Chinese culinary practices much. And I never did figure out what happened to the rest of the camel.

Love and kisses,
Bob


**Explanatory Note:** The Clever Reader will note an 18 month gap between the last letter and the following one. The Even More Clever Reader will note that I seem to have magically changed from being an energy executive into being or trying to become a Movie Magnate. How are these related? Not particularly well—in theory or in practice—except that they were both interesting.

By 1996 I was a tiny bit tired of developing power plants in all the unattractive nooks and crannies of the second and third worlds. Power plant number 23 just wasn't quite as gripping as power plant number one. I wanted a break or a breather and because AES had done well since going public, I was able to afford some self-financed time off. My colleagues in the AES leadership, Roger Sant and Dennis Bakke, finally agreed that I could leave but only if I consented to join the Board of Directors. Since I had long wanted to be on the Board, and since I had a major amount of AES stock in my personal portfolio, and since being on the Board actually paid a salary for not that much work, I said, "Sure" and "Thank you." The senior team gave me a nice party and I packed up and departed.

My goal in sailing off into uncharted business waters was two-fold: first, to avoid doing anything that had any relation to energy, as I wanted no conflicts of interest in whatever it was I was going to do now, and second, to learn new stuff. And boy, did I! As the letters that follow should clearly document.

Read on...

# ten

# i wanna make some pictures

March 1997

Dear Dad,

You asked how Linda, my Harvard-trained lawyer wife, and I got interested in the movie business when I left AES, and what happened, and why we aren't interested anymore. All good questions, and maybe one that could be made into a screenplay; let me think . . .

We try to learn the business.

Our first idea was that it would be good not to make movies (everybody knows how hard that is) but instead just to finance them. Although at the time we were only clear on one of these; it turned out that we actually had those two key ingredients so necessary to participate in the film industry: money and a desire to lose it.

Once we decided to become moguls, it seemed like a good idea to find out how movies were made, what things cost, the answers to the general questions of "who does what to whom and what do they get for it" that once determined can be used to characterize "business." or maybe all human contact. Our belief was that we should start with independent films, since they cost less and seemed to need money more. Mel Gibson can get financed in a film where all he does is eat a cheeseburger; Parker Posey can't. Whoever she is. Fortunately, our newfound interest corresponded with the annual running of the mother of all independent film festivals, Sundance. As you probably know, this whole thing was organized by Robert Redford—who as far as anyone can tell has never actually appeared in an independent film—and named after his Utah ski resort, Sundance, which is where it is not held. The ski resort is named after his character in *Butch Cassidy and the Sundance Kid*, which made him a lot of money and was also not an independent film, and by the way had nothing to do with skiing or Utah. It was a pretty good movie, though, and the above associative thread is provided to indicate that the movie biz is not necessarily about consistency, clarity, or logic.

So I call up the Sundance Film Festival and ask about buying a ticket. Ha hoo! I am calling in December, the festival is in January, and the festival person laughs uproariously. It is long since sold out. In fact, it is now such a big deal that as soon as the tickets go on sale, all the Hollywood studios buy them up. No one appears to think this strange for an event that started out with such a strong counterculture bias. The festival does now reserve some small portion of the tickets for the "non-industry" sector of the public, i.e., people who just like movies. Very important to remember your roots. I speculate idly on how you prove that you are *not* part of the industry and thus eligible for such tickets. Is there a special non-Hollywood card that you buy? Are you part of the industry and thus disqualified if you own one hundred shares of stock of Paramount? If you subscribe to *Entertainment Weekly*? You're clearly disqualified if you subscribe to *Variety* or *The Hollywood Reporter*, of that much I'm sure. Anyway, it doesn't matter since all these non-industry tickets are also sold out, all seven of them.

But I know how to do these things. I ask to speak to the "Director of the Development Office." Small digression: dealing with nonprofit organizations, as I have for the last several years ever since being able to make an interesting charitable contribution—and for some groups interesting is pretty small—you learn that nobody in the whole place works at raising money. At least not by title. The money-raising people are all working in "development." I don't know why it is called this—some misplaced Victorian sensibility about how crude it would sound if you actually had to admit that you actually did ask people for money? Businesses have people called "chief financial officer" or "vice president of sales," but nonprofits perhaps come from a gentler era. Oh well.

The development lady is very nice, which means she doesn't laugh uproariously at my request. I suggest that we could be a sponsor of the festival. This again, in nonprofit secret squirrel lingo, generally means an interesting amount of money ($10,000 and north) and is often quite well received. Not here—all the sponsorships were sold out within a week of their availability date. "Well," I suggest, "can I sign up for next year?"

"No, we only begin taking applications for sponsorships in September."

It turns out that the stupid organization is so well funded that you have to apply to give them money, and they turn away contributors without special qualifications. Money is no longer just money to them, egads! This is the dream of every nonprofit in the world, or at least the dream of their development offices. Again one wonders oddly why they don't take some more money and run more festivals and support more independent film-makers. Market forces seem to be on their side. But, sadly, they aren't asking me for advice about organizational strategy or financing possible expansion plans.

Stymied by trying the normal tactics, I resorted to an old standby: begging and pleading. The program includes not only actual movies but also a bunch of seminars held during the festival: how to make a movie, how to market a movie, etc., including one called "how to finance an independent film." I had wanted to go to the whole thing, but this last session seemed especially on point.

"Can I just get a ticket to the financing seminar?" I whined. She relented and said that she couldn't *sell* me one—all sold out, of course— but if I came by the office of the festival she'd leave me one, on a complimentary basis.

So on the appointed day I flew to Salt Lake City, drove up to Park City, found a parking place (not easy), found the festival office (crowded and busy and disorganized), and after a certain amount of processing, and moving, or being moved from one staffer to another, I actually got my ticket to the finance session. I was even on time—actually I was fifteen minutes early, since I had forgotten how easy it was to get to Park City from the Salt Lake airport.

It's a good thing I was. When I got there the auditorium was already full, and I got one of the last seats. I sat down, took off my coat, and looked around. I was dressed in official AES casual attire: khakis, blue button-down collar oxford cloth shirt, cashmere v-neck sweater, engineer boots, polished. Observation number one: I am highly overdressed. Standard garb is baseball cap (for some reason worn in the traditional fashion, bill forward), plaid flannel shirt unbuttoned and not tucked in over white undershirt, jeans (long and baggy and black), and hiking boots. Alternate is black sweater over the same white undershirt. Well not the same as the guy in the flannel shirt but one very similar. Observation number two: I am the oldest person in the room by at least ten years. Observation number three: I have the shortest hair of anyone in the room, and I am no longer in the Army reserves, so it ain't that short. Shorter than most of the women and all of the men. I do not have a ponytail, but many do, both sexes. Observation number four: No one else seems to be taking notes in a Coach portfolio using a Montblanc pen. *Who are these people?* Perhaps I am in the wrong meeting.

The lights dim, the panel members troop onto the stage, and the moderator introduces them. They seem quite impressive: six people, including several with "president" as their title, nobody less than a senior vice president except for one lawyer, and even he gets to be a managing partner. They all also do seem to work in the industry, and to be successful at it. Standard industry panel proceedings then proceed. Each person makes a ten-minute talk, but with no slides, to my surprise. How do you do that: make an industry talk as part of a panel and not have any slides? I've never heard of such a thing! I take careful notes. Everybody seems to be saying pretty much the same thing, to wit:

First, you have to assemble the package. Now in movieland the "package" means you have to own, own the rights to, or otherwise control a script. Not just an idea for a movie, an actual 80 to 120-page document with all the words and scenes written down. The panel members say it with something close to this level of detail. I am grateful since I know nothing, but I suspect all these other movie pros in the audience already know this. It is emphasized several times that this is important. Seems clear to me and really pretty obvious. How do you make a movie without a script, at least as a logical starting point? I have seen some movies that seem to have been made without one, at least when they started filming, but this is clearly not a good idea.

Second, you have to assemble the rest of the package. Tell us, children, what might that entail? Well, you need a director to sign on and promise to do the movie, and you need at least one or two stars to also sign on and thus be in the movie. Editorial note: the movie industry, as a business, is organized a bit like the construction industry. Every movie is a new project, and you have to assemble the team of people to make the movie from scratch, each time. On the labor side that means everyone is self-employed and does project work. At the end of each project you find yourself unemployed again. This is a very efficient way for an industry to work, but brutal and competitive. It also means that the scheduling of projects is quirky and demanding. If Sean Connery isn't available because he's in Tunis working for George Lucas, then it doesn't matter that he promised to be in your movie and you want to start shooting right now. Thus the need for the package to have pretty strong commitments, as close to contractually binding as you can get.

Third, you need a budget. What will it cost to make this little darling of yours? This also implies a shooting schedule and a shooting location since it's hard to construct a budget without knowing where you will be shooting (New York is expensive, the Arizona desert is cheap) and for how long. Interestingly, the actual physical cost of the film is a material portion of the budget. But I find the need for a budget vaguely reassuring.

Fourth, once this is all nicely put together, then and only then do you sally forth to the possible sources of financing. Every one of the six panelists said this, and several said it a couple of times: you only get one shot at this with financing people, so you have to have your package assembled,

polished, and ready to go. Don't expect to get warm mentoring and guid-
ance and a request to come back next month when you have things better
organized. These are busy people, and they hear a lot of movie proposals,
like fifty thousand a year. I idly worked through this in my head, and
assuming they aren't working weekends, this is 227¼ proposals a day.
Maybe that's not a real number, but I am prepared to believe that they
do get a lot. The sources of this financing: a limited number of specialized
independent studios, a couple of banks with specialized film finance units,
any rich friends you have, and that is about it. Remember, these are $2 to
$10 million films, and this is a hard range to find financing for anything.

It all made sense to me. Actually, after about the third explanation
of the steps listed above, the small lightbulb flashed over my head and I
said to myself, "Shoot, this is just project financing of a power plant all
over again. Except instead of a script you need a set of plans, instead of a
director you need a construction company, instead of actors you have a fuel
supply contract, and in our case it's nice to have the market risk handled by
having somebody to purchase the power. And always you need a budget—
how else do you know how much money you need to raise?"

I spent the rest of the session confirming my understanding, and
sure enough the remaining three folks all said, clearly and forcefully, the
same things noted above. *I've been doing project financing for fifteen years*, I
thought. *I can understand this.* And I see why they're saying what they're
saying. The words were different, but I clearly recognized the melody. I felt
quite pleased.

The panelists all finished, and then they opened the floor to questions.
First question, from flannel shirt: "I, like, want to get this really great
concept I have for a movie financed. Who should I talk to first, a studio or
one of the banks?"

Polite response: "Do you have a script?"

A: "No, but I got this dynamite concept."

Panelist: "Really, you need to have the whole package assembled, you
need to have a script, you need a director and the actors, you need a careful
budget, etc."

The next sixteen questions were, I swear to Jerusalem, variants of "I got this idea for a movie, how do I get it financed?" The panelists were wonderfully polite and consistently answered in the same fashion, emphasizing that you only get one shot, it has to be a good one, and you need it all together. I, however, after about the third stupid repetition of this same dunderheaded question, wanted to leap out of my seat, grab the person by the lapels of his or her plaid Pendleton shirt, shake the bejesus out of the dope, and scream, "Weren't you listening, you moron? Where have you been for the last ninety minutes? Were you looking for the 'I Have a Dream' seminar and wandered in here by mistake? Pay attention!! Stop asking these questions!!"

The last question was the best. Black sweater over white T-shirt: "I got this, like, concept for a movie I want to get funded, but my question is different." *Thank God*, I thought, but too soon. "Part of my concept is, I think, like, that Meryl Streep should be, like, one of the stars, but should I tell the studio that, or, like, will they just steal my idea?"

That really was the question. Again, the saints on the panel responded, politely, that they weren't sure that the idea of using Meryl Streep as the star of a movie could really be thought to be that original, and maybe first he needed to assemble the package, get a script, etc., and then maybe he actually could get Meryl Streep interested. I myself figured that this clueless person had as much chance of nabbing Meryl Streep as I had of being appointed head of the Mormon Church. I also began to have just the tiniest inkling of a doubt about my new chosen career—were these chowderheads the people whose films I was seeking to finance? Could it be these unattractive folk with the poor tailors, the short attention spans, and the inability to process and retain simple information were in fact . . . FILMMAKERS? Yikes.

---

We educate ourselves some more.

Linda said we needed to go to the annual market of the AFMA (American Film Marketing Association) held each year in March in Santa Monica. This group is made up of both folks who make independent movies and the people who buy them, other than the studios. Linda knew about this gathering and this association from her days in the Commerce Department when this was one of the industries for which she was negotiating trade treaties. Her task was to try to get their product into foreign markets. In point of fact, most countries limit, to a greater or lesser extent, the number of US films that can be imported into the country. Pretty weird, no? I think the number in China is twelve. What made this assignment even more challenging was the fact that, since our market is quite open on these matters, she didn't have much to trade. So much for the background. The important part is that a week in March in Southern California didn't sound bad to me, and I had some lovely new black clothes to wear for the occasion, so I said yes.

Parenthetical interjection: Here are some things that no one tells you about the movie business, and you therefore have to find out by asking dumb and even embarrassing questions, usually repeatedly.

I was good at this, the dumb question part. Much of the language in Hollywood is misleading and uninformative. Of course, so are the movie trailers. Right now, you're probably asking yourself, "What does a studio do?" Or maybe, "Why am I reading this letter?" Never mind. Well, first off, a studio doesn't have any studios to speak of. This isn't gibberish. I don't think they even have studio beds. They just have offices. There are seven of them: Universal, Disney, MGM, United Artists, Fox, Warner Bros., and Paramount, plus DreamWorks, the first new "studio" in fifty years, except they don't have a studio really, either. It doesn't matter that they don't have studios, because movies are no longer really made in studios anyway. And it's too expensive to work in a studio in Hollywood—cost of living, housing, unions, nowhere to park, everybody trying to go to the same hot restaurant—it's a nightmare.

Studios are financing sources for equity, not debt; they are not lenders, and thus they end up owning the product. They are also the ones who distribute the movies to the theaters. Financing, in very broad terms, can come before the film is made (but only if you have your package together, as we have learned previously), or if somehow you have gotten the money together otherwise, a studio can buy the finished product and distribute it. This is known as a "negative pickup deal" and for the first eight times I heard it I couldn't figure out what was negative about it. Then Linda told me it was the physical film itself to which they were referring. "Oh," I said. To slightly further confuse matters, there are a bunch of arrangements that can be made in between, where the filmmaker can keep some or all of the ownership of the film but negotiate a distribution deal with a particular studio. Who then gets how much of the revenues thereby (hopefully) generated, who gets what costs paid in what order or priority, who keeps the books, etc., all are complicated issues. In many senses the studios have huge power, because without them you can get your movie made, maybe, if you have enough money, but you can't get it into any theaters.

To return to our story: because we knew we were going to go to this conference or industry meeting, I started casting around to find if any of the banks we dealt with at AES were also in the movie business. As luck would have it we were meeting with CSFB (Credit Suisse First Boston, a bank put together by the merger of Bank of Tokyo and Societe General—no, just kidding), and I asked about the movie financing business. One of the guys said he thought they did have some people in LA who did that. "Great," I said. "I'm going to be out there in a couple of weeks, and I'd love to meet with him and talk with him. But would you please make sure to tell him that I'm *not* a crackpot. I don't want to meet Meryl Streep, I don't intend to dress entirely in black, I don't have a screenplay that I'm desperate to get made into a movie, and I'm unlikely to ever wear my hair in a ponytail. I just want to treat the financing of independent films as a business." He promised to find out and call and he did.

Parenthetical interjection the second: Just what is an independent film?

Good question. About five hundred movies a year are made in the US and go into "theatrical release." More are actually made than this, but when they aren't "released" they suffer the dreaded fate known as "direct to video." Yes, that's why when you roam the shelves of your local Blockbuster, unable to find *Return of the Jedi* or *Gone With the Wind* or even *Die Hard Goes Hawaiian*, you see all these other titles and say to yourself, "I never heard of that." And indeed you haven't. Of the films that do make it into theaters, about 80% are made with the blessing of and financial underwriting of the studios. The rest get financed somewhere else and are generally therefore referred to as "independent" although they may well be distributed by a studio. Only it's more complicated than that. As the cachet of being an "independent" film has increased (more Oscars: *Leaving Las Vegas*, *The English Patient*; better reviews, more edgy, better critical acclaim, but not, we hasten to add, better economics or revenues, although sometimes better profits as in *The Full Monty* and *The Blair Witch Project*, both of which were made for next to nothing), the studios have all set up branches or divisions to finance independent films: Sony Pictures Classics, Fox Searchlight, Miramax (bought in by Disney), etc. "Aha," the careful reader will cry, "but that means that they're really not 'independent!'" True. But they are still called independent films because it's thought to be good marketing. All is not necessarily what it seems in Hollywood. Better you learn it now than later.

We're in Santa Monica. We arrange to meet the CSFB banker, a nice young man named Eric, for dinner at a restaurant along the ocean called Ivy at the Shore. Unknown to us, truly, is that this is a very trendy restaurant, at least the Beverly Hills version is—so trendy that it is the venue of the restaurant scene in *Get Shorty*. Wowee! Obviously our banker contact is impressed, because he shows up wearing small diamond earrings, studs of course, in each ear. First time I ever saw a banker do that, I will say. Normal pleasantries are exchanged, and the secret handshake takes place so we are both assured that we speak the arcane language of finance. Then I make my disclaimer: "I want you to understand that I'm *not* a crackpot. I don't want to meet Meryl Streep, I don't expect to dress entirely in black, I haven't written a screenplay that I'm dying to get produced, and I am unlikely to wear a ponytail. I just want to treat the financing of independent films as a business."

"Let me get this straight," says Eric, gently. "You don't want to meet Meryl Streep, you aren't gonna dress all in black or wear your hair in a ponytail, you don't have a screenplay you're dying to see as a movie. And you think you would like to treat the financing of independent films strictly as a business?"

I nod vigorously, and smile in a responsible financial fashion. "You might be a crackpot," he says.

---

**Our education continues.**

We go to the market. So do about five thousand other people. What is involved is half the people there, let's call them Group A, have a bunch of movies to sell, or lease, or rent, or sell the rights to. Each of the members of Group A takes a room or a suite of rooms in the Loews Hotel at the beach, and everybody who wants to buy, lease, or rent the rights to show these movies, call them Group B, pays the requisite fee to get a conference badge. The Group A people stand around in their rooms, all equipped with big TVs playing videos of their offerings, usually just the trailers. And the Group B guys wander around looking at the product and asking whether the television rights to this for pay TV have been sold for Poland or South Korea. Then they negotiate a deal for said rights. Movies are sold horizontally, if you will, in the following order of desirability: theatrical exhibition (just what it sounds like), pay TV, video rental, video sales, broadcast TV. I know all TV is broadcast, that's just what they call it. The movies are also sold geographically, country by country. Maybe this is vertically. To make this more complex, the movies themselves are never in fact sold; what is sold is a license to play or show the movie over the medium and in the geography discussed, for a defined time period. The studios, or in this case the independent distributors, still own the intellectual property that is the movie. Seems funny to call a movie "intellectual property," but it is. We walk around, at least me, pretty confused at first, since no one gave me the lovely explanation I have just given you. We were neither buyers nor sellers, not A and not B, so what were we doing there? Mostly getting propositioned.

I thought that might drag you into the next paragraph. Since we had registered with the "financial" section of AFMA we had a different color name tag, green as it turned out. Nicely symbolic. So every strange person who wanted to make a movie, or was allegedly in the process thereof, sought us out and hailed us: "Bob and Linda!" thus proving they could read name tags, but little else. "Boy, I've been looking for you guys all over!

I really need you to take a meeting with me. I've got twenty killer minutes in the can! You're gonna love this one, it's like Godzilla only it's in medieval England, but with a kind of lesbian twist to it . . ." I kid thee not. They really talk like that. Maybe they've seen too many movies themselves. Usually the accosting person was male, had a silk shirt open down to the navel, surfer blond hair, and a good tan. Weird. Remember, we were nobodies in the movie biz, and nobody knows us from Adam, we had never financed movie one, we just said that we wanted to and could. All you could be certain about us was that we could afford the fee to attend the market. But that was enough. It was like we were a salt lick to a bunch of deer. I began to rethink my vow not to dress entirely in black. Maybe then no one would be able to see me, no, wait, that's in Kabuki, not the movies. Or at least I could say, "I'm sorry, I'm actually Mr. Hemphill's agent; just send us your screenplay and we'll review it . . ."

———

And continues.

On one of the days of the market, they had a lunch just for the financial folks. All the financial sector members were there, and it was a small lunch, with all of us fitting nicely at two tables for eight. This perhaps should have been a clue. One of the nice bankers attending took us aside and explained that he only did "gap financing," which I eventually figured out had nothing to do with clothing stores? Although there were a lot of people around wearing khakis. This guy's bank puts in the last money needed to make the film, thus closing the 'gap,' and since he is the final key to the puzzle, he gets a terrific deal, and he gets out first. But remember, he says to us, here's how it works: one movie out of twenty makes a fortune, it costs ten million bucks, and after you count everything it generated three or four hundred million. Nice return, huh? We nod. But the other nineteen don't even make back their costs. Unless you're taking first money out, your investment goes away, your money never even comes back to see you, or sends a postcard, or says thanks. Gone.

"Well, why not just finance the one in twenty?" we ask.

Knowing laughter. "Nobody knows how to do that," he responds. "And even good scripts end up as lousy movies. And good guys, gifted guys, geniuses, make crap moves. Steven Spielberg made *Amistad*." It's a persuasive argument. Other people repeat this same calculus to us, in about the same order of magnitude numbers. We begin to rethink being financiers. Although the idea of a lesbian Godzilla did seem sort of interesting, except who knows what sex Godzilla is anyway?

---

**We change course somewhat.**

Our story so far (just like those Buck Rogers serials that used to play on Saturday afternoon matinees before the feature): only the studios and idiots put equity into movies. Very well, we can't finance the gold mines themselves, because the miners don't appear to have much idea where to dig, can't recognize gold when they see it, and have no clue as to the refining/smelting process, as we have now learned. Then we'll finance the guys selling the picks and shovels! This, by the way, is a tedious cliché in the venture world and has now been applied to every industry in the Department of Commerce's SIC code. The VC shorthand is "tools companies." Of course it could be argued that Microsoft just sells tools, so there's at least a grain of wisdom here.

But who makes movie tools, at least who does that will talk to us? The special effects guys! We read several articles on "Digital Hollywood" and "Silicon Valley meets the San Fernando Valley" or Sunset Blvd vs. El Camino Real, etc., and thus, having easily developed enough expertise to give away money, set off again for California armed with a list of such companies to visit. The big ones, of course, are already financed: Pacific Digital Image and Industrial Light & Magic (founded to work on *Star Wars*; made Spielberg's dinosaurs) are the best known. But there are lots of little guys, and they seem eager to talk to us. Money opens so many doors.

We meet with a few of them, companies with nondescript names, mostly not with "data" or "technology" in them. They are doing wonderful stuff. Most are five- to ten-person businesses, armed with a bunch of $5,000 Power Macs (the low-end guys) or $250,000 Silicon Graphics boxes named SG A-3000 or something, which are a lovely metallic purple (the higher end). And they would mostly welcome some investment, although we never even got close to talking amounts and terms. But as a business model to invest in, it stinks.

The guy making the movie, usually the director, breaks up his movie into "shots" that need digital effects, either enhancement or something from scratch. Or he may just inadvertently screw something up, run out of time, or light, or money for that shot or that location, and brush it off with the all-purpose expression, "We'll fix it in post." The first several times I heard about something getting fixed in post, I had in mind some small town in Arizona where film was mysteriously repaired, but then Linda said it was just shorthand for "post-production," so I felt silly.

But to continue: sometimes it's not a mistake. For example, it could be an actor performing safely in front of a blue screen, and the digital effect is to fill in the terrorizing or remarkable background behind him. No, I don't know why they use blue, probably some Kodak sort of thing. You remember all the '30s and '40s movies where the two folks are sitting in a car, inevitably a roadster, driving someplace, and the road recedes behind them, except you could clearly tell that it was two actors sitting in a car that wasn't moving (despite the occasional turning of the wheel) with the "road" being projected on a screen? This is the same thing, except much enhanced, and added after the fact rather than shot in place. Or maybe Stallone is sweatily climbing up a steep cliff face so he can shoot some bad guys on the top. It's filmed with him climbing, all right, except he's also hooked up with a rope being held by somebody on top of the cliff. This doesn't look so exciting or dangerous. So afterward one of the "shots" is for the digital guys to go in and take the rope out of the frames and substitute in a rope-sized slice of the background which they lift/duplicate from the background right next to the rope. This is very clever work called "compositing." It saves a lot of wear and tear on actors, doubles, or stunt guys.

Or take the actual example where the director is making a movie about solar cars racing in Hawaii, but while he was there burning up his limited budget, he shot the film because he had to, only it was cloudy the whole time. Only Marlon Brando gets to wait six days for the waves to be right, and he only got to do that back when he wasn't fat. To fix this the director has a digital effects house composite in bright sunny skies for the crucial scenes. But, and here's the rub, they compete these digital scenes out to all the effects houses to bid on. Nobody gets the whole movie; it's all piece-work. And you have to make a fixed-price bid, even though what you are being asked to do is sometimes not fully specified. But there are many hungry small competitors since anyone with a Mac and some software and a bit of computer training can set himself up in the business. Because there are so few guys making movies, the movie guys can get terrific deals on the work from the special effects houses. This is a lousy investment, of course. And more to the point, all the special effects people we met mostly dressed all in black and had ponytails. And after a while they admitted that what they *really* wanted to do was make films, not just do special effects. Yikes. Unclear if they also wanted to meet Meryl Streep. These guys probably wanted to meet Pamela Anderson.

We retreated back to Washington, where they don't make movies, at least not much, and where we only finance B-1 bombers, the mayor of Washington's cocaine habit, and other useful stuff, to reconsider our approach. This was turning out to be harder than we thought.

More on the quest for meaning later. First I have to go rent *The Producers*.

Love and kisses,
Bob

# eleven

# sharks to the left, tourists to the right

June 1997

Dear Dad,

Disregard the heading on the fancy stationery, which would make you think I'm in Arlington. I'm actually sitting here on the island of Huahine, in French Polynesia, in the living room of an elegant and idiosyncratically designed two-room "fare" (pronounced *fah-ray*.) The view of the small bay, the really truly no-kidding turquoise water, the white sand beaches, the bougainvillea out the window, etc., is quite delicious, and the wind is at about gale force. This house is constructed in typical Polynesian style, or at least in some Westerner's romantic idea of typical Polynesian style (Polynesians would probably not have put a house on a sheer cliff face) of totally native materials to include a pandanus leaf roof, beautifully layered and woven.

What happens in a wind of any consequence, in addition to the charming tinkling of the shell wind chime, is that small bits of the 100% authentic native materials of construction form a gentle and continuous rain out of the ceiling and on to all flat surfaces. This is coupled with the occasional gecko droppings on same surfaces. Ah, the romance of

Polynesia! Of course, you may remember some of this from Hawaii, especially the geckos. I do not, however, remember the remarkable winds and
the bits of roof lying about of a morning. As one of the gracious local
Tahitians explained it to us yesterday, "If no wind, then rain." Seems like a
limited menu of choices to me. Fortunately Linda brought along a bunch
of long-sleeved shirts to protect herself from the sun. Also fortunately they
are all men's size small and so can also be used to protect one from the cold.
At this moment the danger of heatstroke is rated quite low.

The island itself is pretty terrific—much bigger and more scenic than
Bora Bora where we first stopped, and which could be categorized in my
book as "Sixteen Views of One Big Rock," and not near as interesting
as Hokusai's *Thirty-six Views of Mount Fuji*. Lovely lagoon, though. Bora
Bora was garrisoned by five thousand US soldiers during the second world
war. The current population of the island is only 5,300, and it's hard to
conceive where they put all those soldiers. It is also interesting to note
that the GIs, probably bored out of their minds, built the airport, the only
paved road around the perimeter of the island, and the only dock and port.
Why exactly anybody thought the Japanese lusted after Bora Bora is not
clear to me, except possibly they wanted to prevent yet another bad remake
of *Mutiny on the Bounty*, which might have been a worthwhile strategic
objective. Here is another thought to keep in mind: any island that you can
ride around on your bike in three hours is pretty small.

We will say this for Bora Bora: the snorkeling is terrific. This was the
first time Linda and I had ever tried this sport—where you jump in water
you've never been in before but which is guaranteed to have in it a lot of
live stuff that hasn't been properly introduced to you—while wearing fins
that make ridges in your feet; a mask that slowly leaks and asphyxiates
you; and a breathing tube that fills up with seawater, which in the process
makes your breathing reverberate in your ears like a bad imitation of Darth
Vader. Yes, it does take some getting used to. But the fish are everywhere,
including swimming right into your mask. And the colors are as advertised—brilliant yellows, and blues, and greens, and pinks, and blacks, and
on and on. Linda took to it naturally and was off in a flash, while I was
still trying to figure out which foot which fin went on. At one point she

paused to stand on a patch of coral, and the angelfish all came around and started sticking their noses (I guess fish technically don't have noses; OK, they were sticking those pointed things on the front of their faces) into the openings on her fins to nibble at her toes. I suppose if you're a lagoon fish and you spend all your time poking around coral looking for tiny bits of slow crustacean to munch on, the idea of big pink toes may be at least worth checking out. Since we were on our honeymoon, I became immediately jealous. However when I tried this later I was unable to hold my breath long enough. Besides, we had to turn the flippers in to the guy who ran the boat.

We also took a four-wheel drive ride around the unpaved roads of Bora Bora, of which there are in fact three or four, no doubt built by the Americans after they ran out of asphalt and anything else to do. These lead up into the hills via routes laid out to go carefully through the middle of giant mud puddles, where the mud was frequently up to the tops of the tires of the trucks we were riding in. I had visions of the two of us and six honeymooning Japanese couples trying to push a five-ton vehicle out of the mud, all wearing our designer outfits and carrying video cameras. Miraculously, this did not occur. The result of all this sloshing and gear grinding was nice views: lagoon to the north, lagoon to the east, lagoon to the west—you get the picture. Linda, who has a better appreciation for this, particularly enjoyed the jouncing around and splashing this entailed and suggested that this would make a heck of a commercial for Land Rover Defender, which is what we were riding in. After carefully wiping the mud out of my hair, I of course agreed.

So far, our collection of Favorite Phrases of Polynesia includes the following:

"The boat, she is coming." (They really do say this; they're not just trying to talk like Tattoo in *Fantasy Island.*)

"The truck, she is coming." (Note some similarity between these first two, both as to phrasing and as to likelihood of the mode of transportation actually showing up.)

"The Chinese peoples owns all the stores."

"The Americans built this for us."

"You want something to eat, you just reach up and pick it."

"We put out the yellow rope in the water, the sharks stays on one side, you tourists peoples stays on the other." (My personal favorite, raising all sorts of secondary questions, such as: Who trained the sharks to stay on their side, and if it's just a yellow rope in the water, how does a shark know at the beginning which side is his and which side is yours?)

The islands are still French colonies, or protectorates, or administrative districts, or some complex thing like that. The guidebook explains unclearly that there has been a sort of a drive for independence, which the French have responded to by setting up an autonomous local government that has all powers of government except for a certain few which are reserved to Paris, e.g., taxation, police, import and export duties and controls, public works, immigration and citizenship, public health, external affairs, and education. I was stumped for what was left to the local folks; trash collection was the only thing that occurred to me.

The language is a continuing source of interest and confusion. Here are some examples:

Our favorite exchange to date: Me, on the telephone to the front desk of our fancy hotel, trying to figure out if the next day will be suitable for a boat trip around the island: "Could you please tell me what will be the weather for tomorrow?" Front Desk person: "What is your room number?"

Favorite incomprehensible explanation of a Polynesian dance: "The king of the village goes to sleep and in his sleep he has a strange dream." Yes, that is actually the entire explanation of the one-hour program. With no further ado, six young women, all wearing bras made of coconut shells (one suspects that these must be heroically uncomfortable since on a day-to-day basis the female islanders seem to prefer T-shirts, and it's not because there aren't enough coconuts around, goodness knows) come to center stage, sit there for a while weaving pandanas leaves into baskets and creating flower wreaths for their hair, then get up to dance what we decided was "The Dance of the Traditional Arts and Crafts." Basically much hand and arm waving and hip moving. They are followed by some young men, all looking surprised to find themselves in the lobby of the Sofitel Hotel in skimpy costumes, jumping about and banging sticks on the floor, followed by a large paper-mache clam carried in by more young men wearing long strands of green bamboo hair. The clam, when it opens, has inside it (no!) yet another island maiden, same underwear, who dances with her contemporaries—something that we think can be interpreted as "I Keep Away from Run-Around Sue." Then all the dancers wander out into the audience and drag back surprisingly willing audience participants who proceed to do "The Dance of the Uncoordinated Gringo." My belief is that this last part of his dream was what the king of the village considered truly strange. For good reason.

Most interesting label on a food product, in this case peanuts in the shell: "Ingredients: Peanuts 100%. These roasted peanuts are specially blended from fresh Tsing Tao peanuts and the finest ingredient into these fresh, delicious." Parenthetically, we found ourselves at one point at a small snack bar on Bora Bora eating peanuts from China and Lay's potato chips from Dallas, and drinking Perrier from France and Coke bottled in Australia (Linda) and beer from Tahiti (me). Pretty global.

The little offshore (but inside the coral reef) islands that are a part of both Bora Bora and Huahine are called "motus," pronounced as you would think. This can't help but inspire one to invent motu jokes:

What is the most prevalent type of transportation on a motu? Motu-scooters. ("Ha! Ha! Ha!" adds Linda, who tolerates this sort of humor only as a matter of politeness.)

Who was the corrupt dictator of the motu's in the Congo recently overthrown with help from Rwanda and Uganda? Motu-butu.

What physical principle explains the fact that a body in motion on a motu tends to continue in motion? Motumentum.

What do the teachers in a motu school use as an explanation for the poor performance of their students? Lack of motuvation.

Where do they put folks who die on the motu? In the motuary.

Additional entries in the Best Motu Joke contest are as always welcomed.

But never mind all that. The real purpose of this letter is to alert you to the fact that the next time we see you, you'll have to look through approximately six thousand photographs and help us pick out the two or three thousand best ones. Be prepared. Oh, and did I mention the eight hours of videos??

Love and kisses,
Bob

---

twelve

# is it socially responsible to explode cats?

November 1997

Dear Dad,

We were ready to go home from the office on Regent Street this evening. Our rental car was parked in a lot about five blocks away; this is downtown London, after all, and parking's not easy. For some reason the garage is in a very small but distinctively Japanese neighborhood. Why there is a "Japantown" next to Regent Street I cannot tell you. It's not anywhere near the Japanese embassy. There are small Japanese grocery stores, a newsstand that carries lots of Japanese newspapers and magazines, and a number of Japanese restaurants.

Linda loves Japanese food for its simplicity and honesty, for the high-quality ingredients that are used, for the freshness of the food, for its elegance of presentation. She does not care for sauces of any kind, as you probably remember. Since knowing her I have had burned into my hard drive the requirement that salad be served with the dressing *on the side*; that anything sautéed or fried is verboten (which kind of knocks out most of my favorite Japanese foods: that tempura stuff, now that's OK); and that sandwiches must be made dry—no mayonnaise, no butter, no nothing. Having lived in Japan with you for four years, I have a less enthusiastic view of Japanese cuisine, but then I'm a midwesterner, and I think fish should be cooked. I can't go into a Japanese restaurant without remembering the John Belushi skit from *Saturday Night Live* where Belushi is playing the chef in the kitchen of a Japanese restaurant -- "OK, they ate the raw fish, now let's see if they'll drink the hot wine . . ."

So anyway, we're trudging up the street in the London damp and wetness; it's pretty dark, and cold, and rainy in the winter, which starts about September 15. My darling says, "Do we have anything to eat at home?" I'm a sensitive guy in general, and besides, it's been a long time since lunch, which was probably not very good: English sandwiches, including my favorite, aptly named "tuna mayonnaise." I can see that we're passing a row of Japanese restaurants, and in fact we don't have much in the fridge, maybe some expired chicken breasts and some milk and, naturally, this is the UK, some Brussels sprouts. Those things keep forever. Also, I know that "Do we have anything to eat at home?" is not a question, it's more of a suggestion.

"Hey, we've had a hard day, how about we just stop and eat here before we go home?" I cleverly suggest. After all, Asahi Super Dry is a terrific beer, and maybe they'll have tonkatsu, Japan's answer to Weiner schnitzel, and I will get points for being a Good Husband.

Offer accepted, we go in. The waitresses are wearing kimonos; they bow and say, "*Irashai-masu! [welcome!]*," like they're supposed to, and the sushi chefs are behind the glass counter, which is filled with various dead fish. The chefs, who are wearing headbands, say, "*Irashai-masu!*" as well. I wonder what the Japanese characters on the headbands mean. Could be: "Eat at Joe's sushi parlor." Could be "Let's kill all the fat, round-eyed fools." Who knows? We sit down at one of the blond wood tables, break apart the wooden chopsticks, and get a couple of Asahi beers. Linda orders her standard sushi order, which always starts with a California roll.

OK, hold it right there—says the Magistrate of International Consistency—what the heck kind of sushi is California roll? What does California taste like? What part of Japan is it in? Is this like "ranch" dressing, which classicists would argue is not a flavor? Could there be "California ranch dressing?" These are questions impossible to answer, like how many Samurai can dance on the head of a pin. In case you didn't know it, "California roll" is rice wrapped around crab and avocado, usually garnished with salmon roe, but Linda asks them to leave that off. Her standard sushi order also includes cucumber roll, shrimp, and *unagi*—smoked eel. And extra ginger and extra wasabi.

The miso soup comes and we eat that, chasing the little cubes of tofu around the bowl with our bulky ceramic spoons, like not very good lacrosse players. Soon the sushi arrives, nicely arrayed on a black pottery platter, garnished with green leaves of some sort. Linda digs in. She eats the first couple of sushi quickly, the shrimp ones so that I won't ask for one. Smart girl. Then a couple of cucumber rolls, then a California roll.

She stops mid-sushi, looks quizzically at the slug of rice in her chopsticks, then looks at me.

"What's wrong?" I ask. I am a thoughtful guy, I can for at least a moment stop motoring though my tonkatsu, a wonderful breaded, deep-fat-fried pork cutlet that would be right at home in Omaha, thus proving that not every food item in Japan is inedible, delicate, weird, or healthy, although most of it is.

"Nothing, no, it can't be," she mutters, then finishes the rest of the bite. She stops again and starts to take a California roll apart. This is possible, but messy. She inspects the unrolled rice and stuff. The waitress comes over, perhaps suspecting that my wife doesn't know how to eat sushi and thinks that you're supposed to take apart every second piece.

Linda says to her, "What do you put in this filling?"

The waitress recites the standard ingredients, rice and so forth.

Linda says, "Anything else? Like, do you by any chance put *mayonnaise* in this?" I laugh to myself. Goodness knows these are Japanese, there are standards, they use only the freshest oils for the tempura, only raw fish caught within the last half-hour; Linda's been working too hard, the climate is getting to her.

"Mayonnaise," says the waitress. It's not clear if she has understood the question and whether she is confirming or clarifying it. Linda repeats her query. The waitress this time confirms it: "Yes, mayonnaise put in sushi," only she charmingly pronounces it "may-o-nay-sa."

Well, I never. I am thoroughly surprised, and Linda is pretty disgusted, and so orders something else, asking pointedly that it be without "may-o-nay-sa."

I ponder this culinary incident: Is it a victory for English cuisine, God forbid, or a simple adaptation to the market? I have to hand it to these Japanese residents of off-Regent Street; they have invented a kind of sushi even a Nebraskan could love. Except they shouldn't call it California roll; they'll get a lot more business if they call it "sushi mayonnaise."

———

Well, this doesn't have much to do with movies, I'll admit. Except that's why we're here. Or at least movie theaters. When last we left our hero and heroine (me and Linda), we were still groping around for the right business idea having to do with movies. As we tried to explore all the options, we decided against financing movies (lose all your money except one time out of twenty), and against investing in special effects companies (lose all your money probably every time), and so we were stumped. Rather than moping around we kind of fell into an interlude of investing in venture capital deals of all kinds and descriptions.

When I went off to Yale I decided that I would take all knowledge as my province. Leonardo da Vinci would be my idol. He invented the parachute and the tank, painted the *Mona Lisa*, swam the Hellespont—did it all and knew it all. Well, maybe not the swimming, I think that was Lord Byron. We hadn't had any renaissance men for a while, and I figured it was about time. Besides, what better place to do so? Yale had other ideas and narrow-mindedly forced me to "major" in an area. Taking all knowledge as my province turned out to be a bit more difficult than I had postulated, as All Knowledge had gotten a bit broader since Leonardo's time. In fact, almost immediately upon arriving in New Haven, I found that All Knowledge was now too big for its britches, or for mine, so I regretfully cut back my ambitious agenda and decided to sacrifice—opera. Hard to do, but something had to go.

Naturally I had forgotten that lesson when I started White Wolf Capital after I left AES. Linda and I were at something of a dead end about the movies, and she was very deeply involved in Enron stuff. They were paying her a salary, so it was churlish to complain too much. I figured if I couldn't do movies, being a baby venture capitalist was as good as anything. What I decided was to take all business plans, any business anywhere, as my province. Sounds sort of like going off to Yale, no? I set myself up in a small office in Arlington, made up the name with my daughter Elika's help, got a friend of Linda's to draw up a logo, had business cards printed up saying "Managing Director" (a title I've always admired although I can't tell you exactly what it means) and hung out my shingle as a venture capitalist. Not that I was very informed about what one was.

I did set two clear goals: first, I wasn't going to invest in any energy businesses. I had been doing energy stuff since 1973, and I had it in mind to learn new stuff, especially stuff related to science and technology. Second, I didn't want to lose a lot of money, rapidly. Always set goals that you at least have a chance of achieving; that's what they taught me in business school. Those two seemed to be reasonable.

So, armed with my goals and my intentions, I sat myself down in my not very fancy office, in a location not known as a hotbed of venture capital activity, North Arlington. More like a cold bed of activity. The closest offices of any consequence were those of the US Air Force Association, your old buddies. This should give you an indication of the nature of the neighborhood. I had a nice view of the new Arlington County jail, from which I was assured jailbreaks were rare. But the office space was cheap, and they gave you a desk and a chair and answered your phone as if you were real.

Then I couldn't figure out anything else to do, so I waited. I drank coffee and read the *Wall Street Journal* so that anyone coming by would be clear that I was a business person, and I wasn't just working for some nonprofit or interest group. Also they gave you free coffee in the offices.

You may be getting the picture that I was a bit nervous about this. Let's review the bidding: First, I had never done this before, didn't know anyone doing it, and didn't know how to do it. I figured I had a shot at being the

Maytag repairman of private capital, sitting there in my office, cobwebs growing on me and nobody calling. I did make a few tentative contacts with people I sort of knew in the community, and I did let people know when I left AES that this was what I would be doing, but shucks, those people weren't entrepreneurs, and they already had good jobs. Having no experience is sometimes a drawback. How do you get started? Do you advertise? Do you stick flyers on the windshields of cars in parking lots? Do you do a mass mailing? To whom? What if you haven't gone to mass in a while? Do you hire somebody to walk around with a sandwich board?

Not to worry. This was a big wrong notion. The demand for money to fund start-up businesses is essentially infinite, and the supply is surely not. No sooner had I proclaimed that I was one of these things, a "venture capitalist," than suddenly business plans started showing up left and right. And center. People stopped me in the hall, asking, "What is White Wolf Capital?" And when I mumbled the words "venture capital" the response was always, "Say, I've got a friend/relative/acquaintance who's got a business plan; would you be interested?" And of course I always said yes, what else did I have to do? I said I had money, and people believed me and asked for some of it. Many people.

I got business proposals from the cousins of old Army buddies, from the best friend of my daughter, from numerous people who stopped me in the hall, from several friends of AES people, and from several AES people who left the company to form their own businesses. I felt a little like I was a studio head in Hollywood and everybody wanted to discuss movie ideas with me. It quickly got to the point where I could have literally spent twenty-four hours a day reading business plans and meeting with people with ideas. Amazing.

The next blinding insight I had (number one being that if you have money, it is not difficult to get into a business whose focus is getting rid of it) was with regard to business plans. A business plan (OK, this is probably a redundant explanation, but I didn't know it when I started) is a very carefully structured document that is, in fact, just what it seems. There are books on how to write them, there are short and long courses you can take on how to write them, there are articles in business publications about how to write them—you get the picture. For some reason, the majority of entrepreneurs I dealt with had carefully avoided all these helpful teaching aids. They usually knew just enough to submit something with "Business Plan" on its cover, but it generally stopped there. As did, with depressing frequency, things like logic, careful presentation, grammar, syntax, and good spelling. Pretty surprising. I quickly stopped reading ones that had spelling and punctuation errors, as well as the ones where I couldn't tell after one page just what in the world these people wanted my money *for*. This saved a great deal of time.

The third insight came more slowly. As you recall, I had decided that of all the things I might invest in, energy would be completely excluded. I didn't want to find myself in any possible competition with AES, and I wanted to get into the high tech business in some way that didn't require learning how to write computer code. Unfortunately energy was the only business area about which I knew two cents, where I understood the technologies, knew who the competitors were, grasped the production and distribution mechanisms, had any contacts, etc. And one rule of venture capital is that, in fact, you can't be all things to all persons, and the folks who do best are the ones who specialize in an area.

I started to figure this out when, at the suggestion of Bart Holaday, my old Air Force Academy classmate, I signed up for something called the "Socially Responsible Venture Capital Forum."

We must now pause a moment and think about this designation. It is generally thought that venture capitalists are a particularly tough—some would say rapacious—bunch, interested in extracting the maximum value from the minimum investment from the poor entrepreneur with the brilliant idea. Not to mention requiring him or her, as a part of the funding arrangements, to mortgage his or her house, turn over his firstborn if attractive, and personally assume all sorts of burdens and obligations to make sure that the fledging business has her or his full attention. I may have been new at this, but I wasn't sure that "socially responsible venture capitalism" wasn't something of an oxymoron. But I liked Bart, and had time on my hands, so off I went to the conference on same. It was in Los Angeles, home of Social Responsibility, and the Laker Girls. Here are some of the socially responsible companies that presented themselves as ready for socially responsible investors like, I guess, me:

» A guy making chocolate in Central America, only not on plantations (bad) but using indigenous people, viz, NOT peons, to go out and harvest the cacao pods from the forest. They were, in fact, making pretty doggone good chocolate (I had several samples) and, more important: a) preserving the rain forest, and b) employing the natives. A quick analysis of this leads one to ask: first, who exactly owns the rain forest that these guys are running around in nabbing all the cacao pods from, and when they find out, will they be peeved; and second, is it "sustainable" (another important socially responsible word) to perpetuate what is essentially hunting and gathering? Or maybe just gathering. There is, after all, a reason that agriculture was invented. But it was hard to ask such questions with a mouth full of chocolate.

» A woman whose business idea was to take butterflies collected in Central America, encase them in resin, and put them on key chains or make them into paperweights. Because these butterflies would be raised on farms and tended by indigenous peoples (read "peons") this was sustainable, since the butterflies, and maybe moths, too—it wasn't entomologically clear—would *not* be collected from the rain forest, and hence it would be preserved. Detail on how much rain forest had to be cut down to create the butterfly farms was not available. Nor was any survey on how the butterflies felt about all of this. No caterpillars need apply. The same people at the conference, the socially responsible venture capitalists, oohed and aahed at this presentation, just as they had at the chocolate one. I tried to be open (and warm and sensitive), but there was a lot of stuff that was similar. I tried to ask someone why farms were good if they were called farms and bad if they were called plantations, and how could both the farm and the no-farm case be saving the rain forest. No one seemed much interested in this question. I then suggested that these two folks could get together and maybe offer chocolate covered butterflies, which by my calculation had to be at least twice as socially responsible. People at the conference began avoiding me for some reason.

» I talked to one of the socially responsible VCs. "What's your best socially responsible investment?" I asked. "Well, I've looked at a lot of companies, examined their records and all, and I've put a lot of money into Microsoft."

» My favorite was a company that made a machine, a sort of radio transmitter/receiver, which you located in the home of an elderly person who you were worried might wander away. You, I note with despair, have wandered away from Hawaii to Olympia, Washington. If only such technology had been available at the time. The potential wanderee wears a smaller transmitter, and when he/she passes beyond a set boundary, the central machine senses this, and in response sends a signal to the receiver on the patient, which makes a kind of strong and no doubt startling buzz. The central unit, busybody that it is, also dials the caregiver and leaves a telephone message that the patient's off to Cleveland. The whole setup was really expensive, and it wasn't clear to me what you did once you lost radio contact with the departee. Could you track him down like a stolen car? Were we talking about LoJack for Alzheimer's here? Or was this just an invisible dog fence for Granny?

It was the end of the second day, I was tired, I had heard a lot of certainly silly but allegedly socially responsible ideas. I found myself at lunch with the wandering patient buzzer guys. Bart Holaday was with me, so I blame him for what followed, at least in part. Old Air Force guys get together, and who knows what can happen? "Would this work on cats?" I asked the company sponsors.

They were temporarily befuddled. Then, like good entrepreneurs, they rallied. "Of course," they said.

"So, like, if your cat started to leave home you could buzz it?"

"Sure," they responded.

"Could you even step it up a little bit and put an electric charge in the receiver?" I asked. "So you could give your cat a mild shock if it went off the reservation?"

There was a slight pause on the part of my conversation partner. "I guess so," the inventor said.

Bart began to get inspired and socially responsible. "How about if the cat went really too far, could there be a small charge of C-4 on the receiver, and could you blow him up?" he chimed in.

"Well, I don't know . . ." they responded.

Bart was not to be denied. "I suppose you could even blow cats up randomly, based on some algorithm," he mused. Every so often us venture capitalists have to use words like "algorithm" even though most of us truly wouldn't recognize an algorithm if it bit us in the patootie, which would be hard for a mathematical expression, but perhaps not impossible. Algorithms are dangerous when aroused.

"Exploding cats, now that would be worth investing in," I agreed. The entrepreneurs looked at each other, and then at us, and decided to skip dessert.

Actually, there was one interesting business there: a woman with a line of decent frozen meals for kids. The current industry standard kids meal is composed of 80% fat, 5% salt, and the remainder sugar. Sort of like eating nothing but potato chips, except with more sugar. She came out of the food marketing industry, had done her homework, and didn't have an inflated idea of what she actually had and what it might be worth. Her name was Fran something or other, and her meals were called Fran's Healthy Helpings. Maybe the name wasn't a marketing person's dream, but this was, after all, a start-up.

I got interested, read her business plan, and with Linda's help did such due diligence as occurred to us, which consisted of going to the super-market frozen food section and buying some of the competition's meals. Holy freezer burn, Batman! The stuff was awful. It was awful because it was a TV dinner, except it was stuff like chicken nuggets shaped into flat pictures of drumsticks, accompanied by macaroni and cheese, ketchup (still a vegetable in these folks' eyes), no other vegetable, and always some variant of tater tots: cylindrical, round, even pyramidal. If your kid isn't a fat, hyperactive whiner on his way to early onset diabetes before this, you feed him enough of this junk and he will be.

Eventually I found myself in Los Angeles, talking to the production guy Fran had lined up to make her meals. I'll bet you didn't know that the production of frozen meals was a small subindustry all its own, and neither did I. Swanson, Banquet, and all those folks who make TV dinners don't actually make them, they sub it out. This guy ran a big factory in LA employing, as you might suspect, a fair number of Latin Americans; it's not a great job. He wouldn't actually let me onto the factory floor, but it's got to be cold. He said he liked Fran and liked her concept, and he got about five calls a week from people wanting to get him to make frozen food for them. Mostly he turned them down, but not her. And then Linda and I met with Fran, and she answered all our questions reasonably, and it didn't take long. We were pretty much set to invest.

But on the plane back from LA, we had a couple of glasses of wine and decided to confront Truth. Wine can do that to you at high altitudes. "Bob," she said (that being my name at the time). "We don't know much about this industry, do we?"

"Well," I responded judiciously, "I had a TV dinner in 1989; I think it was one of the Mexican ones."

"But we don't know how the distribution channels work, we don't actually know if there is a distribution channel; we don't know what trade publications to subscribe to, we don't know what trade shows to go to; we don't know what it costs to make this stuff or to sell it; we don't have any sort of mental model of how things work in this business."

I had to admit that she was right, as well as being beautiful. You set me down with a power plant proposal, and I have twenty years of accumulated experience, seasoned liberally with bias, prejudice, and inappropriate anecdote to apply to the evaluation process. Here we got squat. I don't even think I bought Elika [my daughter] a TV dinner when she was a kid, and that was a couple of years ago. "Do you suppose we should be a little more focused?" I asked. "And if so, on what?"

"You remember *The Graduate*?" she asked.

"Sure, but do you really think we should do plastics?"

"No, you silly person, but my one word for you is 'movie theaters.'"

Clearly she'd been thinking about this, and so it began to appear that we weren't through with the movies yet.

———

Back in Washington, we had a friend of a friend arrange for us to have lunch with a guy named Milton Herson, a movie theater expert and veteran who had been through the entire business. He had built up his own chain of theaters, sold them to Loews, was a vice president for them, helped manage the integration of Loews and Cinemax, then went into the government and was head of the Government Services Administration— Uncle Sam's real estate manager—and was now semiretired. But he knew everything about the cinema business, all the things we didn't know. He knew how much theaters cost to build, how much they cost to operate, how to get the best deal from the distributors, how to keep your employees from stealing you blind, what the margins on popcorn and Coke were—all that stuff. Combined with what we knew about international business, it seemed like a natural fit.

To better explain what we were about, I need to give you two sets of data that you can then interrelate, and if I've done this right you'll see how we got to the UK. We slowly compiled this understanding over a period of time by talking to people, going to trade shows, and mostly asking lots of stupid questions. This took us probably the better part of a year. We have sadly discovered that to learn about a new industry, you can't just swallow a pill; you actually have to do a lot of work and spend a lot of time. Imagine my disappointment. And it's always like picking up a novel and starting to read it at the fifth chapter. You can tell that people are doing things to each other, but it takes a long time to figure out why. But enough whining; let us begin. Set of facts number one, which pertain to how the movie theater business works:

» Bums in seats: the good part. Movie theaters are not about movies; they're really a real estate business, only you have to sell the real estate—the seats—every day (well rent them, actually), unlike an office building where you can get people to sign a twenty-year lease. In an office space lease you pay, for example, $37 per square foot per year, then you get to have a nice office that you can use all the time if you want to.

You go to the movies, they rent you the seat, which entitles you to a space of about 22 inches by 40 inches, or six and eleven one-hundredths square feet, for about 100 minutes, the average flick being 90 minutes long.

You, the movie attendee, are paying $7 a ticket. When you go through the numbers in office rental terms this is the same as renting office space, not for $37, but for $6,015.71/square foot/year. This is 163 times what an office made out of the same space would pay. Of course, the people in the office don't get to sit there and watch Arnold Schwarzenegger; they have to work. It's an interesting price differential, no? And bear in mind that constructing theater space is not hugely more expensive per square foot than building office space.

» Bums in seats: the less good part. Office trolls rent the space 24/7/365, as they say in the customer service business. You movie patrons, fickle lot that you are, rent the space very temporarily, so the real number to focus on is not the $6,000 and change listed above, it's the occupancy rate. As in, what percentage of the time are the seats actually occupied? But wait, listen to what the thin and crotchety person residing in the back of your head, wearing a green eye shade, sitting at a desk lit only by an unshaded light bulb hanging down from the ceiling and manipulating a calculator, says: "You can't show movies 24/7/365, so occupancy rate has to be calculated based on how many times per week or year you can actually reasonably expect people to come to your theater." How many shows per day, in other words.

And he's right, as he always is. This number turns out to be two times per day during the week and maybe four times per day on weekends. Five, if you really push it. Folks just don't go to the movies at nine o'clock on a Tuesday morning. They should, and the world would be a better place if they did, but they don't. So each seat can be rented about eighteen times per week, maybe at the most twenty. Theaters do well to maintain a 50% occupancy rate—nine or ten sales per seat per week. And this is hugely, gigantically dependent on, I'll say it, the quality of the movie being shown! Over which you have no control.

» "Well, then, I'll only show the good movies." Actually you, the theater owner, do have some control, only not as much as you would think. The physical movies themselves are in the control of the studios— Disney, Fox, Paramount, MGM, DreamWorks, United Artists, Universal, and Warner Brothers—who, as I have mentioned in other letters—aren't studios anymore, they're just gigantic Blockbusters. What they do is rent their movies out to the theaters, known in the trade generically as the "chains," because the individual movie theaters are generally owned by a series of larger corporations: Loews, Cineplex Odeon, Carmike, AMC, Edwards, United Artists, and Regal in the US, and some of these plus some others overseas: Village Roadshow (Aussies), Ster-Kinekor (South African), Golden Harvest (Hong Kong), and so forth.

Here's how it works: the studios have control of the movies because they own them outright or have exclusive distribution deals for them. But they need the theaters to show them. They rent out the movies to the theaters, but on a share of the ticket price basis. What is neat about this is that, as a theater owner, YOU HAVE NO INVENTORY COST. In simplest terms, you put *The Madness of King George* in one of your auditoriums, and if nobody wants to see it, you don't owe the studio a thing. You send them back the movie, say thank you, and spool up *Julia Roberts Loves Some Loser, III* and away you go. You are, in essence, getting your movies on consignment. You and the studio split the general revenues fifty-fifty, although human beings being what they are, much complication has been introduced into the formulae. For example, 80% for the studios, 20% for the theaters the first week, then 70-30 the second week, then 60-40 the third week, and so on. It's all a negotiation, but it's rather like the frontier knife fight where the two guys are chained together. The studios need the theaters, the theaters need the studios. Hence history and relationships play a big part in this. Not every theater got *Star Wars* and there's a reason for that, and it's not all just revenue split.

» Revenge of the theater: the invention of the multiplex. This is the coolest thing we learned about theaters. When you and I grew up, we went to the movies and it was one building and one show. Big marquee out front, popcorn inside, red carpeting, the odd statue of some Egyptian goddess holding a light fixture, the works. But everybody went to the same movie, because there was only one auditorium and one screen. In about 1964, some genius at AMC decided that there was not necessarily a law of God that said that you could only have one "screen" per location, and invented the multiplex, starting with four screens or auditoriums. But that wasn't the brilliant part. What they did was set it up so they had four auditoriums of four different sizes; say 400 seats, 300 seats, 200 seats, and 100 seats. So when they opened a new movie, they put it into the 400-seat auditorium. Depending on how well it did, they gradually moved it down until in its final week it was playing in the 100-seat venue. Now I have been to the movies a bunch, as have all God-fearing patriotic Americans, and though I pride myself on being a pretty analytical guy, it never occurred to me to think about auditorium size as a part of the moviegoing experience. And I don't know anybody who walks up to the ticket window and says, "I'd like to be in the two hundred-seat auditorium, please, but I don't care what the movie is." If you make all theaters equally comfortable, who, for goodness sake, is going to care? As the movie wanes in popularity, the theater owner just moves it down to a smaller and smaller auditorium and puts the new release in the larger space. It has no effect, really, on the quality of the customer's experience. Pretty neat, huh?

» So where's the real dough? Generally, the tickets pay the rent and the concessions make the return. Every moviegoer, on average, spends one third of his ticket price on concessions: the classic popcorn and Cokes. You no doubt have noticed how much popcorn costs in a theater? Well, it's only about a 600% markup over cost of goods sold. Same for Cokes, which are largely water and ice. Concessions are a very big deal and a very big (perhaps the only) profit center in the theater. And no, you can't bring your own popcorn from home.

———

That's how it works: you get your inventory for free (the movies) so you have no carrying costs, no risk of having bought fuchsia outfits for your clothing store when this year it's chartreuse; you hire minimum wage labor, and not many of them; you sell popcorn and Cokes for far more than they cost; and it's all cash, so you haven't got any credit worries, no uncollectable bills from customers who skip town. Keep a good relationship with the studios, you get the best movies, and you fill the seats. You fill the seats, you get the best movies. Just make sure you don't build a theater that's too expensive or in the wrong place. These last, of course, are basic real estate laws.

Now for the second set of facts: Eastern Europe, land of opportunity.

We made a bunch of trips to Eastern Europe on the theory that there weren't many theaters there. This was a good theory. In 1996, despite five years of freedom, democracy, and the capitalist system, there wasn't much of anything there. Just old decrepit buildings, poorly dressed people, not much traffic on the streets, and those ranks, and ranks, and ranks, of twelve-story blocky apartments. Warsaw, Budapest, Bucharest, Prague, Bratislava, Kosice, Sofia. We went to all of them, looking at existing theaters and sites for new theaters. Illustrative example number one:

It is a cold, rainy Thursday evening in Warsaw. We are researching the movie theater biz, so after spending all day looking at sites, we decide to go to the movies. We find a downtown theater named "Na Provisyky" (meaning who-knows-what in Polish, maybe "The Majestic") where a movie called *The Juror* is playing starring Demi Moore and Alec Baldwin. Basically it's a lousy movie and did poorly in the US in theatrical release. Also it's playing in English with Polish subtitles.

We interrupt this narrative to discuss the subject of subtitles versus dubbing, a key issue in the industry outside the US. I know you'll be interested as well. As beginners/outsiders when we first started investigating the business, we asked dumb questions. We got, to our surprise, even dumber answers in many cases. For example: Why, we asked, are movies first released in the US, then rolled out slowly across the globe, first Europe, then Asia—who knows when they get to Africa. You release *Independence Day*, you get all this free advertising, it's on the cover of *Time* magazine worldwide, yet you can't see it in Hamburg until November. It's featured on *Entertainment Tonight*, or CNN, or any global TV program—and there are many—and you lose all that name recognition and free advertising value in Singapore and Buenos Aires because the movie doesn't come along until months later.

Well, we were told by several people all wearing straight faces, this is because the Europeans want to see what kind of box office the film does in the US first, then they decide whether or not to see it. We looked at each other. "You know, you're right," said Linda, "I can't count the number of times we've been to the movies in London or Paris and saw all those folks standing in line with their copies of *Variety*, looking up the box office numbers in the US so they'd know what to see."

Now back to our main question and answer: Why aren't all the movies dubbed; why use subtitles at all? Well, knowledgeable industry insiders said to us: that's easy, it's because Europeans like to practice their English when they go to the movies. We got this answer more than one time.

It's hard to know how to react to this. I am a big fan of English, given that it's my best language, some would say my only language, although I claim French and Spanish as well. I surely can believe that people in Europe are so serious and so oriented to participating in the global economy that they welcome the chance to try and read difficult-to-see subtitles when they go out on Saturday night to see Bruce Willis. Education is so important. If only Americans had the same opportunities.

The truth, it turns out, is far simpler. Subtitles are much, much cheaper to put on movies than dubbing, by about eight or nine to one. And when it's specialized languages like Czech or Slovak, nobody bothers. It's not a big enough market. Interesting sub-note: almost all Disney movies are in fact dubbed, but this is not because the Disney folks want a better cinema experience for their patrons, but because they recognize that they want to attract a lot of kids, and the little buggers can't read subtitles. Aha.

We now return you to the cold and rainy night in downtown Warsaw. The theater was poorly lighted on the outside—actually there were neither lights nor a marquee. We had been informed by the concierge at our hotel that the movie was playing and that the theater was open, but when we got there you sure couldn't tell that from the outside; it was dark and there was nobody around. But we checked and the theater did turn out to be open, so we bought tickets from a surly ticket booth person. We looked into the small, dimly lit lobby and saw no one. There was a very limited concession stand, again not lighted, looking like a candy counter with no one behind it to sell you some Jujubes or Sno-Caps. "We're probably going to be the only people in the stupid theater," I said to Linda.

"Yes," she said, "not so many people wanting to practice their English tonight." We went off to get a quick beer at a nearby bar and came back about five minutes before the show was supposed to start. Still nobody around. We walked into the auditorium. Bazongo! It was packed! There were literally only two seats in the whole theater. We were quite surprised and impressed. And the movie really was a stinker.

Illustrative example number two: Wednesday night, Budapest. I was on my own, looking again for theaters and sites. This time I went to the old part of the town to see a movie, Bernardo Bertolucci's *Stealing Beauty*, a nice Italian arty number with Jeremy Irons. Probably anything with Jeremy Irons qualifies as arty, since I don't think he's ever actually made a popular movie. And I'll bet my truck he's never been in a movie that grossed $1 million, the Hollywood magic number.

The building was crumby, with an uneven wooden floor, unwept and dusty. There was limited lighting and no concession booth at all. And wooden seats, just like in your third-grade auditorium—remember those? I'd sure never seen them in a theater before. The movie began, and I watched it with vague interest. It was about a bunch of Italians, in Tuscany, in the summer, sitting around talking to each other, swimming naked in their swimming pool, eating and drinking outside in the golden Italian sunlight. Really not so interesting, even the naked parts. After a bit, I slowly began to notice that something was nagging me about the movie. Other than the total lack of plot. Finally I figured out that it was not in focus, except the out-of-focus part was around the outside part of the screen. The entire image wasn't out of focus, just the 20% comprising the edges. I promise that Bernardo, artiste that he may be, did not shoot his movie partially out of focus. Some combination of screen, projector, and perhaps projectionist were at fault. In the US, legitimately enough, within about two minutes the genteel patrons would all have been yelling, "Focus, focus!" Not in Budapest. And once again, the theater was jammed, packed full, not an empty wooden seat in the house, focus or no. We were convinced.

Soon to come: We discover Prague. No, it wasn't lost, that's just a figure of speech.

Love and kisses,
Bob

# thirteen

# the uk is not the us, even though both names start with "united"

March 1998

Dear Dad,

Once we decided to be movie theater moguls, I began flying back and forth and back and forth from D.C. to Eastern Europe, trying to find sites to build a theater or theaters for sale. Eventually we tired of single-handedly supporting Richard Branson, although Virgin Airlines is really pretty great, and they give you gray sweat suits to wear when you fly "Upper Class," a nice touch although a sweat suit doesn't bring out the best in every figure. After some debate we bought a house and moved to London. Well technically, we bought a house, moved to London, and then bought another house. More on that later. We first thought about actually moving to Eastern Europe, since that's where we were focusing our efforts and negotiations, but we weren't ready to be that adventurous. And we thought, foolishly, that the UK would be pretty much like the US, only closer to Budapest. Physically, that is. The closer part was right.

Ahh-hoo-ho-ha! It's a furrin' country over there in the land of the big-eared prince with the horsy girlfriend and the dead princess with the divorce and a rose named after her. Here are just few of the more curious things we encountered.

Where's Walmart (and Staples and Giant, etc.) when you need it? Boy, are we spoiled in the US when it comes to shopping. Or maybe we are just particularly good at it. Shopping may actually be one of our National Talents. What they don't have in the UK is, well, it's a long list. How about:

*No place to park.* No place to park. No place to park. I think you get my meaning. London was never designed with the automobile in mind. It is a charming city of neighborhoods. The one we lived in was Hampstead in North London, home of Charles Dickens when he was alive, and lots of other famous people who I can't remember, mostly arty and many dead. I suppose technically that it's no longer the home of the dead ones.

Each London neighborhood has a shopping area called a "high street." But it's just a piece of London street connected at each end to more street, with lots of traffic on it (coming from both ends as it happens), and the stores all right next to each other, and a few on-street parking places, always taken, and no parking lots. I say again, no parking lots. You're supposed to walk everywhere and carry everything home by hand. This may explain why all the stores sell things in little tiny portions. Lots of single cans of beer. A single chicken thigh. A single wing, for goodness sake. Not, unfortunately, a single Brussels sprout.

This probably worked OK when everyone had a wife who stayed home all the time and could walk to the shops each day. And had big shoulders from carrying home each day's provisions. Or in Hampstead where there are big and grand old houses, where everyone had servants who could walk to the stores each day to get the master a drumstick and a beer. And nobody drove their cars there. Maybe they rode in on their horses. And this goes for everything: hardware, furniture, clothing, books and magazines, etc. All these stores are on the High Streets, not in malls where they belong. Very cute looking but lousy to put up with if you actually have to live there.

*No place to buy stuff efficiently, even if you could park.* What there are not, are the "big box" retailers. No Kmart, or Walmart, or Mattress Discounters. And when you're outfitting a new house, that's exactly what you need. Here's a good example. We needed some beds, because we had a big house and it had a lot of rooms in it, as big houses tend to unless they're gymnasiums, and we figured we should put some beds in some of them. We searched the yellow pages and found "Mattress Superstore." We were new in town, but this sounded like just what we were looking for. So I jumped in our rented car and drove forever. And got to, yes, another high street, with a little storefront-type store with a big sign over the top of it that said "Mattress Superstore." I suppose I should mention that there was no place to park but it might be redundant. The superstore was about the size of a 7-Eleven.

Later we discovered that the recent fashion in retailing in London was to call yourself a "superstore," even if you were selling hot dogs out of a pushcart. We never actually saw "Frankfurter Superstore" but it wouldn't surprise me if there were one. Actually we did find one big box store. Near us was a Toys "R" Us with a big parking lot. At one point I actually talked to one of the guys who developed that store for Toys "R" Us. He was a Yank, and like all us folks from the US who go abroad to try to do business, he had been indoctrinated that he was an insensitive American clod and didn't know anything about foreign countries, and so he had to listen carefully, not violate religious taboos, try to fit in, not point the sole of his shoe at someone, remember that Thursday was a holy day on alternate months, and generally understand the needs and customs of local people, ad nauseam.

When he was laying out the plan for the store, his local consultants all looked at him and said, "Why do you need such a giant parking lot?" And they looked at his hiring plans and said, "Why do you need so many people?" When he explained to them that the parking lot was for people to drive to the store and be able to park, and that the people to be hired were so he could be open and operate on normal commercial hours with decent staff coverage, they informed him that this was not how things were done in their country. Waste of money, no one would come to shop at night, nobody would drive there and park, and everybody took the tube or taxis everywhere. Fortunately he persisted, and the place was jammed, parking lot and inside, every time we went by. Even at night, until 10:00 p.m. when it finally closed.

*Even when you find a place to buy stuff, it's not open.* When do people who work actually have time to shop? This is not a trick question. Yes, after work, as in, after 5:30 or 6:00, or on the weekends. Here's my favorite example: Say you are, oh, let me see, how about the most famous retail name in all of the UK, you operate a big fancy department store in down-town London, right in the heart of the upscale tourist area, your facility is one where everyone who comes to the UK would like to go shopping and probably buy something with your logo on it to take home and show their friends and prove that they've been to London. Surveys have been done which conclude that "shopping" is among the top three vacation activities of everyone, even the French. Given the above, here's the riddle: when are you open, and who are you? The answers should be that you're open late every evening and of course on the weekends. And that would be the answer in the US. But in the UK, you close every evening promptly at 5:30, except for Thursday evening when you are open until the unheard of late hour of 8:00. And you're closed on Sunday. By the way, your name is Harrods. This is not just a peculiar exception because the owner of the store is mad at the English because they won't let him become a citizen, so he's punishing them by not letting them shop at this store. It's the pattern all over London. And it's probably worse outside of town. Maybe it's because the BBC secretly controls the country and wants to make sure everyone is home watching awful British television in the evenings, and especially on Sunday. It's hard to get enough of those "panel of experts" TV shows. Although I liked the gardening ones, except I missed the car chases and explosions.

*No business services.* Is there a real person named Kinko? I don't care; I love him even if he's imaginary. You can get copies of stuff made even on Christmas! It's great! It's convenient! It's pretty cheap! If you have a rush job, they'll do it quickly! They'll let you use their computer and printer and won't get mad at you even if you have a virus on your disk! They even have one in Olympia, that God-forsaken place where you live! They don't have any in London! Or anything like it.

We went into the Quicksey Print store on Regent Street, near our offices, after we'd been in town about a month, because we needed copies of a set of presentation slides to take with us to a meeting in Prague. All we wanted was twenty copies of a fifteen-page presentation, printed and bound, and we already had the originals. Cover page was color, the rest black and white. "Rush," we said, even though we had a couple of days before we were to leave and were therefore prepared much sooner than normal for us. Our standing rule is always to change the slides as many times as possible, up until the very last minute.

"Righto," said the cheerful attendant. "Have these for you first thing next Tuesday." It was Monday.

"You mean tomorrow?" we asked, although technically that would have been the "next" Tuesday.

"Oh, no, man, Tuesday week. You wanted it 'rush,' right?" We left, stunned. We called Instantie Print, Rapidie Print, Fastie Print. No dice, pretty much the same answer. Other business services were the same, as in nonexistent. No car, or limo, or cab service that you could set up a credit account with. No Staples that would deliver an order of office supplies the next day. You couldn't even call up American Express in London and get them to send you over your tickets for Warsaw; you had to go to their office to make the reservation. We finally figured out that you could call American Express in the US (collect on their nickel), make a reservation, buy the ticket, and have them FedEx it to your office in the UK. And all this was simpler than trying to buy a ticket from the same company at their UK offices. Maybe this is globalization, but it's a funny and inefficient kind.

*Omigod, the food.* Yes, the war is still on, Nazi subs control the seas, nothing is getting through to our brave British compatriots but canned peas and Brussels sprouts. Or possibly there's a storm coming and everyone has rushed to the stores in preparation for five days of 100-mile per hour winds and torrential rains, trees uprooted, bridges washed out, roadways flooded, no one able to leave his or her house for fear of being struck by flying debris. The UK is popularly known for having not so great a national cuisine, although there are now a number of very good restaurants in London. But try to live there and shop in the supermarkets. Go on, I dare you. Here's what you'll find.

Weird Design Fact Number One: the stores are big, and some even have parking lots. Yes! At last! Inside they have really wide aisles, big enough that four shopping carts can pass abreast should they ever need to. Maybe it's a fire regulation. I myself rarely encounter four shoppers abreast who wish to pass by each other. And they actually can't in the UK because of Weird Design Fact Number Two: the design authorities persist in requiring that all four wheels on the shopping carts rotate. You've been through Heathrow; it's the same on the damn baggage carts. What this means is that you can't actually steer your shopping cart or your luggage cart very well as it tends to go off sideways. Eventually you find your-self still gamely going north to south, but your shopping cart has rotated itself into an east-west direction, although all four of its little wheels are going north to south. By the way, this is not a European thing; maybe it's something to do with the Commonwealth, although I don't remember this perversion in Australia. But I digress.

Weird Design Fact Number Three: the shelves in the stores are all nice and low so that as you walk along them you can actually see over the top into the next aisle. Now this may be genteel and gracious and all that, and it does allow you to converse with acquaintances one aisle over should you encounter any in a talkative mood, but if you think about it in terms of stuff, as in "a store is a place to buy stuff," it's not great on the stuff axis. What you have is a lot of room and not much stuff.

Personally when I am in search of graciousness and gentility and random chats with friends, I don't usually think of going to the grocery store. I go to a grocery store to buy stuff, normally stuff related to, containing, or in some other fashion having to do with food. And because the stores are laid out so inefficiently, there isn't much food for such big stores. We calculated, roughly, that for the same square foot of retail space in a US store, you got at least 80% more merchandise. And no meaningful decrease in politesse. There are other peculiarities—the low fat items are labeled "half fat" and the not low ones are labeled "full fat." At least they're truthful.

But back to the stuff. Store shelves do not seem to be restocked other than every time the British win the World Cup. Linda went "shopping" at our local Sainsbury's one evening about 6:30. This is not a task she enjoys, and why I ever consented to subject her to it I cannot imagine. But there she is, it's early evening (although in the UK in winter the sun goes down about 3:30, but the weather is the subject of another letter) and she has her little list with her and is dutifully trying to check things off. But she can't, because they don't have anything.

We weren't trying to buy swallow's tongues, or rhinoceros filets, or hundred-year-old Lafite Rothschild burgundy. Just items like milk, and juice, and bread, and chicken, and lettuce, and tomatoes, and paper towels. Finally she managed to find the store manager. "Is there a storm coming? Like a hurricane or something?" she asked.

The manager seemed puzzled. "No, I don't believe so," she replied.

"When do you stock your shelves?" Linda asked.

"Every morning, first thing," the manager responded. "What is it you're having trouble finding?"

Waving her list in the face of the manager, my wife demurely, but with some agitation, said, "Everything!" It was true. There was an entire fixture with rows of shelves for bread, and on these same shelves a grand total of one loaf of bread resided. All the fresh vegetables were essentially gone, except of course the b. sprouts. Very bad idea of first precepts on how to sell things, like rule one: keep the shelves stocked.

One other paradox—all the fresh food seemed to spoil within twenty minutes of getting it home. So you couldn't just go and load up for the week. All those shelves, no shelf life.

It wasn't just the food stores. When you went to the office supply stores, which you had to since they didn't deliver and you needed a cartridge for your Xerox machine, you had to drive forty-five minutes to get to the store and then spend twenty minutes trying to find a parking place. This transportation feat accomplished, you then found that they did have the cartridge sometimes, but they only had one. So you had burned two hours to buy one thirty-dollar Xerox machine cartridge, which would need to be replaced in two weeks. You would have bought a crate if they had had such unthinkable quantities available. No chance.

And then there was British Telecom. We wanted to get both of our names listed on the phone in our home, since we spent some time working at our office there. Even though we had four lines, BT was unwilling to list more than one name in its directory service even if we paid them to do so. We offered untold riches, but no dice. They had no limit on what your name could be, however, so I eventually announced to them that the name of the subscriber was Linda Powers Robert Hemphill. They thought that was fine, and that's how we were listed. Strange, huh? I was sure they'd make us hyphenate the last name. On the other hand, for some reason they hooked one of our lines up to what had apparently been the alarm system line and then never billed us for calls on that line and number, ever, of which there were quite a few since this was the line we used for our fax.

Many other interesting things have happened to us here, not all the result of the peculiarities of the British retail system. Like the first time I washed some clothes. I have actually been doing this for some time. Not the same batch of clothes but performing this relatively uncomplicated household activity. I sort of like it—it's orderly and you can see accomplishment. Not like vacuuming, which is hateful, and you can't ever see any results unless you've spilled flour all over the rug. When I lived in a slightly decrepit town house on Capitol Hill as a young bachelor, my roommate and I didn't have a washer and dryer so I had to go to the Laundromat. Eventually I figured out that the way to make this most efficient was to have a really large amount of underwear and only go there about every four months. Yes, and still wear a clean pair of underwear every day in case I was in a car accident and they took me to the hospital to examine my underwear. This is the first thing that happens to accident victims, as we all know.

Well, anyhow, you roll into the Laundromat, which all look the same everywhere—after all, how many ways are there to arrange a lot of washers and dryers?—carrying five or six olive drab laundry bags, mostly an Army inheritance, full of 120 pairs of underwear and socks and T-shirts, and load up about seven washers at a time, go to the Safeway next door, buy lots of beer and an entire chicken, come back, and put all the wash into several of those gigantic dryers, and open a beer and read the *Post*. You're probably done in an hour and a half, and now you don't have to come back until Easter. Modestly I must declare that I am a person who has thought deeply about laundry and am skilled therein.

In our new UK house with the cute garden and the history of having belonged to a Russian count, I figured I would do the laundry. I had not brought 120 pairs of underwear with me. Got the wash part done in our swell Miele appliance, somewhat small compared to any US stuff, but then all of Europe is small when you really think about it, except the Eiffel Tower and any French person's regard for himself. Then I encountered the dryer.

Since this is Europe I am sure that there are EU standards for the symbols used not just on the roadways but on consumer goods as well, since God forbid you use English for the labels on the dials. None of this "more dry, less dry, Sahara" kind of stuff; nope, just cute international symbols that are easily recognizable and interpretable by all sophisticated humans. On this particular dryer, on the knob that seemed to indicate how dry you wanted your clothes to be, there were six choices: one, two, or three round things with teeth, basically a representation for gear wheels, and one, two, or three slightly ovoid things with a point at the top that clearly were the symbol for natural gas. Remember those advertising campaigns, "Choose clean burning natural gas for all your cooking and heating needs"? With the little blue gas flame at the bottom of the ad? Very distinctive and inter- esting that it has been picked up as an international symbol for dryness. Not so clear what the gear wheels have to do with things, but the gas stuff is clear. So I pick three gas flames, clearly the highest heat and thus the driest level for the clothes, and go off and make dinner, probably pasta or perhaps one chicken breast and some sprouts.

I come back to get the clothes, and they are damp as anything. "Dang," I say to myself since Linda is not with me, and there are not other visitors that I know of about the premises. I reset the dryer to the three gas flames, punch "start" again, and go back to either do the dishes or work on my critique of Kierkegaard, I forget which.

I return to get my clothes and they're still wet, like somebody has left them out in the rain. "Darn and heck, stupid German appliances," I mutter, then reset, repunch, and retreat to the study to try and figure out which sports page articles are about soccer and which about cricket. This is harder than it seems.

I return to the dryer and things are still damp as damp can be. The dryer is clearly broken, and in the morning I call a repair person. After a month and a half one actually shows up when he says he will. I explain that I have set the dryer at the three gas flames for really DRY, but what I got was really wet, so perhaps the control logic is goofed up. "Maybe a fried circuit board," I suggest helpfully, although I have not the slightest idea whether this dryer has circuit boards, whether they get fried, whether they control dryness, or whether instead it's a function of three alternating chipmunks buried deep inside the machinery. Then again it could be the heating mechanism, burners, no doubt on the fritz. All service people value help and advice like this.

The repair person looks at me curiously. "Do you have the operating manual?" he asks.

"Well I'm sure it's around here somewhere," I say, "but clearly this is a mechanical and/or electrical problem. The dryer isn't responding to the control setting." I go dig up the manual, which is a booklet whose thickness is a result of the same four sentences of instruction being written in the seventeen official languages and dialects of the European continent.

"Well, here's your problem," says the repair guy. "These three round things . . ."

"Yeah, gear wheels; what can that mean?" I interrupt helpfully.

"Those are suns," he says, "and these other things that look like gas flames are actually drops of water. So what you've been doing is setting the dryer to the maximum wetness setting, three drops of water, not the maximum dryness, which would be three of these sun things. Besides," he adds helpfully, "it's an electric dryer so it doesn't use gas." He departs, thirty-five pounds richer, but I can at least finally dry my laundry, which has been sitting around wet for so long that it's slightly mildewed and I have to wash it again anyway. Boy, though, you set that dryer to three suns and you can just about burn up your clothes! Fry an egg on your blue jeans! Good thing I wasn't drying anything flammable.

Other technological triumphs abound, a chronicle of the joys of moving to a foreign clime and surmounting a myriad of obstacles. Some were easier than others. Take electricity, for example. As you no doubt remember, I am an Electricity Expert due to all my experience, first for four years at TVA (The World's Largest Electric Utility Owned by the Government Located in the Tennessee Valley), then by my sixteen years at AES, where our business was to build power plants and make and sell electricity. Never mind that when we started the company none of the three of us could do much more than spell electricity correctly two out of three times, and we surely had never built a power plant (although I had driven by several) and never sold one kilowatt hour to a single solitary customer.

Thus as an electricity expert, I was able to tell, when I got to the UK, that their electricity is different from our electricity. How did I make this startling technical deduction, you may ask? Well the plugs are all different, which I have found in my dealings with electricity on a professional basis is a very good clue that maybe more parts of the system are different as well.

As a second clue I note that all the UK guidebooks, in the section on electricity, say "Different here!" Plus so did all the expats that we talked to. "Don't forget," they would say upon being introduced to us, "the electricity is different here!" We certainly weren't electricity illiterates, we knew this, and after a while it got sort of repetitive. Like, "Don't forget, drive on the left." I do note that the helpful Brits now have painted signs at all the crosswalks, on the road as you step off the curb, saying "LOOK RIGHT!" with a big white arrow pointing, in fact, right. Of course, if you're not focusing directly down on your toes, you won't see this sign until it's too late. But they're trying.

One of the helpful pieces of information our friends gave us was that you had to change all the plugs on your electrical items and lights, but that you shouldn't bother doing this on the appliances because they wouldn't work anyway. However, the lights would, only you needed to get UK lightbulbs, because if you tried to use US ones after you had changed all the plugs, then the lightbulbs would explode.

This seemed sufficiently dire that we never tried it. OK, I did have a sneaking, little-kid sort of interest in seeing if this were actually true, under a controlled setting, such as with me in a bomb-proof bunker fifty feet away. The new lightbulbs, surprise to say, did in fact fit right into the US lamps. And they worked, once you changed the plugs. I must note that this is no small feat of standardization. The traffic's not the same, the money's not the same, the food's darn sure not the same, the climate is not the same (unless you have been living in your bathtub with the shower on turned to cold), the system of government is not the same (they have a Queen), but the lightbulbs still screw into your US lamps.

When I was a draftsman, a million years ago in Lompoc, California, they taught me something about a standard called the "International Screw Convention." I am not making this up. It has to do with screws and nuts and bolts all fitting into each other no matter where you purchase them. And all the screws going in if you turn them clockwise, no matter which side of the equator you're on. Power plant guys have a not very euphonic saying on screws, "righty tighty, lefty loosey," which I object to because: a) it doesn't rhyme and thus relies for its mnemonic effect solely on alliteration, and b) it assumes that one will naturally equate "righty" with clockwise. As in, the top of the screw is the direction of rotation that matters. Anyway in the UK it appears that the International Screw Convention applies to lightbulbs. I didn't buy any nuts and bolts and try out the rest of its impact.

To return to our saga: one evening early in our tenure in the UK, I find myself downtown at our offices in Regent Street. Pretty cool address, although the offices were what's called in the trade "serviced offices," which means you rent an individual office for a really high price, and they give you some loathsome furniture, and then overcharge you for using their copier, etc. But you don't have to negotiate and sign a long lease, or rent your own space, or buy furniture, or hire a receptionist, and so on. Actually it's a reasonable arrangement, especially if your needs for space are small, as ours were, and you want to get going quickly and expect a very small staff, as we did. After all, all our investments were going to be in Eastern Europe.

Anyway Linda hadn't yet arrived in the UK (always good to send out an advance party) so I am in the process of setting up our office. I succeed in unpacking my computer and then in plugging all the wires, and cables, and with assorted connectors into the correct apertures, which is not easy if you are only an electricity expert and not also a Computer Expert. The damn things aren't even color-coded, although it was helpful that not every cord will plug into every receptacle. Then, having reconstructed the octopus that was the computer/monitor/keyboard/printer/fax machine, and hooked up all its component parts to each other, correctly I think, I need to turn it on.

I have a plug adapter with me, but these are dangerous items. They solve the problem of not being able to plug your electric whatever into the wall socket of the Beljickistan electric system, but they are just that—they got no innards; they don't translate anything into anything. I know this. Fortunately, I had also as part of my equipment a surge protector.

But also, I take the extra step that all us experts take; I actually look in the computer manual. I do realize that this is a direct violation of the "Guy's Guide to Life," Rule 1: never ask for directions; and Rule 2, never read the manual. But it's a foreign country, so I figure I can get a dispensation. Sure enough, it says that this dandy computer can accommodate either 110 volts, the safe and reasonable US level that everyone in the world should adopt immediately or 220 volts, the dangerous and unreasonable level that the UK and other miscreants insist on firing through their system, frying numerous infants unlucky enough to be born with the defect that allows them to actually stick their fingers into electric sockets, three fingers in the case of the UK. It's a really bad mutation, but self-correcting. "Aha!" I say to myself, highly pleased. "I have an international computer, I can operate on any electricity anywhere!" I won't take the time at this point to discuss the confusing issue of fifty cycles vs. sixty cycles, which is another component of retail electricity that also varies and has something to do with how fast or slow your clock runs and is frustratingly independent of voltage. Besides, I barely understand the voltage stuff, so forget the cycles. Anyway, I am golden, I am ready, the UK is ready, so I plug in my computer, with surge protector, turn it on, and BLAM!!

This is an inadequate written representation of the sound of a small explosion, which is not the sound you are anticipating in your office at 6:00 on a Sunday evening when it's all dark out and everything. In fact, it's now dark out, and in. Equally interesting, there is that unmistakable odor of singed electrical things coming from somewhere inside my office, although since it's suddenly awfully black I can't tell just where. Fortunately I have a lot of windows in this office, and all the Regent Street street lights and store lights are still on (a good or bad sign, depending) so I can sort of see that there is at least no raging fire in my office, and the computer hasn't exploded into pieces spewing shrapnel everywhere—I probably would have noticed—or melted into a puddle of plastic and electronics which I might have noticed if it got on my shoes.

But we also don't got no eerie grey glow on the screen, nor that wonderful sound of Windows announcing itself with a set of chimes. I begin to suspect that Something Is Amiss. See, all that expensive Ivy League education wasn't for naught. It also seems clear to me that whatever has happened, or more truthfully whatever I have done, is unlikely to be fixable by 1) me, or 2) anyone I could call. I also don't know anyone to call, and besides they might ask me what I was doing when night fell on the offices. And it's Sunday evening in the Land That Service Forgot. I carefully pack up my stuff and leave feeling my way down the hall. There seem to be no lights anywhere in the building, although I would swear there were when I came into the office. And the elevator, for some reason, seems to have ceased running. No matter, we're only on the fourth floor, I can take the stairs.

I come back to the office on Monday, later than usual. Everything seems to be all right. No "Wanted" posters up for whoever shut down the electricity of the building. I admit that I am skulking a bit, ready to run for it if confronted. "Say, didn't I see you coming in here about five o'clock last night just before we had that big electricity problem?" But the elevator works, the lights are on, and no one is looking at me funny.

I call up the Compaq hotline in the UK and ask them about electricity. "Doesn't this computer, Model SK 20000f47, Q-prt-1076234 have a dual electric capability? Didn't I read that in the manual?"

"Oh, yes sir," says the cheerful call center person, probably Irish since lots of EU call centers have located there. "Faith and begorrah it does. What seems to be your wee problem?" I explain that I have fried my computer, omitting the part about shutting down the entire office building. You can't tell who might be listening. The call center lass is most helpful. "There's a sacrificial circuit breaker inside your computer that cuts out and protects the rest of your computer, should you be so unfortunate as to have a surge," she says.

*Surge*, I think to myself, *how about tidal wave?*

"And," she adds, with delicacy that I do appreciate, "as the manual states, if you find yourself in a country with the higher voltage level, all you have to do is push the red button on the back of your computer from the 110 volt setting to the 220 volt setting. I think you'll find both settings clearly labeled. Then you'll be having no problems. And we can ship you the replacement circuit breaker in the overnight mail. If you are familiar with computers, you should easily be able to install it yourself."

*Fat chance*, I think. If I were familiar with computers I probably wouldn't be needing this replacement part. I struggle for some last hope of self-respect. "Am I the only person to ever have done this?" I ask forlornly.

"Ah, goodness no, we get calls like this every week," she responds brightly. "Don't worry, we'll get you fixed up good as new. Or at least your computer." Call center humor.

So much for the office. What about our house? When we left the US, as I said, our plan was to rent a place for a year or so, just to make sure we liked it and everything worked out; and besides we were in a hurry to get over here. So now we own two quite expensive houses and rent none, so what transpired?

On our first serious house-hunting trip, we arrived, and then had to figure out how to find a place. We asked for a referral from the AES folks in Richmond (the town west of London, not the capital of Virginia) and got hooked up with a person who "specialized in Americans." We are, apparently, a different species. Probably it's because our electricity is different.

We spent our first weekend looking at houses to rent in the nicer parts of London: Kensington, Chelsea, Knightsbridge. We saw a truly wonderful place with a nice garden on Cadogan Square. At the end of two days of diligent looking, we came back to our hotel room, sat down, kicked off our shoes, and looked at each other in disbelief— and not because there were holes in our socks. The rental prices of decent houses with small gardens were 3,000 to 4,000—which isn't nothing, but it wasn't in dollars a month. It. Was. In. Pounds. Per. Week. Read that again. Then multiply by 1.6, the exchange rate. Yes, your eyes do not deceive you, and it's not that you have forgotten how to multiply in your old age: $4,800 to $6,400 per week.

And the house on Cadogan Square, we were informed, had just received an offer for 15% above the absurdly high (3,950 pounds per week) asking price. I went off to Prague, and Linda went home to finish up at Enron and cogitate.

We went through this drill, singly or together, several more times, but it wasn't that we had just been unlucky. We changed real estate agents, hooking up with a lady named Ironsides, just like the Raymond Burr series only she wasn't crippled. She did look a bit like Raymond, had he been a tall, unattractive, and vaguely stallion-faced English woman. Didn't matter; prices stayed the same.

Finally we settled on a nice place in Holland Park, for the paltry sum of only 3,200 pounds per week. And it had, as everyone was proud to point out to us repeatedly, an AGA cooker in the kitchen. I was not possessed of any AGAs that needed cooking, but that wasn't the point. This is a dang fool contraption that for some reason, not ever fully explained, is very expensive; made out of a lot of cast iron cleverly covered with enamel in unattractive dark tones; and is always on—yes, always on—so your kitchen is always very hot, even in summer. It's made by the Swedes as a nice joke on the rest of Europe and considered extremely trendy. Perhaps nude cooking is sweeping the continent. All those flashing knives would make me pretty nervous. Never mind.

We decided to have it taken out and they said sure, we'll take it out and store it, but you have to pay for the new stove. Then came the lease. We had been asking for it for some time. We had already agreed to the outrageous price and the departure at our cost of the stupid AGA. Finally they gave us the lease and we read it. This was a bad mistake. Then we made several comments, which was a worse mistake, like inserting the odd "reasonable" or "not unduly" or some very minor changes to change the lease from 110% landlord/zero tenant to a much more balanced 102% to zero; there was nothing about changing the economic terms at all. Guess the response: "No, and if you're the kind of tenant who is going to insist on reading the lease, you're probably not the kind of tenants that we want." And they withdrew the offer to rent us the place. No kidding. Could I make this up? And we hadn't at that point even become electricity criminals.

It was a wholly poopy experience and burned up lots of time, and we didn't even get to see that many neat places. So much for spending your weekends looking at houses as a leisure-time activity.

We got mad, hired yet another real estate agent, and went looking for houses to buy. Our perfectly reasonable theory was that if we were going to be paying that much money to rent, we might was well purchase a house and build up equity. We settled at first on a very nice house in Little Venice, somewhat north of Kensington and Hyde Park, but a neighborhood with an actual—no kidding—real canal running down the middle of the road. Ain't a lot of these in London, and one, in fact, with European-style canal barges tied up along the sides and people living on them. I never asked about plumbing, but I'm sure they had some, and electricity hookups.

It was a nice house, lots of bedrooms, great garden, and a community park and tennis courts in the back, hemmed in on all sides by the other houses, so none of the riffraff could use it. It only lacked a greenhouse in the back, "conservatory" as the Brits say, but there was plenty of room for one. And several other houses already had them. So we signed on, disregarding the small agreement we had to sign at closing with the Little Venice Garden Amenity Company Ltd., the tender of the garden in the center of the square.

It was sort of a surprising agreement in that it obligated us to pay our portion of the communal dues to keep up the garden, about $300 per year, and included, if we did not, a first mortgage interest on our 2.7 million pound property. In pure legal terms, this gave them the right to seize the property and sell it at auction if we were late on a quarterly $75 payment. Hmmm. Oh, yes, and then there was that little bit of language about how they had to approve any changes to the house's exterior. "Oh, that's not a problem, that's just so you won't put up any clotheslines or such," said our realtor. So we said OK, we're strangers here, if that's all it means, so be it, although the language is rather broad and unspecific.

We hired an architect, got plans drawn up, got a decorator to start replacing the carpet and curtains, and put in our application for a conservatory. We had to get approval from the Planning Committee of the district, Westminster, and our architect handled that easily. We needed the Garden

Amenity Company Ltd. to sign off, which in truth meant a meeting of the Planning Committee of the local folks. But it's the UK, right, and I actually sort of thought it was a regulatory requirement to *have* a conservatory and that we might be out of compliance.

Weeks and weeks went by, carpet was installed, interior walls were rearranged to make the bedrooms more sensible, bathrooms were rearranged, but no meeting of the local Planning Committee. Then the meeting. And decision. Disapproved. With additional comment: "The committee is not required to discuss the reasons behind its decisions, and as a matter of practice does not do so, nor does it choose to do so in this instance." Oh, yeah, and no appeal rights. Unbelievable. What about the first amendment, or the right to bear arms, or the Magna Carta or something? Isn't this the birthplace of Common Law and the House of Lords? I was pretty piqued, and Linda was downright furious. We decided to see if we could buy a different house and sell this one to a large Serbian basketball player with loud girlfriends, or a surly rock star with a serious cocaine habit, or maybe a family of 120 Pakistanis. But some partner at Salomon Brothers rented it instead for an outrageous price. So it goes. And we moved to Hampstead, to a house that already had a conservatory. Of course, it leaked and wasn't heated, but never mind that; we showed them that Americans can't be pushed around.

Love and kisses,
Bob

# fourteen

# they have bacon-flavored popcorn in the czech republic!

May 1998

Dear Dad,

Well, here we are in the midst of packing crates and chaos, with guys in blue jumpsuits wrapping up the china and putting it into boxes so it can be lost or broken. What can this all mean? Could it be that we're moving? Again? Did the Brits deny us our God-given right to do something else? Well, yes, we did want to cut down a tree, and that has had to go to the Borough Planning Commission for approval, which seems a bit much, but no, it's not that.

And it's not that travel in Europe doesn't have its amusing moments, to wit:

I was on the phone to American Express trying to get a ticket arranged to go from D.C. to the Czech Republic (Czechoslovakia to all of us old-timers), except they separated into two ethnic bits. It was a relatively amicable divorce by international standards, no UN forces necessary, no massacre of thousands of parties. This should have been a good example for the Serbs and the Bosnians and the Herzegovinians and such, except they were in the back of the class talking and have now had to stay after school because they were all killing each other at recess. So the place is now two five million-person countries rather than one ten million-person country. I cannot tell that this is an improvement other than easier to spell. I tell the nice travel specialist lady located in some Call Center in Phoenix, or Orlando, or Wichita, or Albany, or Portsmouth that I need to go to Prague, the capital of the Czech Republic. Since I have done this before I suggest that I can go most conveniently through London, or through Amsterdam, but that there are no direct flights from Washington. "Where do you want to go, again?" she asks.

"Prague, in the Czech Republic," I say, "spelled P-R-A-G-U-E."

"Oh," she says, "well, let me just take a minute here to look up those flights for Pray Goo."

"OK," says I, losing hope.

Another day, another agent. I need to go to Warsaw, and then after that to Budapest, and then back to Washington. There is much consultation, and many bad suggestions on the part of the agent, who was clearly unfamiliar with anyone wanting to go to such weird places. If it wasn't Pittsburgh, he wasn't having any of it. Finally in exasperation, he says, "Well, I can't get you any flights. All the flights go to Warsaw, but I can't find any that leave."

I pondered this. Could it be that all the world's airliners eventually ended up at the Warsaw airport? Could this be how Boeing, and Airbus, and McDonnell kept demand for their products high? How unobservant I was, having been there a number of times yet never seeing all that shiny aluminum stacked up around the edges of the field.

Norman Mailer, America's reigning male bad boy intellectual, wrote a book in the late '60s called *Why Are We in Vietnam?*, a matter about which he knew little but felt called upon to opine. Naturally it wasn't really an explanation of that particular unsuccessful involvement, but I've always liked it for being an especially misleading title. So I thought about calling this letter "Why Are We in Eastern Europe?" except we did have a reason, sort of. As noted inconclusively in earlier epistles, we thought movie theaters in Eastern Europe were a killer idea. Theaters there are, to paraphrase Thomas Hobbes, old, dirty, and few; and the demand for cheap entertainment is decent and growing, the economies coming along, and there's no competition. Not an entirely bad analysis.

The first cities we identified were Warsaw, Prague, and Budapest. Maybe that's not all that visionary since these are the three best cities in Eastern Europe. But they all met the McDonald's test, my own particular analytical framework for telling you when you should make a consumer-driven investment in a new country. It works like this: Count the number of McDonald's in the capital city. If one or fewer, don't invest. If two or more, investing is okay.

Why is this? We think about it this way. If they have two or more McDonald's, then you know a number of things about the county:

» The folks there have enough money to afford Big Macs on an ongoing basis. This is in the same range as movie tickets, so there is enough disposable income to support a theater. Provided that your patrons would rather be entertained than fed a hamburger.

» Property rights exist. As in, you can own a site or get a lease. The locations where the McDonald's are certainly haven't always been McDonald's. This is pretty important for a business like theaters, which is largely real estate. I note for the record the enormous amount of press the one (count them, one) McDonald's in Beijing and the one (also count them, one) in Moscow received, for a very long time. If such a thing is that newsworthy, that says all you need to know about the investment climate.

» Contracts work. A lot of the McDonald's business has to do with contracts with suppliers. They want and need local suppliers, and they won't go where they cannot get contracts that are enforceable. This is considered by us boring business persons as a good thing to have.

» Blue laws allow you to be open enough hours to meet demand and pay the rent. Probably self-explanatory. People go to the movies at night, mostly. Curfews are considered problematic unless running from seven to nine in the morning.

» A labor market exists and allows you to hire young kids with no unionization threats and have them work peculiar hours. Quite important for both McDonald's and movies.

» You can take money out of the country, real money. If you're a McDonald's, you have to be able to pay those franchise fees and pay them in a convertible currency. This is also nice if you have to pay the studios for the movies they send you.

» They don't hate Americans. No small matter if in your theater you will be playing mostly American movies, which you will, because we dominate the market for this particular class of goods. Bad example: big problem in India for Kentucky Fried Chicken with lots of anti-American sentiment. I don't think they ever did open a restaurant. And it wasn't even cows (sacred to Hindus) or pigs (anathema to Muslims) they were trying to fry. As far as I know, no religion in India considers the chicken to be sacred. Didn't matter.

---

Having determined that each of our target cities met this rigorous test by personally having Big Macs and fries at each location, we set out looking for either properties to develop or theaters to acquire and renovate. The first proposition we got introduced to was a movie theater in Prague planned for a park on the east side of town, the location of the major conference/exposition center. It was a fairly good site with access to parking and to mass transit, which are both quite key for theaters in these sorts of cities where not everyone yet has a car; it just seems like they do. The only problem was that the developer was a movie maker, an artsy one at that, not a cinema guy, and he was linked up with some oh-so-modern Czech architects who wanted to make a bold architectural statement. Their business card was printed on metal. I have determined that this is, in general, not a good sign. In keeping with the newly free EE spirit of modern design, they had designed the theater in the shape of an octopus with a theater in each of the eight arms. Now I will be the first to say that typical Bolshevik architecture was horribly awful and atrocious, with the awfulness of its style matched only by the quality of the workmanship. And this was not a Bolshevik design, for sure. However, it had about a hundred things wrong with it.

First, they had made each of the auditoriums the same size, so no

managing of audience size as the movies wound down in pop
to our earlier lesson on the invention of the multiplex. The bun...
was also designed for just about maximum heating and cooling load since
it had almost the largest possible amount of outside wall and roof area
per cubic foot of interior space, and thus the largest heat loss per cubic
foot that you could possibly design. As may seem obvious, most heat loss
is through the walls and roof of a building. The most perfect design for
minimizing wall space to internal space is, therefore, a sphere, but these are
hard to walk around in and it would make the screens all curved; so the
next best choice is a cube or its close friend, a rectangular parallelepiped,
not an octopus. Don't you just love those words from geometry that are so
hard to work into conversations?

They also wanted to use fancy new unproven technology spanning large
spaces with glued wooden beams, which seemed risky to us. Your patrons
will be testy if they're watching Bruce Willis and the roof falls down on
their heads. They may even demand their money back. The octopus also
offers no good way to do ticket sales, or concessions, or manage traffic
into and out of the theaters. But we had many, many negotiations, signed
a letter of intent of sorts, and even brought in a real theater architect to
critique the goofy design. Oh, and did I mention that the site was city
property and the entrepreneur, although he said he had a lease, never was
able somehow to actually come up with such a document that he could
show us? We did like the site a lot, so we spent too much time and money
on this idea, but we were learning.

Then we got introduced to the two guys who had done Prague's first
(and EE's first) real multiplex cinema, called the Galaxie. Seven auditoriums of varying size, 1,053 total seats, and occupancy levels (seats sold vs.
seats available, calculated on a weekly basis) that were truly astounding,
usually as much as 75%. US cinemas do well to get to 40%. This sort of
validated our feeling that there was a market here. And the owners, Peter
Kot and Miro Brocko, wanted to sell us a half interest. Our potential partners were actually Slovaks, not Czechs, but they came out of the movie
biz. Under the old regime they had run the distribution business for films
all through Czechoslovakia, so they knew that part. After the fall of the

wall, they had wangled the lease on an old Bolshevik cultural center in the heart of a bunch of those ugly apartment blocks on the far eastern edge of town, right at a metro stop. Somehow they had gotten a loan from a German bank for about $1 million to renovate the cultural center and turn it into a multiplex. They had done an excellent job of constructing and then operating the place. We were charmed, we liked them, it was an almost Western-type theater, and Peter spoke good English. It turned out that he had been in the diplomatic corps until his brother defected to the West, and in retaliation Peter got yanked back and made to find work of a nondiplomatic nature. So we bought a half interest for $500,000 and became real, no-kidding, movie theater owners. We were so proud.

We did do a certain amount of homework on the deal, including hiring Deloitte to do the financial and accounting due diligence. This experience was very interesting. At one point in the process we got an anguished call from Peter. "These people you have hired, they are meeting with us and asking all these questions, and asking for all these financial informations, and for all these documentations we don't understand it. We thought you *liked* us!"

I finally figured out that capitalism had been around these former Warsaw Pact countries for only about five years, so that no matter how old or experienced the "business person" you were dealing with, he only had five years of business experience. Hence we were dealing with an entire nation of twenty-six to twenty-eight years olds, in a business sense. And Peter and Miro had never been through "due diligence" before. But they had enough market sense to sell "ham flavored" popcorn at their cinema. Actually it tasted sort of like bacon.

Prague, which I don't believe you have ever been to, is a beautiful city. Unlike much of Eastern Europe, it didn't get totally destroyed during WWII, being declared at a certain crucial point in time an open city. Hence the Germans didn't blow it up and neither did we, and neither did the Russians. I think the Italians had retired gracefully by then. It is full of beautiful and well-preserved old buildings, many dating as far back as the fourteenth century. The river Vlatava runs though it, the streets are narrow and crooked and essentially medieval (designed for horses and carriages, not cars), and you can walk comfortably around most parts of the downtown. Because there wasn't a lot of vacant real estate, there is very little Bolshevik architecture, as our partners referred to it. The nasty blocky chunky apartment blocks are a prime example. There is, inevitably, some, but mostly not in the center city. I really liked going there.

After this marvelous success with the Galaxie, we were pretty energized and decided that we knew what we were doing (hah!). So we next spent a lot of time in Budapest looking for sites for a new cinema. Budapest actually had three multiplexes, all a bit more recent than the Galaxie. One was in a cheap strip shopping mall and looked just like you could find it in the outskirts of Muncie, or Petersburg, or Huntsville. The second was in the top floor of another shopping mall, this one a new three-story one with a parking garage, and the cinema was also quite well done. The third was a renovation of an old single screen theater in the downtown area, exquisitely done, but they spent way too much money to make any sense and it had no parking. It was the city's money that had been used for the renovation, and the city still owned the theater as a junior partner, but the cinema's management had magically become the majority owner. We never could quite find out just how the new guys had acquired a majority ownership in this cinema without putting up any dough, or why the city had footed the entire bill for the renovation when it was only the part owner. Many equivalent transactions occurred during this time that were not necessarily in accordance with the Official Western Handbook of Privatization. On the other hand, things did move out-of-state ownership into private ownership one way or the other, mostly the other. On balance this was probably a good thing, although it would have been a better thing for it to have been done more openly and equitably. So it goes.

We eventually came across a site on the outskirts of town, in the northeast, where a group of Belgian developers were planning a major new shopping center. We liked the shopping center model, because shopping centers need "anchor tenants," and movie theaters are good ones. Thus you can usually negotiate some favorable lease terms, and most important, you don't have to bear the cost of the parking lot yourself. This may not seem like much, but parking lots cost a lot, not just the land but also the stupid paving, and lighting, and landscaping. We futzed around for a while with another developer but finally landed on the Belgians as having the best site. Unfortunately they had never heard of us. In fact, they had never heard of the Galaxie, our Prague triumph, and it was unclear if they had ever heard of Prague itself or the Czech republic. They didn't seem to get out much. For all these reasons, we couldn't get their attention.

Finally, after resorting to our fallback tactic—abject begging—they agreed that they would allow us to meet with them so they could see what we wanted. Well they knew what we wanted, but we were engaged in a strange courtship here. They had a very good site and site control in Budapest, and they knew it and we knew it. On the other had, they needed tenants for their very good site, and the better each individual tenant, then the more attractive their project became, and the more rent they could charge the next tenant to sign up for the next store. Additionally, Nieman Marcus probably wasn't in the cards, and they did at the end of the day have to rent the space to somebody, so they couldn't just sit and wait forever. Being a real estate developer is a tricky business and requires, it turns out, some pretty acute business sense, timing, luck, and so on. Kind of like life. We wanted to be one of their anchor tenants, and we had what we had initially assumed was the only necessary qualification: money. But that was naïve on our part, especially when we figured out the impact that the anchor tenant had on the marketability of the rest of the space. The landlord/developer legitimately needs the anchor tenant to know what he's doing.

Finally it was agreed that we would go to their headquarters in Belgium and meet with their key folks, sort of to present our case, and only then, if someone judged that we were worthy would we actually be allowed to enter into commercial negotiations for the site. A bit of a drawn out two-step process, but they had the site and we wanted it.

It was cold and rainy in Brussels, but that's no surprise. I have been there a fair number of times and it is always thus. No wonder Belgians have no sense of humor, eat a lot of frites, and drink beer. I guess they got the headquarters of the EU as a consolation for the worst climate in Europe.

So there we are, all dressed up, sitting politely with our architect in the very severe, very minimalist modern conference room, no windows—actually it was in the basement of their building. Soft ceiling spots, black felt wall coverings, black conference table, black leather chairs, but uncomfortable ones, and little tiny European cups of coffee to drink. The meeting starts out with us giving them our pitch: who are we, why we want to be a part of their project, what can we bring, and our experience. We had to inflate that last part a bit. It turned out to be a good thing that they had never actually been to the Galaxie as they wouldn't have easily recognized it from our description. Our architect was along to help us present what our plans would be for the site. It is worth interjecting here the interesting lesson that I learned at AES: all business is sales. There is almost always more involved to any business relationship or transaction than just money, and you always need to sell yourself to the other guy, even if, as in this case, you were trying to give him money.

The Belgians listened politely to us, but with no clear reaction. They didn't like our jokes much, either, although the atmosphere was not sufficiently warm or chummy that we tried to be very amusing. Then it was their turn, and they started with an explanation of who they were. Their company, something or other Belgique, was an independent real estate development entity with three or four shopping centers in operation, including several in what used to be East Germany and one in Belgium, but they had started out as a diversification move on the part of the Belgian utility, Tractebel. I perked up at this since Tractebel had been our first foreign partner at AES, and together we had bought two power plants in Northern Ireland. They had handed us a standard package of their corporate materials at the start of their part of the discussion, and as they went on about what they did, I started to idly leaf through their Annual Report. And I got pretty surprised.

"Hey," I blurted out like the dumb American that I am, "here's a picture of Freddie! Freddie Loeb! He's your Chairman, huh? That's pretty terrific. He is very smart and one tough cookie."

The meeting abruptly grew silent. I sensed that perhaps I had made a misstatement, so in typical American fashion decided to blunder wildly ahead. "We worked with Freddie when he was at Tractebel, when we bought the Northern Ireland power plants together, when I was at AES," I explained to a largely uncomprehending audience of Belgians who we knew not at all. "I knew he had retired, but I didn't know where he had gone to. So, he's your Chairman, eh? Give him my best regards when you see him."

More silence from the Belgians as this outburst is digested. "So you know our Chairman, Mr. Loeb?" says the senior Belgian.

"If he's the same guy who used to run Tractebel, I do indeed," I say. "Please feel free to discuss this with him. I am sure he will remember us." Fortunately I had always been most respectful to Freddie, although AES's general relations with Tractebel were terrible; they and we were absolutely incompatible partners, and we both found this out very soon after the marriage. But this bit of entirely unlikely recognition of events past completely turned the meeting around, and the Belgians were very much more interested in what we had to say from that point forward. You never can tell when those old electric utility guys will get into real estate development or even the Eastern European cinema business.

Given all this terrific start, why are we moving back to the US? Once we got past the first screen with the Belgians, who did check with Freddie, who did remember me, if not fondly then at least with enough respect to encourage them to negotiate with us, we then started the real negotiations. We spent some more money on designing the theater, showed them plans, asked for their input, all the while asking them to give us some idea of what they thought the site was worth. We were looking to own the actual ground the cinema would sit on, called in the trade a "pad site," probably because what you own doesn't extend more than about a foot beyond the concrete pad you pour to put the theater on. But they wouldn't tell us, and put us off, and kept on wanting to discuss other things, other parts of the potential agreement: how much parking they would build, how much of the parking lot maintenance we would pay, allocations for taxes, utilities, and the like. Finally, after literally three or four months of discussions, they gave us their price for the pad site: $12.3 million.

Very big gulp here. Linda and I just stared at them in disbelief. This was for a not very big piece of ground. I doubt that they had paid that much for the whole one hundred fifty acres. And we needed maybe half an acre.

We went home and ran some numbers. Excel is a wonderful program for making up spreadsheets in that it's easy to use and you can explore very quickly what happens to the economics of your project when you change variables. The key things we were interested in were ticket price and how many tickets per week we could sell. The site, and common sense, constrained us as to how many theater seats we could build, and as to how many shows we could run, as in, nobody goes to the movies on a weekday morning, not even in EE. We knew what the existing ticket prices were at the other theaters; we knew how much concessions each patron bought on an average visit based on our Czech cinema. We had rules of thumb for occupancy rates from both the US and from Prague. And we knew rough construction prices for theaters, so we knew our capital investment. I put together the model, which really wasn't all that hard, which was a good thing since I had never done it before. When you're a big utility executive, you got other people to do these things for you. You just critiqued them.

I played with the model for a bit, tried changing this and that to see how things came out. Unfortunately, they always came out poorly. I checked all the equations, all the assumptions, verified with my hand calculator that something silly wasn't going on inside the computer. It wasn't. Finally I said to Linda, "OK, I've got this figured out. All we need is for each of the six million residents of Budapest to come to our theater every two weeks and we can break even. Of course, to accommodate this we will need a theater roughly the size of the Empire State Building, which may be hard to permit. Viewed in another way, we need to take the average weekly attendance of our Prague theater and multiply it by two hundred in a site that will have only four times as many seats. This will be challenging."

The numbers didn't work. In fact, even if the crafty Belgians had been willing to *give* us the site rather than charge us twelve million bucks, it still didn't work. The lazy Hungarians just wouldn't get up from the TV and come to our cinema in throngs—movement not seen since the Turks invaded, and the Turks didn't plan to come back week after week. Of course, we didn't expect to pour boiling oil on our patrons, but we did want them to pay for their tickets. As cinema development goes, the Budapest episode was somewhat of a disappointment, a big stupid waste of time and money, but fortunately not a waste of the size of money that $12 million is. I will say that being asked to write a check for that amount of your own money does make you think.

It made us think about changing our line of work. So we are.

Love and kisses,
Bob

# fifteen

# please carry chocolate with you at all times

July 1998

Dear Dad,

We have just arrived from the UK for a week in Maine and haven't seen any lobsters yet. The snow is mostly gone, at least in those areas receiving more than six hours a day of direct sunshine. It's not raining, though, but that doesn't mean that it's not a strange place. Yesterday we went to a local crafts fair, and at one of the booths they were soliciting donations for the "Rockport Demonstration Family Farm." I asked what exactly they were about. It was explained to me that they needed to raise a large amount of money to give to people running a demonstration small family farm, which was demonstrating the economic viability of a small family farm. The money was to support this demonstration. Huh? I decided that I would not give them either: a) a lecture on the basic economic principles of capitalism, b) advice on logic, or c) money.

But never mind that. There are a few more thoughts I have had, reflecting on our recent international experiences, and I wanted to share them with you before I forget them, or my computer breaks, or Linda tells you what really happened.

Does Language Matter? You spent several hundred years studying Japanese, so you know that this is a throwaway question. When we flew to Korea on JAL, the fancy menu they gave me indicated that one of the choices was "Ham slices, sprinkled by chopped nuts." It could have been true. But we have other examples.

» It was just after we had closed a particularly tough deal, but one with great importance for AES, and we had finally done it. I was in New York the day after the closing, pretty pooped but quite elated. Before heading back to D.C., I decided I had earned a reward for all the hard work. I found myself in Barneys, the Madison Avenue very high class but not weird men's clothing store. I further found myself in the sports coat section. Quelle coincidence. I found myself with a nice, European-accented but professional salesman, who was very helpful. We tried on several jackets, I expressed likes and dislikes, and then he said, "Ah, I have just the right jacket for you, a zeenia," and he wandered off to get it from another part of the store. *Well I have been away from the clothing biz for a while,* I thought to myself, *but I didn't know that there was a line of clothes named after one of my favorite flowers, the "zeenia."* Nice touch though, sort of whimsical.

The salesman returned and tried the jacket on me; I liked it, and I bought it. As he was writing up the transaction, I looked more closely at the label, which said Ermenegildo Zegna. *Aw, rat butts!* I said to myself. *Is that how it's pronounced?* All these years I've been telling people at cocktail parties and at work how much I admired the clothes made by Mr. Zeg-na, as in Peg-ma. So much for sophistication. Should have stuck to Armani?

» David (my brother, your son, you probably remember him) took his family to Mexico for the first time several years ago. He's always been good at languages, speaks Japanese and Chinese, both of which are not your everyday, I would like another beer, where is the bathroom, the dresser of my aunt is on the hat of your uncle, kind of languages. And he spoke some Spanish; figured it was more than enough to get by. Naturally he assured his two skeptical daughters and his tolerant wife that they'd be fine, didn't even need a phrase book, he'd been there before as a college student, had a fine time, not to worry. I don't think he said, "Don't drink the water," but they probably knew that.

First day there they are having lunch in a small very Mexican restaurant, and David is discoursing on the historical fact that the Aztecs invented many important food items, or maybe discovered them, whatever one does with important food items. For example, turkey, hot peppers (although not Tabasco sauce), and most important, chocolate. "In fact," he said, "as I recall, Mexican chocolate is still among the finest in the world, even if the Belgians don't agree. We should have some, you'll see. It ain't Hershey's."

Thus self-inspired, he calls the waiter over and says, "Señor, chocolate por bebida para mi familia por favor." Which of course means, "Chocolate drink for my family, please, sir."

The waiter politely considers this request and then says, "No hay chocolate." ("There is no chocolate.")

"Sort of ruins the effect," says David to the girls. He turns to the waiter. "Esso es el pais de la navidad de chocolate." ("This is the country of the birth of chocolate," or possibly "A large international oil company is the country of the birth of chocolate.") "Chocolate es el fondacion del cultura de Mexico." ("Chocolate is the foundation of the culture of Mexico." Possibly overstated.) And then, dramatically, "Porque no tengo chocolate?"

The waiter regards him curiously. David continues, "Porque no tengo chocolate, la bebida de los Aztecas, la bebida de los dios?" (The drink of the Aztecs, the drink of the gods).

Another quizzical look, an almost Gallic shrug of the shoulders, and the waiter shuffles off to the kitchen. At which point David realizes that his Spanish is more rusty than he thought, especially his use of verbs in terms of case, and what he has just said is not "Why is there no chocolate" but instead, several times, insistently, "Why don't *I* have chocolate?" Hard question for the waiter to answer. Don't Americans always carry it with them?

» I am in Paris, on a trip that includes meeting with a number of French banks and European power equipment suppliers so we can try and make sure we will have both money and stuff to buy with it for our next AES plant. It's the last day, and I am staying for some reason at the Bristol, which is a really lovely and elegant hotel in the 8th arrondissement at the end of the Rue du Faubourg Saint-Honoré, the high fashion shopping street close to the Ritz and the Place Vendôme. The Bristol has a lovely interior courtyard garden with a conservatory to one side of it where they serve breakfast, tea, and such. It might actually be an orangerie if only I knew what that meant. Anyway, us Americans would call it a greenhouse. But what do we know? It looks out on the garden and is a very attractive setting indeed.

I am meeting there for breakfast a Senior Vice President of the Banque Nationale de Paris, one of our favorite banks, since they have lent us a lot of money, and we have high hopes of continuing this fine relationship, maybe even getting them to lead a transaction instead of just participating. The banker appears at the appointed hour wearing a finely cut three-piece gray flannel suit, elegant silk tie, gold cuff links, highly polished black shoes— the whole bit. I am wearing a button-down collar shirt from Lands' End. Oh well.

We engage in some pleasant chitchat, and then the waiter comes to take our breakfast order. The banker says in perfect English, "I would like the continental breakfast with orange juice and coffee." Well, we are on the continent.

I took French at Yale, I've been here almost a week, I can ride the subway, I know how Europeans think Americans are slobs because all they can speak is English, so I say, "Por moi, le même chose, parce que jus de pamplemousse." ("For me, the same thing, except grapefruit juice.") I am particularly pleased to have remembered the word for grapefruit juice since I can't see any particular connection between *pamplemousse* and grapefruit. Orange juice, for example, is *le jus d'orange*, which is not so difficult.

The waiter pauses, looks at me for just a second or two longer than what might be necessary, writes something down on his pad, and trundles off. When he returns with our breakfasts, everything is in order. We finish our finance chitchat, wish each other well, and I check out and go to the airport to fly home. About half an hour into the flight I sit up, drop my book, and say, "Oh heavens!" or something stronger. I realize that what I had said to the waiter, right in front of the French banker that I was trying to impress with my linguistic skills, was *not* "For me, the same thing, except grapefruit juice," but rather "For me, the same thing *because* grapefruit juice." I guess it's fortunate they brought me any breakfast at all.

———

Food in the UK, part two. It's not necessarily as bad as I said in a previous letter. Well, yes it is. But it's not all the Brits fault, and there are some redeeming features.

1) You are close to the not-very-good wine producing regions of Europe. No, forget about the Côtes du Rhône, and Burgundy, and Châteauneuf-du-Pape (Castle of the pope's nose—always struck me as a strange name for a wine, or for a house for that matter). We're talking less well known, by an order of magnitude. We were in Sainsbury's, one of the "supermarkets," and I was in the wine and beer section. Naturally they have no cold beer. Of course now that I understand how cold the silly country is all the time, the concept of warm beer becomes clearer to me. Also they have no German beer, which seems an unnecessary hangover from the unpleasantness of the '40s. They do have Belgian beer, which is not too bad, but no light beer of any kind, not even Amstel. They have an array of cheap wine, none of it with twist-off caps.

We decide to do an experiment. We buy a bottle of wine whose label says "Sainsbury's Bulgarian Merlot." It costs one pound. That is $1.65 of America currency at current exchange rates. We take it home. It does not explode in the car. We open it. The fumes do not poison us or drive us from the house. We drink it. It's not bad! Those Bulgarians may have lousy police and not be much of a high-tech mecca, but somehow they make pretty good wine, and cheap. The Moroccan High Atlas Cabernet Sauvignon with a picture of a tiger on the label is not as good. And also costs $2.50. Take that, you former French colony.

2) Ham is called gammon for no reason we can figure out. You almost need an English/English dictionary to live in England on a daily basis. Gammon indeed. But once you decipher this, you can make good-old Nebraskan ham hock and beans just like in Nebraska. Whether this is a good thing for the world depends on your regard for this heartland dish,

which as you remember Mom despised. I must add, as a culinary note, that the dish is enhanced when served with Tabasco, as are so many things.

3) You can get turkeys here for Xmas, courtesy of the Mexicans, one supposes. Only they come with their feet on their legs. The turkeys, not the Mexicans. I have tried to deduce the reasons for this. Yes, I know that one reason is that the birds originally had these very same feet on these same legs, so that's not the question. Why leave them on? What is gained? Who is advantaged? Is this a labor saving step? The Chinese eat the feet and no doubt consider them a delicacy, but even they cut them off and cook them separately. Nobody else I know eats the feet, and in truth there ain't much there to eat. Is it to prove that this is actually a turkey, and not instead perhaps a chimpanzee or an elephant? It could, of course, be a grouse or a peacock or a titmouse for all I know. The feet don't really give much away, except to prove that it's not an exceptionally large duck. I am mystified by this, and besides it looks gross. But we soldier on.

What you can't get is Pepperidge Farm stuffing in those handy cellophane packages; just add broth and away you go. But we are determined to have, for all these family members who are spending Xmas with us, a real turkey. So we buy two and also two chickens, also with feet still conveniently attached. At this point you are no doubt pausing in the course of reading this letter, looking up thoughtfully at the ceiling, and saying to yourself, "Well, if he thought the feet were that offensive, why didn't he just cut the danged things off?" Good question. You ever tried to cut off a turkey's foot? Those babies are attached, let me tell you. There's bone, and tendon, and muscle, and several titanium rods deeply embedded in and supplementing the skeletal structure. A knife won't do it, although it is good for cutting your finger deeply as you wrestle with the turkey's foot. And we don't have a chain saw or a hacksaw. So I gave up.

Instead I pursued the stuffing, made the old-fashioned way with stale bread crumbs, sage, etc. What I couldn't do so well was make the turkey broth for the stuffing, since the turkeys didn't come with necks, giblets, and all that unattractive internal stuff. The chickens did; nice little plastic package stuffed inside the breast cavities of the birds. But not the turkeys. Some tradeoff—feet but no neck.

We ended up with enough stuffing for the breast cavities of both turkeys and chickens and used the chicken neck and lungs and so forth for the broth. I was secretly hoping someone would eat the turkey and remark that it tasted like chicken. We put all four birds into the two ovens, more or less deciphered the temperature settings, which are in centigrade not Fahrenheit, and went off to the drawing room to open presents, drink coffee and champagne, and be generally celebratory.

Time passes, and the smell of turkey wafts from the kitchen. Also the smell of high-temperature industrial waste disposal processes. I ignore this for a while. Everyone else does so, politely, as well. Eventually I sneak into the kitchen "to baste the turkeys" and try to see if we haven't taken out the garbage, or a cat has died in the closet, or some shrimp shells have been left in the washing machine, or just what it is that is starting to smell unreasonably bad. No luck.

This continues for several more hours as I more and more frantically look everywhere in the kitchen for the source of the offensive odor, and the family members who are children and thus have no manners begin to say things like, "Eww, what's that smell?"

Finally the turkeys, and chickens, and everything else are done. The turkeys, when removed from the oven look great, but they smell like dead muskrat mixed with polyvinyl chloride. It is now unfortunately clear that the odor is localized in and emanating from the two turkeys. I smell the feet, foolishly. Maybe athlete's foot for turkeys? Not there. I poke around some, naturally in front of everyone waiting hungrily and politely. I peek into the neck cavity of the first turkey and sadly discover there the missing neck and giblets, nicely wrapped up in a plastic sack, which has also nicely melted a bit into the turkey and has also obligingly drooled some plastic into the roasting pan. I do not believe that this will enhance the gravy. I do not believe it will enhance my reputation as a terrific cook. Although Linda's dad, a real trooper, volunteers to eat the turkey anyway, we decide that it's a good thing we have the chickens. We set the turkeys outside in the rain and dark (it is 3:00 in the afternoon), carve up the two chickens, give everyone lots of potatoes, and corn, and string beans, and open several more bottles of Bulgarian merlot. And besides there's always dessert.

Cold climate survival tricks: we just got here to our small cottage in Maine. It is late May and time to get ready for "the season," which is what people call that extremely brief period when the ice is mostly gone from the lakes and rivers, the mosquitoes have been reduced to feeding only after four in the afternoon, and there are actually growing green things about waiting to be eaten immediately by the deer. This period lasts from the week before the Fourth of July to the week after it. We are here early to "open the house," although as far as I can tell, what this consists of is unlocking the door with your key, walking inside and turning up the thermostat, throwing out the moldy cheese and liquefied lettuce left in the refrigerator from last year, and putting on a jacket.

No wait, there's more. Since we decided to spend more time up here, we have moved one of our cars here, the Mazda Navajo, a Japanese car with an Indian name made by Ford in Michigan and looking suspiciously like an Explorer. At least you can get parts. What I have cleverly done to make this car weather the winter is remove the battery and keep it inside the house where things are heated, at least heated to fifty degrees, which is approximately two hundred degrees warmer than the rest of Maine. I know about electricity, and I know that batteries don't do well in cold. But now it is time to reequip the car with its battery so we can run around doing errands, like buying more cheese and lettuce.

Linda kindly offers to help, even though we all know that gals don't know nothing about cars, especially the parts of cars that reside under the hoods. "Sure," I say generously. "You carry the battery and I'll get the tools."

I pass the first test of manly automotive maintenance by actually being able, on the third try, to raise the hood. Don't know why these Japanese Indians from Michigan insisted on making it so hard. We then place the battery in its battery location, designated by being the only place it will fit, and besides there are these two electrical cable-looking sort of things with clamp/fitting connector doodads on the end that you have to hook up to the battery. I think.

The connectors have two-piece arms that can be loosened or tightened, with a hole in the middle for the battery terminal post, and bolts on the ends to tighten the fittings once they are on the posts. Very simple and straightforward mechanical design. Various things also seem to be colored red and black but not in any order one can make sense of. The only problem is that one of the fittings is real loose, and the other is clamped down so tight that it won't even fit over the battery post. But Man, the Tool-using Animal, is prepared. First I tighten down the loose fitting with several wrenches of some sort and only manage to draw blood from one knuckle. The too-tight clamp is a bit more of a problem. I have to first loosen its bolts, then try to pry it open with a big screwdriver so it will slip over the other battery post.

"You're putting these in the right places, right?" asks my wife, as I wipe blood and black car goo fetchingly across my forehead.

"Yes, of course," I respond somewhat testily. "Remember, I took the battery out of this car." I don't have to add that I am a Guy, I have been to Guy School, and thus I have an inherent knowledge of automobiles, professional football, and beer. It's sex-linked and genetic.

The clamp is now as loose as I can get it, and it still won't quite fit. So I take the Principal Guy Maintenance Tool from my bag: the hammer. I believe that if you can't fix something with a hammer, then it's probably broken beyond repair and you should just give up and buy a new one. I whang away at the connector until it finally sinks down around the post. "Nothing to it," I say with an air of modest triumph. "Let's see if she starts."

We get in the car, turn the key, and hear a distinct and fairly loud *pop* from the vicinity of the engine, and then nothing. Not even dashboard lights or the seat belt indicator will turn on.

When I get out and open the hood the unmistakable odor of electrical bad stuff comes gently wafting out in the chill May air. "Must be the generator or distributor," I opine to Linda, as these are the only two other pieces of automotive electrical equipment whose names I know. "Guess we'll have to get her towed in. Winter in Maine is pretty hard on cars."

Linda has meanwhile been unfairly, although productively, using her female wiles playing dirty by idly thumbing through the Owner's Manual. She quietly shows me the page in the book on replacing the battery where it does say—in typical Pearl Harbor, Custer's Last Stand sneak-attack fashion—that the battery posts are different sizes, of all things! Not only that, the doggone connector clamps are also different sizes! And, worse luck, these two sets of different sizes are made to match, and what you are supposed to do is put the clamp with the big opening on the big post and the clamp with the small opening on the fan belt. No, just kidding on the small battery post. But are they different colors, I ask? Are they different shapes, like one square and the other round, which would be a real signal that a normal human could figure out and act on? No-o-o. Well, I ask you, how do they expect a person to know this important information if all they do is put it in the owner's manual? No wonder America is returning to American cars, even if they are mainly made in Mexico.

Love and kisses,
Bob

# sixteen

# because we're french and you're not

October 1998

Dear Dad,

Since you couldn't come with us on this trip, I thought you might appreciate a recounting of our adventures on what we have taken to calling our Whitman's Sampler of the South of France, or "If this is Tuesday, it must be the medieval walled village of Mugance de Crallone, famous for its antique market (held on the day before you arrive or the day after you leave), its colorful festival of St. Valerie the Impetuous (held only once a year six months before you arrive), and its hand-painted *cranpustoules* (which turn out to be lime green toothpick holders in the shape of a head-less body of a housefly made in China where perhaps they should have stayed but instead are here and, sadly, are widely available)."

### Day One—Tuesday, October 20

Linda's mom and dad are already in France and we are to meet them there, then travel about. But first the rest of us have to fly over. We get to the airport one and a half hours early for our flight. You have traveled with us, so you will appreciate how completely unlikely that statement is.

Well we have gotten tickets for Elika, her husband Rich, and baby Leo, and these are coach tickets, and so we have, in a burst of good sportsmanship, also gotten for ourselves coach tickets. Actually, that's not the exact truth. We did make business class reservations, but American Express lost them in their computer and they expired (the reservations and not, unfortunately, American Express). It probably had something to do with the year 2000. When we tried to rebook, the rate had changed, the airline had changed, the geography of Europe had apparently changed, and a business class seat was now $6,500, vs. $500 in economy. All of Linda's and my Scottish blood boiled up, and we decided on these tickets. Me, I am worried—it's been about eleven years since I have flown in a coach seat on an international flight. I have visions of the scene in *Titanic* where the folks in steerage can't get out of the sinking ship because they're locked in. "Don't try to carry too much stuff on board," I helpfully warn Linda, "they'll be mean to you." She refrains from reminding me that she has actually been on an airplane before.

Rich is along, which is delightful. His freelance cameraman job has prevented him from making lots of these trips with us before. OK, it has prevented him from making *any* of these trips with us before. He was actually supposed to be shooting a documentary about jaguars, alligators, and snakes in Costa Rica for *National Geographic*. First the jaguars and then the alligators got edited out of the script, so Rich decided to let the snakes go. Time will tell if this was a wise decision.

We get our boarding passes, and the desk people check our incredibly heavy luggage without a murmur of complaint. I am traveling with my Hartmann hang-up bag packed so full that it is not folded over; when buckled it is actually round. Elika helpfully refers to this as "The Pumpkin." Linda has done all the work of arranging hotels, flights, etc., and is carrying all the guidebooks for everybody, the computer printer, and much else, and has luggage weighing several hundred pounds as far as I can tell. Fortunately it's arranged in only two of those nifty black bags with wheels and handles, the kind that 94% of the traveling public has (the other 6% having Hartmann hang-up bags, except not as round as mine). Trying to be helpful at the last minute before we leave, I fret about having someone, by mistake, pick up her luggage off the carousel rather than their own. Linda seems serenely unconcerned. "Just pick it up," she says. I get it. It's a different strategy than covering the sides with stripes of yellow tape, but nonetheless effective.

Once on the airplane we discover several things: 1) Leo, my eleven-month-old grandson, has decided to make friends by grabbing each seat armrest as he is pushed down the aisle in his stroller. He makes many friends of the people already in their seats, but as this process is a bit time consuming, rather fewer of the people behind him in line. 2) Linda is right again and there is plenty of room in the overheads. 3) They don't charge you for beer on the flight! This seems remarkably human. 4) The food is about the same as what they serve in business class, and they give you FREE BAD WINE! Actually this is a sad commentary on what has happened to business class, rather than evidence that United Airlines is suddenly in the hands of an international charity.

### Day Two—Wednesday, October 21

We land at the Charles de Gaulle airport in Paris, a nifty round building that looked pretty modern twenty-five years ago when it was first opened but looks a little bit dated now. Most of us are feeling gritty, sleepy, and out of sorts—the standard feeling for getting off an overnight flight to Europe, but Elika is awake and cheerful. "I read the history section of the guidebook on the plane," she happily announces. "Now I know who Charles de Gaulle is." All that money spent on all those good schools.

How can you be sure you're in France? Getting on the airplane to Nice in front of us is a middle-aged woman with several medium-sized duffel-shaped carry-on bags. I get a temporary fright when I see a dog's head in one, and think for a moment that that is all there is. The head moves, however, and it becomes clear that the rest of the dog is in the bag with only his head sticking out. No one else seems to think this odd. Then I see that cradled in her other arm is another bag with a dog's head similarly arrayed. Once we're on the plane I make Linda (she's sitting on the aisle, after all) get up and see if the woman has put one or both of the dogs into the overhead. I amuse myself with visions of the flight steward announcing,

"Please be careful when retrieving your bags from the overhead compartment, as some dogs may have moved during the flight." Linda reports that the dogs have been disposed of under the seat and in the woman's lap. She also suggests that, since I am simply fooling around, rather than responding to a potential in-flight emergency as she for some reason interpreted my request, I handle all future such reconnaissance requests personally. "Doggone," I mutter.

At the Nice airport we get one of our first examples of the "things are smaller in Europe" syndrome. The van we have reserved, "for seven people," will hold maybe seven children, small ones who don't fidget and don't mind being friendly with their neighbors. No such seven children exist on the planet, of course. It will hold no luggage at all. Our group has adopted the American plan for luggage: if you can carry all your bags, you haven't packed enough. We renegotiate—luckily—and rent the only big white diesel van in Nice at the last of the four rental car agencies at the airport. And this is the off-season.

With disaster narrowly averted we hit the road driving over from Nice to Cannes through one of two situations: 1) On a freeway where, although we are driving about 100 kilometers per hour (pretty fast in a big van, I think), we are being passed by people driving 700 kilometers per hour. Maybe they're all Germans used to the autobahn, but I can't tell because they go by in a blur. 2) We drive down little tiny streets with cars parked elbow to teakettle on each side. These streets are not intended for big white diesel vans driven by first-time American drivers. Whew.

We stop for a nice long lunch on the Croisette, the main boulevard in Cannes that runs along the ocean. It's famous for classic hotels on one side, beaches with starlets in bathing suits on the other—at least during the film festival, which unfortunately is in May rather than October. We eat at the Carlton Hotel, a truly grand Cannes landmark, in the Bar des Celebrities (I probably don't need to translate that for you). There are pictures of celebrities on the menu. Nope, not Albert Schweitzer or José Saramago, the recent Nobel Prize winner for literature from Portugal. In fact, nobody that l'Academie Francais would approve of. Yes, egad, it's American movie stars including, of course, Bruce Willis. Is there no escaping this? Elika gets almost all of the pictures correctly identified (including *both* Arquette sisters, which is quite a feat) but misses on Catherine Deneuve, the only French person in the group. *Quel dommage.* She is entitled to a free lunch for this feat and orders the *plateau des fromages*, which to our disappointment does not turn out to be a flat-topped mesa constructed out of cheeses but just an ordinary bunch of cheese. Rich and I have several Kronenbourg beers, which somehow taste better sitting in the late afternoon sunlight looking out over the Mediterranean than they do in New Jersey.

Our ultimate objective for the day is a hotel in the small French town of Trigance, so off we go. It is about forty-five miles north of the Cannes/Nice area. The freeway takes us about halfway there, and once we get off, suddenly we are on narrow mountain roads. "Is this the Alps?" asks Linda's mom. Good question, 'cause it sure is steep, rocky, and mountainous. Of course, since the chief attraction of going to Trigance is to see the nearby Gorges du Verdon, which is supposed to be a big steep canyon, I finally begin to put two and two together. Mrs. Hemphill didn't raise no total dummies, even though one of us is a bit slow.

We get to Trigance, located in the very dark, uninhabited, and mountainous countryside and it is, as advertised, a castle built in the ninth century on the top of a hill. Fortunately it's also well lit and well signed so we can, in fact, find it. The host is very pleasant, and carrying the luggage up several thousand uneven stone steps is good exercise, and the dining room is still open. Leo gets mashed potatoes and some excellent cream of spinach soup with crevettes for dinner and plays drums with the silverware on the table, but is generally quite well behaved. The rest of us drink several bottles of very good (*"fort et sec, non léger"*) *vin rouge* and are almost as well behaved. Especially given that we've all had about two hours sleep in the last thirty-six hours.

### Day Three—Thursday, October 22

We wake up when the phone rings. It is the room service people calling diplomatically—as it is nearly 11:00— to inquire whether we are planning to have our breakfast. They are gracious enough not to add "ever." They do tactfully remind us that breakfast usually ends at 10:00 as had been explained to us the evening before. This is most cooperative of them, and we appreciatively say, "Yes, thank you." I explain to Linda that French people take food very seriously and would never let anyone go hungry. This turns out not to be a prophetic remark.

This important matter having been resolved, Linda looks out the window and first thinks that it's cloudy glass, then figures out that it is, in fact, extremely thick fog. This may make the gorge viewing harder. Fortunately after we shower, dress, eat excellent chocolate croissants, and drink strong French coffee, the fog has gone away and it's a beautiful day. God just wanted us to sleep late, bless His heart.

We are not the only ones slow to roust ourselves. It turns out that spinach soup with crevettes is not Leo's favorite, and he has been throwing up all night. He redeems himself, however, by taking his very first unaided steps on the ramparts of the hotel, overlooking the extremely cute ninth century French stone village at the base of the castle. Despite the fact that our party is armed with approximately 2.7 cameras per person, no one records this momentous event on film. This leads one to consider the existential tourist question: If you don't have a picture of a place, have you really visited it? It seems unlikely that we will have this problem.

We eventually load up into the van and stop at the "Snack Bar" in th village, where the French patroness informs us brusquely that they do not have any food for a *bébé*.

*"Pommes frites?"* Elika asks hopefully, since a) this is France after all, and b) it's written right there on the menu in plain French.

*"Non,"* the patroness replies. "I am a restaurant, not a store," she adds helpfully. The real message, of course, is: I'm French and you're not. "Go to the market in the village," she tells us.

We take the big van through the very narrow streets of the village to the market, which, sure enough, is *fermé* (closed) until 5:00 p.m. Leo, strapped into his car seat, is a pretty good sport about it all.

We set off undaunted on the circular route to the Gorges du Verdon, advertised with remarkable restraint by the French as "the Grand Canyon of Europe." One might have expected them to bill this one as "the Grand Canyon" and that little thing in Arizona as "the Gorges du Verdon of the

US." The road is narrow, and winding, and full of switchbacks. Soon we come to a remarkable overlook, the Balcons de la Mescla (we never find out who he was or whether maybe this was just a reference to fancy salad), and sure enough it overlooks a big, narrow, and deep canyon with a beautiful, very green river (the Verdon, appropriately enough, which means "green something") at the bottom of it. The hills are sere, and rocky, and craggy, and extremely impressive. This is not very far off from the most interesting rugged landscapes of the American West, just a touch greener and a bit less high, but no less steep, rugged, and beautiful. We are all impressed. We find at this stop, handily, a small *relais*/souvenir store/snack bar, and they have suitable *bébé* food (bananas, hot dog in croissant, apple juice) so we are provisioned.

We drive for the next several hours along a very narrow, very twisty, very high up (compared to the bottom of the canyon) road along the canyon's edge. Remarkable views, generally unobstructed by guardrails. Fortunately very little traffic, as the driver (me) is being quite cautious so as not to plunge us all over the edge to our deaths. Eventually we get to the canyon mouth where there is a big lake (Lac de Sainte-Croix), which is also beautiful and a striking cobalt blue. And nobody is on it. Or in it. You can just sense, however, that in August the place would be crawling with tour buses and tour bus denizens. Very good timing on our part—beautiful weather (mid-60s), the advertised bright blue Provence sky, leaves all turning on the canyon trees. We eat a lunch of sorts in the town of Moustiers at the top of the lake and then get back in the car to drive on the same quality road on the other side of the canyon. Even fewer guardrails, more exposure, higher up—very remarkable and from time to time scary. Just to liven things up, at one of the most exposed hairpin turns with the biggest drop-off right from the edge of the road and no guardrails at all, in the waning afternoon light, we run into a herd of goats. Not little cute Heidi-type ones, but pretty big goats with large horns and attitude. As in, "We're walking along this road and we don't care about no stinking van of no Americans." We slowly inch the van forward, honking the horn. Goats are unimpressed, ignore us, and continue to mill around. Eventually they got out of the way, but on their own terms. This is not a good road to drive under with anything but the best conditions, but it does give you an unparalleled view of a natural feature of unique beauty. And some pretty tough goats.

Back at the hotel, we all rendezvous for dinner, delighted to be alive, and this time have three bottles of wine and no goat cheese.

During the course of the meal, we discover a wonderful side dish, which is totally new to me. It is on the menu as *pommes lardons*, which isn't especially descriptive in that its literal translation is "potatoes small bits of bacon." We didn't even have the sense to order it specially; it came as a side dish to something else. It is small new potatoes completely wrapped and baked in a piece of bacon. Being as we are from the Midwest where bacon and potatoes are two of the four major food groups, I can't believe I have never heard of this dish before. We order an entire other plate of this delicacy and everybody helps devour it. Even Leo, although with only two teeth he's not so good on the bacon yet. But he is willing.

### Day Four—Friday, October 23

We get up at a more reasonable hour than the day before (or perhaps less reasonable, it all depends on your point of view), pack, load up, and take off for Aix-en-Provence, one of the larger and more famous towns in the area. We now pause in this narrative to interject a personal note of confession. Despite having taken two years of French at one of the best universities in the US, I have always thought that this city's name was pronounced "a," rhymes with "hay." Imagine my embarrassment to find that it is actually pronounced somewhere between "eggs" and "aches." This does, however, open up terrific possibilities for bad puns, long a feature of these sorts of trips. This ugly tendency had already manifested itself the previous day when we saw a rabbit running across the road. The French word for rabbit is *lapin*, pronounced "le pan." Hence the following:

What is it called when a bunch of French rabbits run around in disarray making a lot of noise? Lapin-demonium

What is the religion of French rabbits? Lapin-theism

What is the name of the French rabbit road that runs from Canada to Chile? Lapin-American Highway

Who is the French rabbit that could fly, never wanted to grow up, and fought with pirates? Peter Lapin

Being on the road to Aix, of course, presented irresistible opportunities as well as a captive audience:

What is the philosophy that Jean-Paul Sartre originated while living in A Major City in Provence? Aix-istentialism

What play did M. Sartre write that embodied some of this very same philosophy? *No Aix-it* (Historical note: Linda, who normally disdains this sort of puerile wordplay, even originated this one. *Resistance is futile . . .*)

What was Jean-Paul's favorite punctuation when he lived in A Major City in Provence? The Aix-clamation point

And when old J.-P. wanted to relax while living in AMCIP, what type of books did he read? Aix-scapist

What is the favorite children's book of kids in AMCIP? *Green Aix and Ham*

Cousin Jim will no doubt be able to add to this brief list.

We arrive in Aix after several hours on the freeway, during which time we are buzzing along at 120 kph (which ain't slow) and we pass only trucks, not one single solitary passenger car. And it isn't because there are no passenger cars on the road; it's because every one that we see is whizzing past us. Every last one. We stay pretty much in the right lane, and darn proud to be there.

When you choose hotels out of books that claim to have only "small and charming" hotels as their subject matter, sometimes you do fine (see previous entry) and sometimes you end up at Le Prieuré in Aix, billed as the former home of the abbot of something at sometime and decorated with an enchanting wallpaper of bright blue corduroy; also bright blue paint, blue furnishings, etc. Everywhere, walls, carpets, even the ceilings. Well, the furnishings weren't on the ceilings. In our defense I note that we tried more highly recommended places in Aix, but were turned down at all but this one. Yes, we knew it was the only two-star hotel on the itinerary. Yes, when they quoted us a rate of $60 per night we were a bit concerned (you can hardly eat at McDonald's in France for that). It was oddly decorated, oddly laid out, and staffed with a couple of folks who didn't seem to realize that they were in Aix, judging by their local knowledge, but at least it was pretty clean and they had hot water. First things first: the water wasn't blue.

We all walked back into town in the afternoon to look around. Aix has a more or less typical but very scenic "old town" in the center, with narrow streets, stone buildings, brasseries, lovely tree-filled squares, ancient fountains and buildings, and other such delightfully French things. Ah, one of the reasons we came here. Linda and I hadn't had anything to eat, so one of us insisted that we sit in one of the squares at an outdoor table of a brasserie and have a couple of Kronenbourgs, *entrecôte* with *frites*, and view the passing scene and pretend to be French even though we weren't smoking Gauloises and didn't have a small dog with us. The other reluctantly put aside visions of an eight-minute meal at McDonald's. Subsequently the tables were turned as it happened that there was, right next to the brasserie, a store featuring the brightly printed fabrics of Provence made into kitchen and table linens of all kinds. They are pretty neat—images of all kinds of flowers, vegetation, vegetables, fruits, even insects, in terrific shades of yellow, red, blue, and green. Linda and I are both suckers for primary colors, so it was an easy sell.

That evening we all went for dinner to another brasserie that had two things going for it: first, it had a *chaise de bébé* (high chair), and Leo, like all eleven-month-old kids, does a lot better when imprisoned in such a device than when crawling around on the floor of a restaurant and picking up fallen *pommes frites*. Second, it was named Brasserie Leopold, so of course it got our vote. We got many pictures of *bébé* being held up beside the sign. As soon as we sat down we asked the waiter to bring out the *chaise de bébé*, which he ungraciously did. God punished him, however, because he could barely figure out how to set it up, got tangled up in it, pinched several fingers, and generally looked foolish—and French waiters don't like this. He did immediately regain his good humor when we asked him to choose the wine. When he brought us our menus Rich turned to Linda, who with her excellent French has been a mainstay in the language department the whole trip, and asked her to help him order dinner. "I'd be happy to, Rich, but the menu's printed in English," she replied. The food was several levels above plain traditional brasserie fare, and the wine was terrific, and when the place got full, which was pretty soon after we got there, it was nice and loud, and nobody cared when Leo indulged in a small amount of shouting and other exuberance.

### Day Five—Saturday, October 24

The next morning was the morning of the famous Saturday market in Aix, famous to everyone except the hotel staff who claimed never to have heard of it. The market fills up about half the center square with a wonderful food market and the other half with what the guidebook says is an antiques market, but what the French realistically call *brocante* (literally secondhand goods or junk, but it does sound better in French), and what we would call a flea market. We wandered around it all morning, and here's what I learned: French bread is different from, and better than, American bread, but a flea market is a flea market the world over.

During the afternoon Elika and Rich elected not to subject Leo to another car ride, so the rest of us drove off out of town on the Route Cézanne, a relatively short ride over ruggedly beautiful countryside, which Cézanne painted a number of times. Pictures of, that is, he didn't actually paint the landscape itself, or if he did all the paint has long since worn off. Cézanne is a very big deal in Aix and he didn't even have to cut off his ear. The route goes toward, and then alongside, a significant stone mountain named Sainte-Victoire, which is a vertical, harsh, dramatic mass of light gray granite. It is quite arresting, and you can see why if you were a painter you might think this area was pretty snappy. After we had marveled at the landscape for a while, fortuitously, a vineyard happened to pop up named Domaine de Saint-Ser. We stopped in and had a tour just for our group (we were the only ones there). The vineyard was picture-perfect beautiful: orderly rows of vines with the leaves of each section of vines turning a different fall color—some red, some orange, some yellow. It looked like an orderly patchwork quilt. Add to this the stone terraces, the rows of silvery leafed olive trees, and the charming English of the young woman giving us the tour on, she announced, her first day at work ("This is where we separate the graps from their boon-chez") and it was hard to beat. We bought four bottles of pretty good wine out of gratitude.

As we were leaving Aix to go on this drive, it was decided that since we were on vacation, it was authorized to have ice cream for lunch. Ice cream doesn't really stay with you. By mid-afternoon, however, we were getting pretty hungry. We decided to get something to eat in the small town near the vineyard, at the Relais Cézanne, which the guidebook explicitly recommends as a terrific place for whiling away several glorious hours sitting on the patio in the sun-dappled afternoon. It neglected to mention that you could sit there getting sun dappled all you wanted, but you couldn't get anything to eat at any time other than the narrow window officially allowed for lunch—12:00 to 2:00. At other times of the day you may *read* the menu, but you may not order from it. We found this confusing, but attributed it to tourist naiveté and the peculiarities of dealing with such a famous establishment in such a famous location. Little did we know ...

Famished, we went back into town and had an early dinner (5:30, no less) at a quite big brasserie on the main boulevard of town. Called Les Deux Garçons, it was a classic bistro with a lot of outdoor seating and two sizeable inside rooms with high ceilings, red wallpaper, gilt cornices, and large mirrored walls. We sat at a marble-topped table and had predictable but fine brasserie food. We even managed to leave a message for Rich and Elika telling them where we were. It turned out that they also had eaten recently, at the same place, and it had taken them two hours to have a salad and a hamburger. They concluded that the name of the establishment referred to the number of waiters on duty at any one time. We brought back some sandwiches for them, and we all sat out on the terrace of the hotel that evening, drinking the wine from the vineyard, eating the sandwiches, and telling stories comparing who had the nuttiest relatives. Linda's dad took the prize for storytelling ability, characterizing one of his relations by marriage as "a ne'er-do-well of the worst sort." Elika, in particular, wanted to know what other sorts there were. It was quite wonderful, except for the occasional roar of the trucks going by on the highway next to the small *charmant* hotel. We went to bed early because our plan was to arise at 6:30 (yes, yikes! 6:30!) and go to the famous antiques market at a small town near Avignon called L'Isle-sur-la-Sorgue.

**Day Six—Sunday, October 25**

The alarm faithfully went off at 6:30. Well, not exactly. Linda got up and found a note left under the door from her mom saying she had found that the previous evening marked the end of French daylight savings time, so it was really now 5:30. This presented something of a dilemma. One of us wanted to roll over and go back to sleep for an hour, but the more principled member of the couple pointed out that this probably wouldn't work, and that even running around the hall waking up everybody to tell them that they could go back to sleep for another hour maybe wasn't a good idea. Up we got and off we went into the dark of the morning, on the road to L'Isle-sur-la-Sorgue. There wasn't a lot of other traffic on the road. Fast or slow.

Linda, our flawless navigator, got us promptly to L'Isle, so promptly that when we got there all the people with stuff to sell were still setting up their booths, putting up their awnings, unloading their trucks, and yawning. There were lots of places to park, though. *OK*, we thought, *no problem, we'll just have a wonderful French breakfast.* After all we are here in what is generally regarded as the Region with The Best Food, in what is often argued to be the Country With The Best Food In The World. How hard can this be? We wandered in to one of the few open brasseries. Can we get breakfast here?" we asked politely.

"Non. Just coffee and croissants."

"Is there any place in the town where we can get breakfast?" Gallic shrug of shoulders, connoting indifference, disinterest, and a negative reply. General meaning of entire exchange: We're French and you're not. So we had coffee and croissants, then wandered around the market at length. Everybody rendezvoused about 11:00 at a brasserie called Brasserie sur-la-Sorgue. Had more coffee. No one could stomach more croissants.

Rejuvenated, everybody but Rich, Elika, and Leo threw themselves back into the market fray. By now it is 11:30. Elika orders an omelet with frites for Leo (important to start the kid early on fried food, after all there is a Midwest heritage here to uphold) and assorted drinks. Waiter returns at 11:40 with drinks. No omelet.

"Omelet?" asks Elika, as Leo is getting more and more restless.

"No omelets until noon," says the waiter. Implicitly he adds, "This may be what is generally regarded as The Region With The Best Food, in what is often argued to be The Country With The Best Food In The World, but you can't have any."

About 1:15 we all regroup at the same location and try ordering lunch. Very long wait, but we now have great fear that since it is clear that lunch is *only* available between 12:00 and 2:00, if we get up and try to go someplace else all the tables will be full and we'll miss our window. See Official Rules of Lunch, above. The waiter finally comes. Linda asks for a sandwich.

"No bread," he says, so no sandwich. While this response is internally consistent, it is worth bearing in mind that France is the self-acknowledged bread capital of the universe, and this is pretty far from the height of the tourist season.

"OK," she says, choosing an almost indisputable fallback, "I'd like the plat du jour, but could I have the sauce *à côté* (on the side)."

"Non." She then asks for two bottles of Perrier for the table.

"No one in France drinks Perrier," says the waiter, "I'll bring you Badoit instead." We view this as a concession on his part, since after all, he's French and we're not.

Late afternoon (when we finally have gotten served—including a basket of bread—and eaten our lunches) and we're on the road to Crillon-le-Brave, truly a great name for a small hill town in Provence. And the hotel, when we arrive, is spectacular; actually it was probably spectacular before we arrived. It's set on the top of a hill in a beautifully refurbished seventeenth century castle with attentive staff, a gorgeous setting with views out over the valley, and excellent large and airy rooms tastefully done with white walls, dark roof beams, and Provencal fabrics. Dinner is very French and elaborate, forcing us to expand our food vocabulary. "St. Pierre" (French) translates to "John Dory" (English), causing one to ask which is the sillier name for a fish and who makes up these names anyway? The maître d' is very patient and gracious, and no one ends up ordering anything weird unless they want to.

### Day Seven—Monday, October 26

Breakfast the next morning on the terrace overlooking the valley is equally exquisite—it's a crisp day but bright with sun. The terrace is made of old stone and has roses, pots of geraniums, a lily pond, and tall pointy cypress trees, and really does look like something out of a Van Gogh painting. The only bad part is that Linda has blocked sinuses, for which I have gone off into the nearby town to procure medicine (or what we hope is medicine, given my less than perfect French). In the course of this humanitarian mission I discover that there is yet another market, this one in the small town of Badoin, and it looks suspiciously like the other two markets we have just gone to. Maybe it's all the same guys rotating around from town to town, carrying all that yellow and brown pottery with them, and all those marinated olives, and lavender soap, and gaily printed fabrics. How much lavender soap can a person actually use in a year?

Fortified with strong French coffee and (finally) cereal—OK, muesli, but it's close enough—we get organized and go off for a tour of the perched villages, a highlight of the area. One of us essayed a few jokes about how those fish got up to those villages anyway.

"Language is treacherous" interjection: at the market the day before, I had suggested that we buy a pretty little bottle of lamp oil with flowers, dried grass and herbs, and other cute stuff inside it, colored a nice shade of light orange. It was also scented—in fact at this particular stall there were bottles of various different colors of oil, all labeled with a different fragrance. But when I took a second look at the bottle I put it back, remarking to Linda that I thought it was pretty darn peculiar that they'd have a bottle with "fish" as the aroma, especially when the others were stuff like *l'orange*, and *lavande* (lavender), and *fleur*.

"What do you mean?" she asked patiently.

"Well," I said, "look here, it's labeled *pêche* from the same word as *pêcheur*, or fisherman."

"Darling," she said, "that actually means 'peach.'"

We visit several villages, and they are truly remarkable, built in medieval times on the tops of peaks and cliffs and the like—quite dramatic and photogenic. We stop for a longer time at Séguret, which has a good restaurant. This time we arrive at the appropriate hour, and the guidebook is correct, so we spend a long languid afternoon with a lovely three-course meal complete with two bottles of the local wine, and through the large restaurant windows, unmatchable views of the cultivated valley, hills in the distance, etc. There are only three parties having lunch, so they are glad to see us and very patient about helping us understand the menu. Leaving, we take many pictures of the beautiful town with its narrow streets, colorful doorways, fountains, etc., and NO people. Boy, are we thankful to be traveling in this popular region at off-season.

Returning to the hotel, we really aren't ready for another serious French meal. However, you have to apologize for such unseemly behavior, or at least it feels like that. The staff at Crillon-le-Brave is wonderfully accommodating and not at all put off and suggests that they can even just send up a plate of ham, bread, and cheese to our room, a green salad, whatever we want. Elika and Rich elect to go off and eat while Linda and I watch Leo and revel in the luxury of *not* having to go through another elaborate dinner.

### Day Eight—Tuesday, October 26

Again we all gather at the entirely sane hour of 10:00 on the exquisite patio of the hotel, and again they bring us a breakfast that is very French but with just enough touches of the rest of Europe to be perfect. We consider buying the hotel, or at least the villa next door. We seriously consider coming back next year and renting a big house for a month and doing scholarly research on the vineyards in the area, and is it true that there are really five hundred different kinds of French cheese. Elika, ever the skeptic, says that as far as she can tell, all cheese in France is either goat, blue, or brie. There is a morsel of truth in this.

But we have to move on to Avignon. We arrive at our hotel, Hostellerie Les Frenes, about 12:30. It is a beautiful old white marble mansion in the suburbs, Montfavet to be exact—sure sounds better than Landover or Arlandria as a suburb name, doesn't it? The house sits triumphantly on a gorgeous expanse of lawn with a white gravel drive leading up to it, flanked by its own allée of plane trees. Golden leaves are floating down in the afternoon sunlight. There are more beautifully maintained grounds in the back, including an understated swimming pool, not a feature the French always do well. It does look fabulous, and because it is our last stop, Linda has arranged for us all to have suites. It is also far and away the most expensive (3,000 francs or $600/night) of the places we have stayed. We check in, get situated amongst a lot of "oohing" and "ahhing," and then all take off for town to explore.

Avignon, as almost everyone knows, is where one or maybe a couple of the popes lived for a while under some sort of circumstances that none of us can now remember—was it the Albigensian heresy or the Heimlich maneuver that had something to do with it? Never mind, it is a great walled town whose focal point is the very large and impressive Palais des Papes, a beautiful structure of white limestone in the northern quarter. The site includes a big, but somewhat dark, cathedral and a wonderful garden on a site overlooking the Rhône River. Clearly visible across the river are several other magnificent medieval castles that we sadly won't have time to visit. We have two missions in this city: see the sites and find some cardboard boxes to pack up all our loot in so we can mail it home. We have collectively got enough stuff that the back of the van has blossomed with numerous white plastic sacks laid on top of all the luggage.

We begin the quest for boxes. We try *boîtes* first, then settle on *cartons*, and Linda adds, "*avec emballage.*" I ask whatever in the world we need umbrellas for, since we have brought three and it hasn't rained but one or two drops. She notes that I have mistranslated and the word means "packing material." As I express amazement at the depth and variety, not to mention the peculiarity of her French vocabulary, she charitably adds that she did have to look that one up. Despite this amazing linguistic dexterity, we are not successful. No one at the hotel can imagine such a need, and when we check with the post office they are equally baffled. Makes the US Postal Service look positively modern. And as for any sort of "Mail It 4-U" place, forget it. The palaces and stuff, though, were easier to find and quite impressive. We decided we would come back to Avignon soon; there was much more to do and see here and we barely scratched the surface. And who cares if they don't have boxes, anyway?

Since we struck out on *cartons*, we adopted a different approach and stopped into a luggage store. Turns out that Linda has had her eye on the bright colored plastic hard-sided suitcases that are de rigueur for all European travelers. She has particularly been attracted to: 1) the jaunty electric colors they come in (lime green, royal blue, bright yellow, etc.); and 2) the very heavy "thump" that they make when slung onto baggage belts—evidence that the crafty Europeans are getting lots more weight into these suitcases than we slow Americans are with our black Travelpro roll-ons. Surveying the luggage store, Linda spies a selection of these suitcases and zeroes in on the most tasteful one, which is an electric orange in color.

"THAT'S IT!" she announces triumphantly to her amazed husband, who was foolishly thinking "small, cheap, dark green duffel bag." We purchase it and walk all the way across town to the Budget rental car agency in the train station where we are picking up a car for Linda's parents who are staying longer, lucky devils. Nobody looks at us twice, but then no cars run into us, either. I am amazed—I'm telling you, this baby is ORANGE. Naturally since Budget is our last stop, we find a large stack of *cartons déménagements* (moving boxes) for sale. Of course they don't sell tape there; for that you have to go to another store. It's complicated being French. Anyway, by now Linda is totally attached to her electric orange plastic suitcase, so the *cartons* are left to their fate.

Returning to our fancy and expensive hotel for our final dinner, we are informed by one of the staff that because we are a party of six (without Leo), we either have to all choose the same thing off the menu, or, if we insisted on making individual choices, then serving us each would take the kitchen a Very Long Time (i.e., more than two hours). Six, remember, not a banquet for sixty or six hundred. And we had reserved dinner three weeks before (for six) and reconfirmed that day at noon. And this at a hotel restaurant where the main courses ran as much as five hundred francs ($100). Does this seem strange to you? Does this seem as if it really is the ultimate in "We're French and you're not?" Do you think there is any conceivable chance that any French person with enough dough to go to dinner there would either a) be treated this way, or b) put up with it? OK, those are loaded questions.

Linda and I proceeded to have an increasingly heated discussion with the owner. He said he was only interested in the quality of service for us. We said some of the things listed above. Then he noted that if only we could speak French and discuss this in French we would understand. Very bad tactic, never mind about the insulting part. Linda replied in French and additional heated discussion followed. The chef came in, the maître d' came over, the French TV crew that was there filming something listened with delight. The owner suggested that Linda was making a *scandale*; she replied that she certainly was, and he hadn't seen anything yet. Finally the owner decided that maybe this little effort to terrorize the Americans wasn't going to be successful; he backed down, said they would fix it, and that it was just a misunderstanding. We all came for dinner and found four, count them, four waiters there, and a complementary bottle of very good (Taittinger) champagne. Dinner was excellent, quickly prepared, and well served. We decided that they were afraid of us, or at least afraid of Linda.

I ordered the *bar de ligne* (another kind of Mediterranean white fish) grilled with *herbes de Provence*. We had been seeing little bags of *herbes de Provence* for eight days, although I for one have never known exactly what goes into the mix. They could be selling bags of dried grass for all I know. Nonetheless one last round of bad jokes was thereby inspired:

What is the favorite movie of people in Provence? *Rosemary's Baby*

What is the principal astrological sign of people in Provence? Sage-ittarius

Where do misbehaving children have to go in Provence? Thyme-out

Sadly, we couldn't come up with any ideas on parsley. This clearly argues for another trip and one that you can come with us on.

Love and kisses,
Bob

## seventeen

# what's that parrot doing on your business card?

November 1998

Dear Dad,

Well it wasn't quite the whole story, that earlier letter about our European adventures other than vacations. I did like the ending though. But there was more to the story, as there so frequently is. I just temporarily ran out of energy. But first, you asked me about our company name.

What's in a name? Why call yourself White Wolf Capital? I had a friend who was forming a new financial firm in New York, and he was going to do some of those peculiar and not-understandable-to-normal- human-being sort of activities like equity-linked derivatives, asset-backed arbi-trage, swap-spread currency hedging, mezzanine round funding, forward put/call trading, and Lord knows what else. He was going to be a merchant bank, naturally. This was during the period when being a merchant bank was very fashionable, the finance biz being no less immune to fashion than other businesses; in fact, perhaps more subject to fad since so much of what is done is intellectual work divorced from hard and frequently inconvenient assets like factories, giant paper machines, oil refining vessels, airplanes, etc. Imagine trying to be trendy in the steel industry—it's hard to suddenly convert a blast furnace into a minimill, not that I actually know exactly what either one of those is.

But this guy was not in the steel business. What he was most agonized about was not what exactly all the things he was planning to do actually meant and whether it took any money to do them, which, by the way, he did not have but figured he could get, I suppose, if he simply uttered some combination of these magic words to people who actually had money and were looking to lose it. Rather, he was most concerned about what he should call the company. We talked about it over several beers, the ideal situation for creative thought, and we came up with the Official Naming Paradigm for New Financial Firms. He was a little chagrined that he hadn't thought to include this somehow in the list of things he was going to do, but no matter. We especially liked using "paradigm" as it did qualify as another word that neither of us actually knew the meaning of, but we could blithely use it in conversations with our peers, because no one we ever ran into actually knew what it meant, either.

First we first spent some time dismissing the obvious name candidates. It appears to me that most financial and many consulting firms are in fact named by the founders after (modestly) themselves. There probably was an original McKinsey of McKinsey & Co., and a real Mr. Booz of Booz Allen, and there damn sure was a J. P. Morgan and a Samuel Chase. But we concluded that this practice was a little presumptuous, although an approach that still finds vast favor. It also suggests to the poet in me a huge lack of imagination. I did suggest that calling his new firm "The Sam Company" had some merit, but I was accused of a lack of seriousness.

The second most frequent choice seems to be an anonymous financial one: Capital Financial Assets being one of my favorites, a name I really ran across. Its beauty is its semi-palindromic nature: it could also be Financial Capital Assets or Financial Assets Capital, etc. We briefly considered whether four words of generic financial non-meaningness would be fitting. How about Financial Assets Capital Ventures? But we decided that while attractive, it would get too long to comfortably fit on a business card. First things first. By the way, if you are a consultant, you merely substitute

"Strategic," "Strategy," "Planning," and maybe a few other words for the finance words, "Development" being another good one.

But our real conclusion was the scheme, and it worked like this: You took a piece of paper and wrote three column headings across the top. Column one was labeled "Adjectives," but these adjectives were selective and could only be colors, directions, and maybe a couple of other limited things like "great" or "small," these latter only in limited circumstances. The adjectives had to be neutral and positive, of course, and not common. "Great" is fine, "big" and "grandiose" are not. The second column was "Nouns" but limited to animals and selected geographic features such as mountain, harbor, peak, valley—you get the picture. Probably not bad karma nouns like chasm, or gully, or precipice. And probably not disgusting animals like pigs, or toads, or shrews, or two-name animals like boa constrictors. The third column was also "Nouns" but even more limited to nouns signifying either money: capital, finance, ventures; or some form of association: partners, associates, and maybe a few others.

So you make your list, then you just scan down it and, like the proverbial Chinese menu (which by the way, as far as I can tell no longer exists despite its position in folklore and everyday analogous speech), you select one from column A, one from column B, and one from column C. Thus you can come up with Blue Water Capital, North Shore Partners, Red Rock Ventures, Green Deer Associates, South Bay Capital, and on and on. All of the above, it is interesting to note, are in fact real companies that I have at one point or another encountered. Great system, huh?

I have given the punch line away. I was in California for some reason and had already decided to leave AES and venture off into venture land, and Elika and Rich had me over for dinner at their small but trendy Venice house. We were sitting on their deck, and the bulldog was slobbering on Rich's pants, and we were drinking Dos Equis, which isn't as good as it used to be since the Mexicans watered it down to sell it to us Yanquis in quantity. We debated the name for my new company, drew up the list, rejected Yellow Dog Partners (too Democratic), thought about Black Canyon Ventures but decided it sounded too gloomy, pondered High Desert Associates (too regional), and had several more beers. This naming stuff is hard on your liver. Finally we decided that we liked "Wolf" pretty well, but the color was disputatious. White was finally selected for its nice alliterative qualities, plus we didn't think there were any white wolves. So there you go. I went back to Washington, found a graphic artist, got her to do a linoleum block for about three hundred bucks; had a printer make a master and some mechanicals; selected a typeface off the computer, Arial black bold if I recall; and sent it to a cheap printer—and away we go.

You wouldn't think that this name would be so hard to deal with. But here's what have I been variously called:
- » Mike Wolf Capital
- » White Golf Capital
- » White Roof Capital

Etc. When I was at AES, we initially called ourselves Applied Energy Services and that seemed equally confounding. We were forever being called Applied Energy Systems, and once were called in print "Appliance Energy Systems," even though we hadn't sold anyone any microwaves or toasters in ever so long. My all-time favorite was when I checked in to a cheap motel late at night in Chicago and found that we had been recorded as "Clyde Energy Services." He was probably the guy who repaired all the appliances.

The runner-up was when, early on as a baby venture capitalist (we were still in our "Can't we do something with the movies; how about special effects?" phase) I went to something called SIGGRAPH. I doubt you could guess what that was if you guessed a very long time, even with lots of clues. It is the annual convention of people who do computer graphics of all sorts. There is much relation to the movie biz but also much relation to science, technology, manufacturing, you name it. Where the name comes from no one can quite tell, and I did ask. Maybe it's German, except it's not long enough.

This particular convention was held in New Orleans in August. It was actually attended by people, which is remarkable in itself, given the climate of the venue at that time of year. Maybe no one had told them. Its location was the Earnest N. Morial Convention Center, which is a great long thing right along the river, named after a mayor of New Orleans who either did something or failed to do something, it's not clear. The number of people attending was unbelievably 25,000. It was composed of 24,999 people of widely mixed races, both sexes, and various hairstyles, all wearing either T-shirts (approximately 22,500 of them) or golf shirts (the remaining 2,499 of them) and all under the age of thirty-five mostly, or forty-five for sure. The other attendee was a fifty-five-year old white guy wearing a button down shirt and a blazer. No tie. I may not have fit in all that well, I can't be sure.

The convention was pretty fascinating and a great way to learn the business. When I picked up my package at the registration desk, I was smart enough to look carefully at my name tag before I put it on. Sure enough, it said "White Wool Capital." But they had the machinery to make new ones right there, so I asked them to, then slapped on the new one they gave me and hit the trade show floor. The funny thing is that we always find we are the only financial firm that goes to such things so we do get questioned a bit. But I really got questioned at this one. At literally every booth where I stopped to talk with someone, at some point in the conversation I would be asked what my firm did. And never an intro-ductory, "Oh, you must be some sort of financial company." I had no idea that any knowledge of finance was so lacking in the computer graphics industry. Don't they at least read *Fortune* from time to time? After the last session, two and half days' worth of nonstop walking the aisles and asking questions, which by the way is pretty hard work since you have to stand up a lot, I returned to my hotel room, tore off my shoes, and flopped down on the bed. I plucked off my badge, and then noticed, to my surprise, that the registration lady had in fact corrected the "Wool." I was now identi-fied as Bob Hemphill, White Wolf Capiton. I began to understand why people had been so confused. But not one time had anyone asked me what a "Capiton" was. I guess they assumed it was some new form of financial thing like an equity-linked derivative.

When we found out that we couldn't be cinema moguls because the economics were so lousy, we decided to become venture capitalists again. At least it was again for me, the first time really for Linda. We changed our name to Toucan Capital and put out the word that we were in the deal business.

It might be interesting to note that the confusion has not ended with this name change from White Wolf. We have been frequently called Two-Can Capital (there's two of us, get it?). We try to explain to people that it's just like the bird, but avian awareness is lacking in the circles in which we seem to move. Even people looking at our business card, which has a colorful and anatomically accurate image of a toucan right next to the word "Toucan," tend to say things like, "That's a colorful parrot on your business card." We have also been called Torxan Capital (our Alpha Centauri branch) and Trican Capital, although not yet Tricorn Capital, perhaps because there's no hat on the parrot. My current personal favorite: Pecan Capital. Ah me.

Just why did we think that we could compete in this business area in Europe, a location definitely not our homeland? Aside from normal Ivy League arrogance, I cite the following examples of continental business practice:

Operations planning: When cash machines (ATMs) were first introduced to Germany, all the German banks decided that the ATMs would be open for the same restrictive hours that the banks themselves were. Thus you could use an ATM for two hours in the morning and another two in the afternoon. And never on weekends. At about that same time Citibank was moving into Germany in consumer banking and it had no such peculiar ideas about "hours" for ATMs. Needless to say this proved to be something of an advantage for Citibank. And they wouldn't take anybody else's card; you had to open a Citibank account.

Customer Service: An English winter is world-class awful. The sun sets at 3:30 p.m., it's cold, and it rains all the time, and there aren't any flowers around to offset the weather. And besides it would be too dark to see them if there were. After experiencing this for 2.7 days, we decided we needed a place in the sun, and so we would buy a small cottage on the French Riviera to get away from all the crapola rain from time to time.

We did some research and came up with seventeen real estate firms, culled from likely places such as magazines with titles like *French Riviera Estates* and *Great Homes in the South of France*. We were clever and sophisticated about this; we didn't pick anybody in Poland, only folks in Cannes and Nice, and only folks who advertised in English and said things in their adverts like "Call us and let us show you our Riviera" or "You need a house here and we can sell it to you." We composed a simple letter in clear English that said something like this: "We just moved to the UK, we want to purchase right away a cottage in the Riviera area, we will pay cash immediately, we are prepared to spend up to 7 million francs (about US $1 million), call or fax us and we will fly down tomorrow to see any appropriate properties. We're not kidding and we're not overly picky."

I thought that was pretty clear. Off went our fax. We waited expectantly. And, of course, the replies flooded in. Actually the two replies flooded in after about two weeks and several more faxings of the same faxes to the same seventeen firms. Two responses. And both said that if we came down to visit, we should call them and they would check around and see what was available. No phone calls, no lists of available properties, no promises of color pictures, no FedExed fancy brochures, no videos, no offers to pick us up at the airport and show us around. *Do these guys know how to sell real estate or what?*

Interpersonal relations: A British guy named David Meachum used to be one of those miscellaneous medium to upper mid-level diplomats, then went into some form of mid-level investment banking. He had known Linda in her Commerce Department days, and then in her Enron days when he had tried to interest her in some of his deals or get her to employ him as a banker for Enron. He heard that Linda had moved to London, tracked her down, and listened to her explanation of our new venture capital focus. "Well," he said charmingly, "that sounds very interesting. I'm going to have to put you back in my Rolodex."

It took us a while to sharpen our focus after regretfully giving up on the cinemas. We spent a silly amount of time looking at buying into an airline serving Namibia, an idea of a rich Saudi friend of Linda's. The principal argument was that there was little or no competition on the route, which was probably true, only the difficulty was that we couldn't, in the end, convince ourselves that hundreds of people a day wanted to fly from Johannesburg to Windhoek. Plus all the numbers they kept giving us never agreed with the other numbers they had given us the day before. And the price we were to pay for our shares of the nascent airline was, strangely, four or five times higher per share than the price that the Saudi had paid about six months earlier. Oh, and by the way, the airline didn't yet have an airplane or landing slots at either airport. There were several pilots said to be interested. I have never been an airline, but I suspect that you have to have an airplane and be able to take off from somewhere and land somewhere else. Good sense eventually overtook us and we passed, but not without much careful analysis, and modeling, and so forth.

We finally figured out that the only deals we wanted to be in were information technology and biotech. And the UK was not the place to be for these, and there wasn't much of a venture industry, and the business services were lousy, and, and, and. So we started making increasingly long trips back to the US and became bit-by-bit bi-continental. Our final inspiration was to mine Eastern Europe for technologies left over from the Soviet days and the Far East for cheap real estate. And to do it with cheap labor. The Asian currency crash had just occurred, so we figured that Korea and Thailand were no doubt ripe for foreign capitalist exploitation, and maybe they had some neat technologies to boot. We made an exploratory trip to Korea where we were very well treated by the government. Linda even got her picture in the paper. We also had a laser technology pressed upon us that could be used for sending telecom signals. It worked sort of, except in rain, snow, fog, or sleet. Plus nothing longer than about a mile. This seemed a weakness except in particularly small and flat countries made out of desert. I also wondered a bit about flying pigeons that flew through the laser beam, but then I don't much care for pigeons anyway, so a few fried ones probably wouldn't be a disaster. We were repeatedly assured that the bit loss (dropped data) of pigeon encounters would be minimal. But the precipitation was a problem.

To get the cheap labor, our inspiration was to run around to major business schools and try to recruit students for summer jobs with this unattractive premise: go to a neat foreign capital, be unsupervised, have your living expenses paid for, get a nice salary, and look for deals. Evaluate them, bring them to us, and if we fund them you'll get a bonus. We did attract interest, I must say. Several people were honest enough to describe this as their "dream summer job." We weren't smart enough to realize that this might not have been a good thing.

We selected seven smart kids: a Hungarian, two Indians, two Chinese, a German, and a Korean. They came from the business schools at Rice, Columbia, UVA, and Penn. Almost all of them already had advanced degrees and some work experience. These folks were not, on the surface, dopes. Before sending them off to their countries we spent five days intensively training them as to what to look for. The message was pretty simple: we are interested in investing in start-up and early-stage companies in the four areas of batteries, lasers, biotech, and telecom. And though one wouldn't think you would have to do this, we did further define just what we meant by batteries, lasers, etc. Moreover, we believed that initially we should avoid computers, software, and the Internet. Interesting factoid: according to a study by Price Waterhouse (who now, after merging with Coopers & Lybrand, has decided that they want to be called PricewaterhouseCoopers, thus strongly competing for the "longest silly corporate name" title as well as perhaps beating "antidisestablishmentarianism" as the longest word in English), last year in the US there was $11 billion invested in venture capital, *and slightly more than half* went into computers, software, etc. This was too much competition for us, so we wrote "computers and software" on the board and drew a big red circle with a diagonal slash over the whole thing. It was a bit blunt, but we were trying to get the point across. The training was finished and off these kids went. Results:

1. We sent one Chinese guy to Thailand. During our training session at the beginning of the summer, his only question was whether he got to travel business class going to his assignment. This should have been a sign. He produced nothing whatsoever, and we fired him halfway through the summer. In truth, Bangkok wasn't ready at that point to face reality and sell off foreclosed properties at any reasonable price. And it is hardly a high-tech mecca. Someone offered to sell us a slightly decrepit shrimp-drying factory, however.

2. We sent our other Chinese kid, Naidong Zhou, and a very smart young German, Christian Stich, to Sofia, the capital of and actually only

decent-size city in Bulgaria. Don't laugh; during the heyday of the Evil Empire, Bulgaria was something of a center of both optical stuff and some high-tech physics. They were said to have some battery technologies and some plant-related biotech worth investigating. And these were both smart and industrious young men.

The problems here were of a different nature. First, we could barely get Naidong through customs despite all the right passports and carefully secured visas. We had arranged an apartment for the two of them to share, and fortunately the landlord was meeting Naidong at the airport. She finally had to barge into the customs hall and literally drag him away from the clutches of the Border Police.

A week later, at midnight, two large, heavily armed policemen banged on our guys' door and claimed that Christian's and Naidong's passport stamps were wrong and that they had to pay a fine. Not at headquarters, but right there on the spot. Christian and Naidong refused. Flat refused. Courageous or stupid, hard to figure, and the "cops" went away.

A week later more cops stopped Naidong on the street in broad daylight and just demanded some money as a "fine." It's not clear for what; maybe being Chinese is a finable offense in Sofia. They asked for 30 levs, and he demanded to be taken to the police headquarters so he could pay the fine. They finally suggested 10 levs ($7) and he reluctantly paid.

We were scheduled that next week to be in Sofia, and Linda was a featured speaker at the First Annual Bulgaria High Tech Conference and Expo designed to showcase Bulgaria's progress in this area and to demonstrate what a neat place it was for foreign investment. We went, we met with our embassy people, we met with the Deputy Prime Minister and explained what had happened; we cancelled our participation in the conference, and we pulled our guys out, and sent them to Hungary for the remainder of the summer.

Even in the one month they were there, harassed and all, what they had found out was that we were too late. All the smart, younger technical folks had gone to the West and probably taken the best technologies with them. The "Research Institutes," and we visited several, were lonely, dark buildings, probably less than 25% occupied, with no supplies, no maintenance for years, and what staff remained were all in their fifties and sixties. It was pretty sad.

3. We sent our most entrepreneurial guy to Hungary. Atilla was an MD by training, but he had started a real estate development business in Budapest with his mother before coming to business school, and he seemed to be the closest of the seven to our way of thinking—about deals, and venture capital, and the like. Plus he was Hungarian. We figured this would help. Remember that we had carefully briefed everybody and trained them on what kind of technologies we were looking for: telecom, batteries, lasers, and biotech. High-tech stuff. The first deal he brought to us, with great enthusiasm, was a factory that was for sale outside of Budapest. It made shoe soles. We pondered this. Shoe soles for high-tech shoes? Shoes to be worn in biotech laboratories? What was the connection here? He was puzzled when we told him this didn't make a lick of sense, and our focus was supposed to be as above.

He went back to the drawing board. His crowning accomplishment was his next proposal. He did a better job of preparing us for this one. Atilla assured us there was a real market need, a dominant position could be obtained, it was insulated from business cycle risk, and it had immediate positive cash flow. He wanted us to establish a chain of crematoria. No, really. We sat for a measurable period in stunned silence after his presentation. He was, after all, a nice kid, energetic, enthusiastic, and a hard worker. He had spent a year at a good business school, and it had been a nice business school sort of presentation, with charts, and graphs, and financial projections. "You know," he added helpfully, "the places where they burn up dead people."

"Oh, that kind of crematoria," I muttered, "not some place with dairy associations." And not a crematorium that used lasers, biotech, or batteries, and darn sure doesn't use much telecom. Finally Linda said, "You know what the real problem with this is? No repeat business."

Slowly, we came to the realization that perhaps our plan was flawed and we needed a new one. Actually, this new plan (summary: let's go home and be venture capitalists there) was disclosed to Linda when we were on vacation in Hawaii having breakfast at one of those little roadside diners they have, this one in Kauai. Linda was having pancakes with coconut syrup, something she had been searching for, and the only thing she really liked about Hawaii. She has been a quite good sport about all this upheaval yet again but does admit that she has lost her taste, temporarily one hopes, for coconut.

Love and kisses,
Bob

# eighteen

# around the world in nine days

August 1999

Dear Dad,

As you probably remember, when I left AES in 1996, Roger Sant, the Chairman, and Dennis Bakke, the CEO, prevailed on me to join the company's Board of Directors. Recently, Dennis generously invited any interested AES board member to go with him on his upcoming round-the-world trip to our plants in Europe and Asia. I dutifully raised my hand. Maybe I should have thought back to those first international trips that Dennis and I made together in 1975 when we were both baby energy experts in the Federal Energy Administration (FEA). International cooperation in energy was just beginning, and the State Department, eager for some help that wouldn't count against their budget, had gotten Dennis to come along to one of the initial meetings, designating him as "US Representative" for the energy conservation part of things. At that very first meeting he got elected chairman of the subgroup. My suspicion was that nobody else actually particularly lusted after the job, but us midwesterners, if there's a job to be done, well then, by dang, somebody's got to do it.

When he returned from the meeting, he immediately told me that since he was "Chairman," he couldn't be "US Representative" as well (a wealth of parliamentary precedent confounds this view, but it was fine with me), and so I had to come along to the next meeting as the US rep. But only if I could remember the names: Dennis was "Chairman of the Subcommittee on Energy Conservation of the Standing Committee for Long- Term Cooperation and Development of the International Energy Agency, a subunit of the Organization for Economic Cooperation and Development," and I was now "US Representative to the etc." Are these government titles poetic, or what? Oh, did I mention that the meetings were in Paris? Seemed somehow more attractive than if they were in Greenbelt, Maryland.

The time for this next Paris meeting came and away we went, but I have to give you some details of how Dennis scheduled this. We'd leave the FEA about 4:00 in the afternoon and catch the 6:30 flight to Paris, overnight and tourist class of course, arriving at Charles de Gaulle airport about 7:00 a.m. It was my first real experience with traveling to Europe as a grown-up, so I didn't realize how they trick you—after the dinner and the movie you're about ready to go to sleep because you know you'll be getting in pretty early, and after all it's 10:30 p.m. Washington time. But it's 4:30 in the morning in Paris and you're landing in two hours. Predictable outcome: you feel like someone has poured sand into your eyes while beating you about the head with an inflated platypus.

We land, get our luggage, and hop in a cab for the OECD offices, a former Rothschild mansion in the 16th arrondissement, a pretty fancy neighborhood that includes the Eiffel Tower and, I have heard, many fine hotels. We roll in carrying luggage at 9:00 a.m. and Dennis immediately starts the meeting. We meet all morning in a windowless basement conference room, usually with interpreters, although frankly everybody actually speaks English. Good thing 'cause we sure don't speak any of the languages of the other delegates. Dennis breaks the meeting at 12:30 for lunch and insists on reconvening at 1:15. Gasps and muttering from all concerned except me. The international diplomat work ethic doesn't exactly relate to a forty-five-minute lunch break taken in the third floor cafeteria. Several delegates begin to rethink their votes in the chairman election and wonder if the bylaws allow for impeachment.

We reconvene at 1:15 and work on through until 6:30. More mutterings and hints of uprising—I am informed in a sidebar conversation that no international meeting anyone has EVER gone to failed to adjourn by about 4:00. Now that I am a big-time diplomat, I get to say things like "sidebar conversation." Since, after all, we are in Paris, I shrug in what I hope appears to be Gallic indifference, even though I am as American as baseball. My oxford cloth blue button-down shirt was probably a giveaway. That and the little plastic sign in front of my place at the table that said "*Les États-Unis.*" I sat down behind this sign after all the other delegates had picked other signs, since that meant it had to be mine. I then spent half the day trying to figure out who "*Allemagne*" was.

Ah, free for an evening of sampling all the legendary joys of Paris! Well, first we check into our hotel, a truly remarkable establishment called Hôtel du Parc de la Muette, which I speculate means "the park of the small kiss, or sigh, or yearning," or some such romantic thing. It's only much later that I learn that *mouette* means sea gull. The Park of the Sea Gull doesn't sound quite as entrancing, does it? In practice what this means is a long, thin five-story hotel with fifteen small narrow rooms, five bathrooms, one shower, and a very French patroness, who sits on the second floor (the hotel is over a brasserie, one of its many charms) relentlessly smoking Gauloises cigarettes. It does have room rates—$15 with shared bathroom—that fit into US government per diems, which at this time are $25 per day, and you can walk to the Rothschild mansion. How Dennis ever found this place I cannot imagine since he's been to Paris only once more than me, but it is clean and very underclass Parisian. And it leaves us with $10 to splurge on the evening's entertainment.

We have a very inexpensive dinner at some local restaurant—it hardly matters, because the food is all pretty great in Paris and it's hard to go wrong. Besides neither of us speaks enough French to have a clue about what we're ordering. Of course I had bragged to Dennis that I knew all about French food, and God was listening. As a result for dinner I end up with blood sausage (oops! a real mistake) and what I thought would be potatoes. In my misremembered Yale French, I had read *pommes en l'air* as potatoes. Actually *pommes de terre* is what I was thinking of. The things on the plate were flat, and white, and slightly crescent shaped, but when I bit into them they were mushy and just slightly sweet. Turns out I had apples. I've never figured out the "air" part of this, and it was long before Michael Jordan, anyway.

"And then what?" you ask breathlessly. Well us stylish and trendy guys decided that for real kicks, nothing beat a night riding the subway. Yes, this really happened. Paris does have a pretty neat subway, and it was at least a tiny challenge and associated triumph to figure out how to buy a ticket in the machines and to figure out where to go and, once there, how to get back to our station, "La Muette" if I remember, no doubt named after the famous hotel in the vicinity. And the other good thing about this wholesome and inexpensive entertainment was that IT WASN'T CROWDED. You could easily get a seat. Well, there's a surprise. And it was cheap. We probably had change left over from the $10.

By the time this fascinating evening ended we were pretty tired, so even the U-shaped mattresses of the hotel didn't bother us, although getting up the steep stairs using those lights that turn on when you hit the switch and then turn off three seconds later (to save electricity, which of course is what we were there for, so it was hard to complain too much) was a challenge. The next morning, bright and early, we started our meetings again, at 8:30 this time. No sense wasting a sunny morning in Paris sitting languorously at a sidewalk café, drinking great French coffee, reading the *Herald Tribune* and pretending that you were a budding novelist instead of a GS-14, when instead you could be in a bomb shelter disguised as a meeting room, listening to the Japanese delegation's confused reaction to the Danish delegation's residential energy conservation proposals.

Dennis ran the meetings until 12:30, at which point (note: without lunch, not even lunch at the actually pretty good OECD cafeteria—a government cafeteria where you could get a small bottle of wine with your green salad and fabulous bread—after all, it is Paris. I repeat, in case you missed it: without lunch) we grabbed a cab, hustled off to the airport, caught the 3:30 flight back to Dulles, flew seven hours in coach, landed, got our luggage, and then went into the office. At which point several of our coworkers would inevitably remark, "Oh, back from your Paris boondoggle?"

Yes, I was warned.

### Day One, Sunday: Washington, D.C. and Over the Atlantic

Flying over to Amsterdam, the jumping-off point for this odyssey, you do get to catch up on your newspaper reading, and you find, if you read carefully, that there are wonderful things happening in your very own city. To wit:

The Saturday before I left Washington there was scheduled a march (for some purpose, probably the same purpose as all marches, a purpose now lost forever in the shrouded mists of time) by a neo-Nazi organization called Knights of Freedom. They got all the permits and elicited the following response: 1,500 special duty D.C. policemen in riot gear including shields and such lining Pennsylvania Avenue, including the head guy, Chief Ramsey himself, also wearing a helmet and carrying a riot baton. Actually he looked like a mushroom head— those helmets really do need to be redesigned. They also cordoned off of twenty square blocks of downtown Washington, had 1,000 regular duty policemen, and 300 park police, many on horses. To this add a 1,500 person anti-Nazi rally addressed by the Mayor of Washington and House of Representatives Delegate Norton. At the Knights of Freedom staging area, however, a grand total of four marchers actually showed up and decided instead that they had just enough for a round of bridge, so they went back to their motel and ordered in pizza. The police chief appeared on TV last night, unfortunately still wearing his cow pie helmet, and was pretty mad. He said that this cost the city one million dollars and he was going to sue the Knights of Freedom. Presumably for the reverse of "demonstrating without a permit," which must be "failing to demonstrate with a permit," a well-known civil offense. Delegate Norton of D.C., no shining beacon of legal intelligence herself, agreed and egged him on. She, however, was not wearing a helmet.

The facts slowly dribble out. The fearsome leader of the Knights of Freedom is a South Carolina college student who has changed his name to Davis Wolfgang Hawke (OK, we'll admit it, that is a pretty great name).

The organization is three years old, has a website and 150 members. Let's do the math: 2,800 policemen divided by 150 members—even if they all showed—is close to 20 cops per marcher. Could this be a tiny over-reaction? Here's the best part. Before Davis Wolfgang Hawke became Davis Wolfgang Hawke, his name was Andrew Greenbaum. His mother, speaking on the record last week, said she doubted that the group would have any such march. To quote the eloquent Ms. Peggy Greenbaum of suburban Boston, "I can't imagine him going down there. Number one, he is a chicken. I don't like to say that about my own son, but he is a chicken." The *Post* article ended before she got to number two. Is this a great country or what?

**Day Two, Monday: Amsterdam and Georgia (the Country Not the State)**

Dennis and I meet up with our other two traveling companions, Hazel O'Leary (AES board member, former Energy Secretary, and all around good sport who has also raised her hand to come along) and Gary Levesley, President of AES Silk Road, the division that has both Georgia (the country, etc.) and Kazakhstan in it. Don't laugh—one of our AES divisions has the Caribbean, Central America, and Texas. Geography is relative. We get into a pretty nifty but small jet, chartered for the trip, and take off for Tbilisi. Four hours later we land at a big, very quiet airport. There are lots of Soviet helicopters sitting around in various stages of undress, several Tupolev and Yak airliners all with "Georgia Airways" on their sides, and no activity. Except, of course, us. AES Telassi is our distribution company in Georgia; it serves the capital, Tbilisi, and surrounding area. Several folks from the company meet us, as do to our surprise, press and TV people. Well we are the biggest foreign investment ever in Georgia and the first major privatization.

Dennis gets asked, "How do you think you are doing here in Georgia?"

"You would know better than I would," he reasonably responds. I tell him that the next time just point out that the lights are on. This is, in fact, a marked improvement since we took over. The reporters and photographers are all very friendly, but one can't help but think that it must be a slow news day.

Except for a short courtesy call on the Chief Minister that is cere-moniously uneventful (other than both he and the Energy Minister say clearly, "Keep the electricity on this winter!"), we spend the next four or five hours getting briefed and talking with the AES people. Mike Scholey, an accountant from Newcastle, is running the company. As we listen, it becomes clearer to us just how bad things were when we took over the company and what a good job Mike and his folks are doing putting it all back together. In essence, the company has been resourceless and leader-less for the last ten years. People have stopped paying for electricity, and illegal or informal hookups are everywhere. Of course the fact we haven't been sending out bills to customers may be a bit of a contribution to the nonpayment problem. Before we bought the company in January, the meter readers were responsible for: a) going to the customer locations to read the meter; b) calculating the bill and presenting it to the customer; and c) collecting the money (always cash). Does it seem like this could possibly be a system leading to some abuse?

Actually it turns out that these jobs were sold to the highest bidder by the middle managers of the utility. All consumption and payment records were kept on ledger sheets, by hand, at the various district offices. Nothing was mechanized, nothing was entered in a computer. A fair number of customers had no records at all, even the cumbersome paper ones. All the meters were at least thirty years old and very easy to tamper with or just plain disconnect. Also they read about 20% low. Disconnecting your meter did disconnect your electricity, but it was very easy to wire around. Meters were installed inside the customer's house, so if the person wasn't home or just wouldn't answer the door, you couldn't read the meter. The capacity of the service was usually 17 amps—your house, in comparison, is probably at least 100, more likely 200 amps. As a result of all this, residential collection rates were in the vicinity of 18%. Word of mouth is that the electricity was only on about the same percentage of each day.

When Mike first pointed out this 18% number, I raised my hand and said, "Don't you mean loss rates?"

"No," he explained, "loss rates were one hundred minus eighteen."

Goodness! This is worse than any distribution system we have ever encountered before. Actually, no one knows any of these numbers with great assurance, because the metering of the power at the substations is also old and inaccurate. Well it sure does leave room for improvement.

In the first district where the AES crew has focused on installing new meters, meter reading by new guys (reading only), regular billing calculated at the district office and sent out by mail, and collections accepted at post offices, collection rates went from 17% to 38% to 57% in three months. This is conceptually simple, but it is hard work and effort. All this is taking place at the same time that Mike is reducing employment from 1,300 persons to 800.

Indications that things weren't great: the typical wintertime greeting in Tbilisi is, "How's your shooki?" This has nothing to do with anything you might imagine and is not even prurient, but means, literally, "How's your electricity?" I checked with three or four people and this is really true. This may be the only place in the world where our product has entered so directly into the language.

My favorite story: to get enough money to fix the system, it is necessary for people to start paying their bills, and to get them to pay, the principal lever is to cut off service. We haven't just gone after the little people, however, because that isn't fair and probably not politically astute, either. And besides, everybody wasn't paying, not just the average customer. Soon after taking over, Mike disconnected, on the same day, the principal government-owned TV antenna, which looms over Tbilisi and the Russian Army base nearby. Seemed like a pretty evenhanded approach. He also disconnected the official residence of President Shevardnadze. It turns out this was two days before a scheduled visit of James Wolfensohn, World Bank president, who was to stay there, and who, rumor has it, is not fond of cold showers. This can be a fun business.

After all this meeting and much discussion of how to apply the AES values in the organizational setting of a distribution company and another press conference (same quantity of news, i.e., none), we set off for a restaurant overlooking the city for a *supra*. This is a traditional form of Georgian banquet that includes much food that just keeps coming and coming, much toasting and drinking, and even a fair amount of singing. On the way there we drove past a monumental silvery metal statue of a woman poised on a hillside above the city; she is a principal symbol of Georgia. Her left hand holds a sword, and her right hand is raised, not unlike the Statue of Liberty, except that she holds in the raised hand, not a torch, but a wine glass. As symbols go, I liked it.

I've been to a few banquets in distant lands where the local cuisine is, uh, memorable, so I had some reservations. OK, the guy at the head of the table did get served the head of a pig, sort of staring up at him, but it was just an honor and he wasn't expected to actually eat it. The rest of the dinner was wonderful: all the food was not only recognizable but excellent—veal chunks with potatoes and garlic, chicken roasted with garlic, spinach and walnuts with curry, flatbread filled with cheese, and *shashlik*, which is grilled beef pieces served on a sword. As we hadn't eaten since breakfast, and it was now 10:30 at night, it tasted even better.

Amidst the toasts and the singing, Dennis took the time to go through a detailed example for everyone, complete with role-playing, of our views of the decision-making process—how a leader in AES has to give up power so the person closest to the decision can make it. This probably isn't normal at a *supra*, but what the heck. We're promoting a process that's not normal in any organization. In fact, the designated head toaster looked mildly miffed at getting upstaged. He clearly wasn't ready to give up power. Dennis was rewarded for his efforts by being presented with his own set of the local costume. First you put on a colorful robe and a brown skullcap, which seems more or less normal. Then on top of this one wears a really big hairy hide envelope that covers you from the shoulders to the floor and is made of badly cured sheep or goat skin. Dennis donned the entire outfit (bear in mind it's August and Tbilisi is essentially Mediterranean, so it was *hot*) and looked a bit like a pillow of sheepskin. A big walking pillow. A big sweaty walking pillow.

Sobering notes: 1) At breakfast next morning, I had a nice chat with the US Ambassador, who is delighted at our efforts and has been a big supporter. We were in the tenth-floor restaurant of the Sheraton, which everyone said was the tallest building and thus had the best view in town.

He took me to the window and pointed across the river at a nondescript plaza, bordered on each side by a two-lane road.

"Right there is where the last assassination attempt on Shevardnadze took place," he said. "People watched it from up here—rockets, RPGs, everything. He was amazingly lucky to get away unharmed."

Note: this is smack in the middle of the city, not in some remote location in the country. Hardly good ambush terrain. The Ambassador added that everyone is sure that it was Russian inspired, but no one can quite explain how Russia would have benefited from a success.

(2) If you look at the map (which of course I didn't do until we were about to land) you will find that Georgia is bordered on the north by Chechnya and by Dagestan, the province of Russia where the Russians have recently been using helicopter gunships and mechanized infantry to shoot up "armed gunmen" who have surrounded a town. I read the entire story in both the Sunday *Post* and the *New York Times* the day before we left, and that was all it said. This could be a candidate for "least informative news story of the year." Who were they? Why did they surround the town? What was in the town in north Dagestan that was worth either surrounding or sending in helicopter gunships to defend?

But I digress. At the meeting with the Chief Minister, he apologized for being preoccupied because he was dealing with the fact that a Russian plane had bombed three villages in north Georgia that morning, causing no deaths but several casualties. The Russians were of course denying this. Maybe they were aiming at the Chinese embassy in Belgrade but using US targeting methods.

3) I asked the Ambassador how he thought the country was doing. I told him the city looked to me like Eastern Europe, maybe Budapest, in 1992, still recovering from decades of socialism. It does have one McDonald's and two Baskin Baskin-Robbins, but nothing else of that nature. He said that their characterization for the country was "stable but fragile." I thought that nicely expressed things.

Traveler's nightmare: the Sheraton in Tbilisi has a fancy type of key system that none of us had ever seen before. The plastic "key" is kind of chunky, and you push a button on the door handle, then wave your key

in front of a particular little panel above the handle, and it unlocks elec-
tronically. This does take a little getting used to. My fellow board member
Hazel O'Leary, after the festivities ended and we stumbled back to the
hotel about 1:30 in the morning, was using her usual system for finding her
room. She has adopted certain traveler's shorthand tricks, as does everyone
who travels a lot. She doesn't try to memorize her actual room number, just
the number of the floor and the position of the room. So at 2:00 in the
morning she goes to the fourth floor, trots all the way down to the end of
the hall where her two-bedroom suite is, punches the appropriate button,
and waves her key around. No luck. She goes to the other door—it's a big
set of rooms—same thing. She tries both doors again, more methodically.
Nothing. She goes back down to the front desk and apologetically asks for
help with her key, noting that it probably is her fault, not the system's. As
she is telling us this story, Dennis and I both think that if it had been us,
we would have been less polite, more along the lines of "Your G— d— key
doesn't work!" There are some gender differences. Or Hazel may just be a
better person than we are. Hazel and the bellman go back up stairs, and he
tries her key on both doors. Still no luck.

"Don't worry, madame," he says gallantly, "I have master key." Sure
enough, the master key does work, only the first door has the inside chain
on it. Hazel doesn't precisely remember putting the chain on one of the
doors, but anything's possible—except you can't put the chain on from
the outside anyway. The master key unlocks the other door, which is also
chained. "Don't worry, madame," says the bellman, "I will get cutters."
Fortunately, Hazel at this point remembers that it was the night *before*, in
Amsterdam, when she was on the fourth floor, and here in Tbilisi she's on
the *fifth* floor.

"Uh, wait," she says to the very helpful bellman, who is clearly in her
thrall, "maybe we should try the fifth floor . . ." We never learn what the
poor sleeping traveler in the room on the fourth floor was thinking.

### Day Three, Tuesday: Georgia and Kazakhstan

An 8:00 breakfast has been set up for us in Tbilisi with the Ambassador,
a bunch of AID and World Bank folks, various government ministers, and
local business people. It's in the restaurant on the tenth floor. Of course

I seem to think that it's at 7:45 on the eighth floor. Maybe Hazel's floor confusion is spreading. At least I'm on time. And lots and lots of people show up, even though a number of them do note that breakfast meetings are: 1) not a Georgian business practice, and 2) maybe not an American custom worth adopting. Given our late dinner the night before, I'm inclined to agree with point #2. But we meet and talk with a number of interesting people, almost everybody goes back for seconds, and only one person leaves before Dennis has finished his talk on AES and it purpose and principals, so it has to be counted a success.

Off we fly to Astana, a city of about 300,000 persons and the new capital of Kazakhstan, landing about 3:30 in the afternoon. We are again in a very not busy airport. Not quite as many broken-down helicopters, but the same very still Russian airliners, only this time they say "Air Kazakhstan" on the sides. We stand around on the tarmac waiting for the bus to take us to the gate, which is all of fifty feet away, but we can't just walk. There are rules. It gives one time to look around, and boy is it flat. Flat and brown. I mean really, no-kidding flat, Kansas without the topography. National Bureau of Standards flat. And quite windy. Our local people inform us that it is windy here all the time, all year long. Astana is a new capital. Hazel correctly refers to it as a "forced capital," a bit like Brasilia. Not clear why President Nazarbayev decided to move the capital here from Almaty. Everyone likes Almaty a lot; it's 1,000 km further south, larger and more cosmopolitan, situated at the base of the mountains, and looks like Denver. Maybe he decided to move it because he could. Did I mention that it's flat?

We're a bit late, so we hurry to our meeting with the First Minister, the equivalent of Prime Minister in the Russian system; he's appointed and serves at the pleasure of the President, whose pleasure appears to be changing these guys about every twelve months. Since Yeltsin has just fired Stepashin the day before, we wonder idly if this gentleman will still be here. He is, and he has arranged for us to meet not only with him but also with Mr. Tokayev, the Foreign Minister, Mr. Balgimbayev, the Energy Minister; and Mr. V.N. Boos, the head of the privatization program. Moreover, what we thought was a little courtesy call is now being carried out in front of TV cameras and other press. The minister begins by suggesting that we not cut off electricity during the winter. Dennis suggests that we should get paid for providing electricity. The minister suggests that we should start up a factory making electrical equipment, because he wants more jobs in K'stan and he's tired of buying stuff from outside the country. Dennis suggests that it's not something we're particularly good at but refrains from discoursing on Ricardo and the theory of comparative advantage. The meeting dwindles away, but politely. Then we go off to the press conference that has already been scheduled. How much learning is still going on in these former soviet countries, and how much damage the soviet system did to them is underscored once again by two of the questions asked of Dennis: 1) What is the purpose of competition? 2) You have come here as Americans to invest in K'stan? Does anyone go to America to invest there? Very interesting.

We finally get back to our hotel, the InterContinental. We decide on dinner in the Marco Polo Room, the hotel's restaurant. It's a gigantic restaurant, about three times the normal size for even a large hotel restaurant, probably close to one hundred tables, all correctly set up with linens and glassware, several bottles of wine on each table, and so forth, and there is no one in it at 8:30. No, that's wrong, there are two waitresses. The wine list includes two choices of local wine with great names: Bigibul Red and Kagor. I resolve to get a fierce dog and name him Kagor. Trying to be charming, I ask for a bottle of same. Both waitresses take this in, albeit a bit tentatively, then go off. Out of the corner of my eye I notice them walking around to all the other empty tables and looking at the bottles of wine on each table. After a long time they come back and say there is not any Kagor. Undaunted we try Bigibul Red. Same process, same result. I am slowly getting the picture. This time I try a simple Italian Chianti. They return, smiling, with a bottle of something French. It looks like red wine, however, so we decide to drink it, whatever it is. "Welcome to Kazakhstan," says Gary, who as noted earlier is in charge of our AES assets here.

### Day Four, Wednesday: Kazakhstan

We get up and meet in the hotel lobby at 6:15, run off to the airport, and fly for an hour to Pavlodar, the airport nearest to our first destination, the Ekibastuz power plant. We use "nearest" in the extremely relative sense of the word. Once at Pavlodar (no, no more descriptions of quiet airports littered with broken-down helicopters, you've had your treats for today) we are driven at 9,000,000 miles per hour for 120 km over a long, extremely straight, reasonably well paved but undulating road to the plant. This takes about an hour and a half, which is plenty of time to note that it is very brown—no trees, no green vegetation—and quite, quite, quite flat. It is truly remarkable, and you can see large distances. We can see the stacks of the plant when we're more than fifteen minutes away. And we're not moving slowly. We could see anything else from just as far away, but there is nothing else to see in any direction. Well a couple of power lines and nearer to the road, the odd cow about every 10 km. Very impressive. Gary notes that K'stan is the eighth largest country in the world in terms of landmass, and that every mineral on the periodic table can be found here in economically productive amounts. Only sixteen million people and none in the immediate vicinity. If there were, we could see them. From a long way off.

The plant is impressive. Eight 500 MW units, all in a long row. It was designed to be part of the Soviet grid and churn out power for the Urals and central Russia. As far was anyone can determine, it's the largest thermal power plant in the world, but it actually seems dwarfed by the enormous brown plain surrounding it. There are a couple of hydro plants in the world that are larger, but even Three Gorges in China will only be 15,000 MW and we all know what a foolish monstrosity that is. The plant manager, a very good guy named Naveed Ismail, remarked, "The Soviets never saw a big project they didn't like." The turbine hall itself is more than 500 meters long—call it five football fields. Hazel and I get a tour while Dennis, who has been here twice before, goes off to talk to an assembled group of 200 employees. The place is fascinating, in a number of positive and negative ways:

» When we took over (exactly three years ago to the day of our visit) there were 7,000 persons working at the plant. Well more accurately, 7,000 persons had "jobs" at the plant, but after a decade of mismanagement and limited to zero resources, the plant could only make 300 MW, not the 4,000 for which it was designed. And, no, that don't hardly take 7,000 people, even if they were making electricity by hand. We are now down to 630 and no contractors.

» There were no tools at the plant. Guys were tightening big bolts (of which there are quite a lot at a power plant, securing flanges and vessels and stuff like that) by: a) welding a piece of rebar to the side of a nut, b) pushing it as far as it would travel, usually a quarter turn, c) using a cutting torch to cut the rebar off the nut, and then, yep, d) rewelding it onto the nut for another quarter turn. No, this is not efficient.

» There were fourteen levels of supervision. Nobody had been paid for six months. Nobody had cleaned anything in the plant (except in water treatment, a separate building which was staffed entirely by women and was, in fact, quite clean) and there was literally a foot of ash and coal dust on all the floors. And needless to say, there was all manner of junk and miscellaneous rusted metal and general crud lying around inside and outside the plant. In the last three years the people at the plant have hauled off *10,000 truckloads* of ash, and coal dust, and junk to the dump. That's real close to ten trucks a day. Amazing. The plant now looks pretty clean.

» Construction started in 1979 and finished in 1984, about the same time we were building Deepwater, our first plant, but Ekibastuz looks thirty years older. There are no computer controls, no signaling or data transmission electronics anywhere in the plant, just the old (1950s) standard compressed air-driven controls and sensors and gauges. People in the control room still pull levers and push switches. "At least we're not too worried about Y2K problems," one of the operators remarked.

» There's an entire bomb shelter underneath one of the plant buildings, complete (when we took over) with water and dried food for several months for everyone at the plant. What the survivors were supposed to do once they emerged, in the middle of nowhere and the plant blasted to smithereens, is less clear. On the other hand, we had something similar at Raccoon Mountain in TVA when I worked there in the late seventies.

» One of the plant's two stacks has a dogleg in it. Really, you can with the naked eye tell that it isn't perfectly straight, but bends out a bit, then bends back. The story is that the stack construction crew got paid too early, then got drunk but kept building the stack anyway. When they sobered up, they noticed they were going off at an angle, so they fixed it by going back toward the vertical at another angle. So much for quality control.

» The basic design is full of other strange things. There is a large coal yard, with all the associated conveyers, and stackers, and reclaimers, and transfer towers, and crushers, and so forth, but it is artificially divided into two halves. One half serves boilers 1–4 and the other 5–8. If something key in one of the two coal yard-to-boiler supply chains breaks, there is no way to serve all the units from just the other system, no crossover capacity. At the same time, however, in some parts of the water treating system, there is quadruple redundancy, flexibly engineered to serve any part of the power plant. It's pretty amazing.

» The design was done at a design institute in Moscow, perhaps by people who had never seen a power plant. For example, the last step in the coal-handling journey is to deposit the coal in bunkers or large silos, generally referred to as day bins, which are right next to and really an integral part of each boiler. From there, the coal goes into grinders for its final pulverization and then is blown immediately into the boiler and burned. The bunkers at this plant are sized so they can only hold a two-hour supply of coal. Yikes! It's like designing a car with a one-gallon gas tank. At our most limited plant we have eight-hour silos, and Bechtel only did that to us once. All our other plants have twelve to twenty-four hours of day bin storage at the boiler. For one thing, this means you can do coal handling during the day shift, top up the bins, and then run all night without anyone working in the coal yard. It also gives you a fighting chance if something in the coal yard breaks. You have some time for repairs before the boilers run out of coal and you have to shut down.

» The Moscow experts also put wet scrubbers in the exhaust gas path in front of the precipitators. These latter are great big boxes in which an electrified field removes all the fly ash (utility code word for burned coal stuff carried along in the exhaust) as the gas passes between large steel plates. This is putting equipment in the gas path in the wrong order and is never, never done, because what you are doing is injecting water into the exhaust while it still has all the ash and coal dust in it. Add water to dust and you get—yep—mud. The precipitators all filled up with this dark wet muck in about the first two months of their life.

There was also sulfur in the coal, which after burning yielded oxides of sulfur, which with the addition of water yields sulfuric acid. This means you had acidic muck, not just your regular garden-variety muck. Not good for metal. After the first total failure, the precipitators were all cleaned out and the acid eaten plates and the containers holding them rebuilt. But at the demand of the designers in Moscow, they were rebuilt in exactly the same configuration. Ran them again, filled them up again, ate up the plates again. The precipitators have been blinded and bypassed ever since. This means that the combustion gases are essentially unfiltered. And you can see the plume from the stack for miles and miles.

» My favorite story: the night they sucked the roof down. Combustion air going into the boilers is drawn in by very large fans—two per boiler—but rather than being placed outside, as all such fans are in all plants I have ever seen, these fans are inside the turbine hall. This contributes to noise in the hall and is not particularly safe. During one of the early winters, the plant was running six of its eight units and it was minus thirty degrees outside. Needless to say, the turbine hall was pretty tightly closed up so folks working inside could stay warm. Orders came from central dispatch to put on the seventh unit, so they began the start-up procedure for the seventh boiler. One of the initial steps is to turn on its two fans. The additional vacuum created inside the turbine hall by the fans sucking air out of the hall and into the boiler first caused the steel beams holding the roof up to bend, and paint began flecking off and falling down all over. Before anyone could quite figure out what this eerily beautiful phenomenon was, a beam failed, a large portion of the roof came crashing down onto the turbine deck, the temperature dropped to minus thirty, all the units tripped off-line, and literally miles and miles of sensitive fuel, steam, and control lines were frozen. The plant aged ten years in that one day.

The AES people at Ekibastuz are doing a terrific job against (as you can see) very large odds and making real headway. It is an impressive crew, and they invited us all back. "Come in the winter," they said, "because when it's thirty-five below around here and the snow is five feet thick, you can drive down the river and the ice fishing is really something." Hazel promised that she would, but I seemed to remember that my calendar was filled up for just those months. Thirty-five below, centigrade. Well, technically, it's only minus twenty-four Fahrenheit. Interesting fact: this is one of the places Solzenyitzen was sent when he was rusticated. He actually worked on the construction of this plant and lived in the small town that houses the miners and plant people. It's a long way from anywhere.

Hectic drive back across the same roads, same views, and we then fly to Ust-Kamenogorsk, which I am assured means "East Town Next to the Mountains." Seems reasonable, because there are in fact some mountains there. Small unbusy airport—see previous three references. Dennis goes off to talk to the people at the new distribution system, and Hazel and I first tour one of our hydro plants there and then get to take the "Director's Intelligence Test." At the local coal plant, which we also have acquired, the plant people have built a new tipper for unloading the railroad cars, generically hopper cars, full of coal. They are justifiably proud of having done this entirely with their own resources and want very much to show it off. Fine, it's what we're here for. We have a tipper at Deepwater, so I allegedly know something about these already. The tipper is essentially a big shed with a large open barrel inside it, with rails running though the barrel into which one inserts a loaded coal car. Sort of like a vertical railroad roundhouse. A railcar loaded with coal is pushed in, big clamps grip each side of it, and then the whole ungainly thing slowly begins to rotate with much groaning, and creaking, and crashing. We two directors are encouraged to stand close to the machinery for the best view. Gravity being what it is, coal starts pouring out into a big hopper below the slowly rotating barrel. Coal being what it is, large clouds of coal dust billow up gently, enveloping enthusiastic dignitaries. No, dignitary. Hazel, no fool, has moved a respectful but still attentive distance back. Not so your first son. Cough, cough.

Our next event is the ritual meeting with the local governor of the "oblast" (state or province) in which these new plants are located. As happens with some frequency in the CIS states, he is wearing a meticulously tailored and quite expensive suit, gorgeous shirt, and Brioni tie. The suit is not only expensive but is also a shade of electric blue not normally found at Nordstrom or in any OECD country. We get lectured about cutting off electricity to poor people by the guy in the expensive suit. He cites the example of a hospital that was cut off while a patient was in the middle of an operation and died. Our guys suggest politely that if that hospital could be identified and the date of the incident specified we would surely look into it. Since we have only had the distribution companies a month and a half, it seems unlikely that we have yet cut off any hospitals. We don't even have a very good handle on who all the customers are and whether or not they are being billed, let alone who is paying and who is not.

This is the equivalent in the utility business of an "urban legend"—alligators in the New York sewers—especially since almost all hospitals and other crucial facilities have backup generators. This is not because they get cut off all the time, but because the electric service to date has been so screamingly unreliable. We are repentant nonetheless and pledge to do better. The evening ends with a dinner with all of our troops, again a remarkable, talented, and dedicated bunch of people. It is at a Kazakh restaurant owned by a Korean lady who specializes in preparing and serving Russian food. I feel very global. As far as I can tell, to make Russian food you take about anything, chop it up, and put sour cream on top of it. This is not necessarily a bad policy. We fly back to Astana, arriving about 12:30, and stumble into our beds.

### Day Five, Thursday: Kazakhstan and India

We have to be at the airport at 4:30 (ugh!) to fly to Madras in South India for a development meeting. We make it groggily onto the plane, then sleep fitfully as we fly over the western Himalayas (K2 and Nanga Parbat rise majestically above the clouds), making a jog to avoid Afghanistan. I am willing to avoid Afghanistan almost any time the subject comes up. We touch down in Delhi to refuel. Dennis has actually been up all night, because we just bought a telecom facility in Brazil and he had to participate in the analyst call at 3:00 a.m. Astana time. Consequently he has also found out that the helicopter that was to take us from Bhubaneswar (our next stop after Madras) to the Ib Valley plant has been appropriated by one of the political parties. He is not charmed by this news and stands on the concrete using the pilot's cell phone, suggesting to our folks in India that the reason that we came to the country is to see the plant and talk to the people there, and he is going to do that even if he has to walk.

The meeting in Madras is cordial. We are courting new partners for a new project in Andhra Pradesh, the state where Madras is located. Much to my disappointment no one is wearing colorful plaid shirts. Or Bermuda shorts. We fly on to Bhubaneswar, capital of the state of Orissa. Six months ago we bought 49% of the existing power plant at Ib Valley from the state government and were promised at least an additional 2% so we could really remake these plants into our kind of facilities. But . . . things happen. The Chief Minister (governor equivalent) had to resign after three American missionaries were killed in Orissa, and elections are two months away, so there is only a caretaker Chief Minister in place. We meet with him and then with several others from about 5:30 until 9:00 and finally come up with a clever way to get movement on the majority ownership issue, consistent with the political situation. In essence we propose to loan the government a big chunk of money, which they need for the budget this year, secured by their interest in the plant. They can elect to repay either in money or in shares of the plant, but technically don't have to face the issue of selling (unfortunately called "disinvesting" in India) right now. It should work, but nothing here is ever simple. We adjourn to our hotel where we have dinner with all the AES people in Bhubaneswar, a group of six or so. We are punchy but pleased.

### Day Six, Friday: India and Sri Lanka

Our people, concerned that they might have to walk the 150 km to Ib Valley with Dennis, have arranged another plane, leaving of course at 6:30, so by 6:00 we are downstairs, checked out, and breakfastless. Our charter jet remains at Bhubaneswar, because the airfield near the plant, Jharsuguda, was built in WWII and hasn't been manned since. For some reason our Austrian pilots don't seem keen to fly into it. Actually I don't know how they would even find it. But the Indian pilots of the King Air don't see this as much of a problem. And they are savvy enough to realize that you have to buzz the strip first to make sure there aren't any cows on the runway.

It's a fifty-minute drive from the airstrip to the plant, and it really is rural and tropical—diked fields just being planted with the brilliant green of young rice plants, narrow poor roads, small villages of brick with corrugated roofs, lots of palm trees, lots of people on bicycles and scooters. It reminds me enormously of Vietnam during the war, except without the war. Better. It's still India, but it's much more bearable than the urban centers like Bombay and Delhi where so many people are crammed into such small, difficult surroundings. Maybe it's the palm trees.

We are more or less in control of the plant, but until we can get 51%, it must continue to operate as a "government" facility, which means hierarchy, bureaucracy, overstaffing, underemployment, and procedure manuals on how to write procedure manuals. On the way to the plant, Julie Gabel, one of the AES heroes who has volunteered for an assignment here, tells me the flashlight story. She is a bright, dedicated young woman with nineteen years' experience in Pennsylvania in utility plant operations, most recently at Beaver Valley. A month or so ago, as part of her job in advising the current operating people, she needed a flashlight to go into one of the murkier parts of the plant. Power plants, even well lighted ones, have lots of little dark nooks and crannies, so this is hardly an unusual need. She went to the tool room to get one, which for some reason is located in another building about five hundred meters from the plant itself. She was politely informed that she needed a requisition form.

"Well, OK, give me one and I'll fill it out."

No, these forms are only available in the procurement office. She went to procurement, also conveniently located not anywhere close to the tool room, in fact, in yet another building outside the main plant. She got the form, filled it out, and brought it back.

"Madame, this is indeed the proper requisition form for flashlight, but it must be approved by your supervisor." She noted that her supervisor was Ross Fredericks, the AES person serving as director of operations, and she was sure that it was OK with him if she had a flashlight and perhaps it wasn't necessary to bother him with respect to a $2 item. No. She caught Ross the next day, he signed the form, she took it back to the tool room.

"Madame," said the clerk, "this requisition form is now fully complete, but I am very sorry to say that we have no flashlights. In addition, you have no requisition form for batteries . . ."

We only had a couple of hours there, and we did the best we could, meeting with small groups of people and trying to explain to them what the place would be like once we were actually able to take over. There is much apprehension and concern about job security. Very few people smiled at us, and only a few were even willing to talk to us. And the ones who would talk were inevitably the senior managers, and then they wouldn't stop talking. At one point Dennis was trying to talk to a group in the control room, and one guy kept interrupting him and wanting to argue loudly about how all this delegation of authority stuff wouldn't work in an Indian context. Dennis had only a short time, was getting increasingly frustrated, and finally turned to the person and said, politely, "Shut up!" I have never in thirty years heard him do anything like this, so you get the picture. It turns out that the person he admonished was the government-appointed General Manager of the plant. Oh well. Hazel is very good at interacting with groups, and even she had trouble getting people to open up. Changing this culture will be real work.

Favorite vignette: we were briefed carefully before venturing out into the plant about how sensitive an issue job security is to everyone. Sure enough, it's the first question Dennis was asked. Just to reassure everyone, he said, "Every one of you here will lose your jobs." He went on to explain that in an AES plant, all the jobs are expanded with cross-training, and a higher level of decision-making authority and responsibility. I think he got the point across, but in any event it was the best "get their attention" line I've ever heard.

Three flight segments later we landed in Colombo, were met at the airport, and whisked off to a dinner sponsored by our partners in our Sri Lanka project, the Hayley's Group. Well whisked off isn't really what we were. The road in from the airport is a classic hodgepodge of small shops, three lanes of traffic using two lanes of paving, bicycles, buses, motor scooters, pedestrians, trucks, motorcycle cabs, and no stoplights. The latter isn't good, because it means no crosswalks, and people darting out into traffic from all along the road. But there are lots of flowers—bougainvillea, hibiscus, plumeria, coral vine, shrimp plant, all the flora of Hawaii, and lots of palm trees. It's beautiful, not at all manicured, but gorgeous, and riotous, and delightfully undisciplined. The shops are all open, people are out purposefully doing whatever one does in Colombo, and things seem cleaner and neater than India.

The dinner, held in the penthouse of the Hayley's office building, was a lovely gesture by our partners. They couldn't have known that our daily routine on this trip includes skipping breakfast and lunch, so we were doubly grateful. Their chairman, Sunil Mendis, is a warm and gracious person, and the relationship seems a good fit. We were introduced to a broad range of government officials along with World Bank and AID people, suppliers, lawyers, etc. The country has a population of only 16 million, and it seems that the senior people across the spectrum of business, politics, government, and academia all know each other. This is a pattern repeated in many developing countries. We finally made it off to bed around midnight.

**Day Seven, Saturday: Sri Lanka and Singapore**

We are in Colombo because our team won a bid to build a 150 MW combined cycle power plant, the first large private sector power project ever in this country. A series of meetings with government officials have been arranged so we can show the flag, demonstrate interest, and maybe help push things along. We get to sleep in, because our first meeting isn't until 7:30 and it's in the hotel. When I get up, I look out the window and am surprised to see that the hotel is right on the bay, and the beach looks beautiful. I think wistfully about skipping the meeting and going out to run on the beach. On trips like these when you come home and people ask you what you saw, if you're truthful you say, "The insides of hotel rooms, cabs, airplanes, airports, restaurants, and conference rooms." Not that I'm complaining, because we do get to see the insides of power plants.

We have a good breakfast meeting with the US Ambassador and the Economic Counselor, both of whom have been very helpful to us. Hazel did suggest to me that she found it odd that I was having both cornflakes and dhal for breakfast. At least I didn't mix them together. Going to our first meeting we note that the streets of Colombo have a bit of

a Costa-Gavras air to them. There are many sandbagged posts at inter-
sections, manned by troops carrying big guns and wearing an interesting
uniform of blue camouflage. Dennis and I try to figure out what kind of
fighting environment you'd have to be in for blue camouflage to be effective. We're stumped, unless the answer is the ocean.

Next we meet with a Finance Ministry person who is quite encouraging, then with the head of the CEB (Ceylon Electricity Board—interesting that it is still called "Ceylon" since nothing else in the country is).
He notes helpfully that the utility really hasn't been reorganized since
1969. No one on our side of the table seems stunned. He also points out
that he can't see any particular reason why there should be private sector
investment in Sri Lanka's power system as long as he can get "soft money."
This is foreign aid money with an artificially low interest rate, usually 4%.
The money, however, always comes with a requirement to purchase the
equipment and construction services from the country providing the "aid,"
and thus the prices tend to be higher than you would get in an open bid
situation. Real world example: CEB is building a plant that duplicates ours
at the same site using soft money, in this case from Japan. Their price is
approximately 40% higher than ours for the design and construction of the
project. A 4% interest rate hardly makes up for this.

The Chairman is a very smart and experienced guy, but he has been
raised in the government owned/monopoly system and sees no reason why
any change is useful. Fortunately soft money seems to be on the way out,
and the political leaders have decided that it should be spent on those areas
where the government has no private sector alternatives. But change will
come here with difficulty. Of course that seems to be our specialty on this
trip.

The highlight of the visit is a meeting with the President, Mrs.
Bandaranaike. We go to her compound and endure a lengthy and quite
thorough check of both our cars, all luggage, etc. Since her father and her
husband were both the victims of political assassinations, we are sympa-
thetic to the interest in security. Plus we don't really want to be blown
up ourselves. We make it through the inspections and wait in one of the
reception rooms of the residence. It is very British—open to the gardens

but a classic drawing room, twenty-five-foot ceilings, yellow walls with white plaster cornices, painted formal arrangements of English flowers in each wall panel. It was no doubt the British Governor-General's residence when the country was a colony, and it has been beautifully maintained. Madame President eventually comes in wearing a striking yellow sari. She is at first a bit reserved (you can see her thinking "Which group of foreigners is this and what do they want?"), but having Sunil with us helps. When her staff serves us some very nice sweet cakes to go along with the inevitable Ceylon tea, and Hazel teases Dennis about his sweet tooth, she visibly lightens up. For some reason this wasn't in the Ambassador's briefing. She warms to us and outlines the enormous problems she's had with corruption and bribe taking, mixed with slowness, recalcitrance, and obstinacy on the part of the existing bureaucracy. She is very knowledgeable about the bid process that we have been through and then insists on asking Dennis several very good questions on the advantages of coal vs. oil, what the mix of an electric system should be, how hydro fits in, etc. We had been briefed that she might go off on a tangent, but she asks good questions, to the point, and listens closely to the answers. Dennis asks her to come visit us in Washington, but she says that she can only have official contact with us until the plant is in construction, because otherwise her opponents will say that such a meeting was for the purpose of receiving her payoff for the plant. This is tough politics. We finally have to leave in order to make our connections in Singapore, but we're all sorry and hope to return. Despite the ugly Tamil war in the north, the President impresses us as a leader truly struggling to move her country forward in a democratic and open market way.

Once on the airplane to Singapore, I focus on the fact that the reason we were time constrained was our connection to the flight taking us to Australia. Hold it, you say, aren't you on a private jet? Well yes, but the private jet portion of the trip ends in Singapore. I knew I had to get myself back from Australia, but somehow I hadn't paid attention to getting from Singapore to Australia. Even though Joan Halbert, Dennis' superb assistant, had conscientiously asked me if I needed help on the non-private portion of the trip and sent me the schedule and itinerary several weeks ahead of time. I ask Dennis hopefully if he has a ticket for me, but that gambit doesn't work. We can't call anybody, because the plane doesn't have an onboard phone. Hmmm. Well, maybe I'll just have to spend the night in Singapore at the Raffles Hotel, where Hazel is also staying, rather than fly on—overnight—to Townsville in northern Australia. As options go, it doesn't sound terrible.

At the Singapore airport, I rush around and purchase a ticket to continue with Dennis along to Australia. We say good-bye to Hazel, who has been a wonderful traveling companion and made a real contribution to our efforts. We get on airplane, fly overnight to Cairns, take a smaller plane to Townsville, a coastal town of about 120,000 in central Queensland, where we have a small plant. Trey Hall, the plant manager, meets us. It's Sunday morning about 10:00 by this time, and Townsville seems pretty sleepy, not unlike us. It's also beautiful weather—Hawaii-equivalent tropical—palm trees, and hibiscus, and all. Trey has a surprise for us—he's chartered a boat and the entire staff of the plant is coming with us to an offshore island for a barbecue. After all, it is Australia; how can there not be a barbecue?

Turns out that the entire staff of this plant is five people, so the seven of us embark for Magnetic Island, about a thirty-minute sail from Townsville. The name comes from when Captain Cook was exploring and naming all the parts of Australia with good English names, including in many instances, his own. When he got to this area, his compasses got goofed up in the vicinity, so he concluded there was something—yes, magnetic—about the place. No further verification seems to have been made, but it is a lovely place nonetheless—semi-rugged, mostly unsettled, one small boat pier, a backpacker hostel, hiking trails, and a number of isolated half-moons of beach, reachable only by boat. We anchor in one and spend a wonderful two hours talking about AES. Dennis is his usual zealous and focused self, but I confess to spending a bit of time watching the sea eagles dive into the jade green water and the waves lap on the sand.

We then motor over to the civilized portion of the island. Lunch has been arranged at the beach lifeguard house, which our guys have been supporting with contributions. All lifeguarding in Australia is carried out by volunteers, and the people running this are appreciative of our help. They give us official lifeguard gear and explain that they are an Aussie version of Baywatch. I look around carefully, but Jasmine Bleth or whatever her name is does not appear. In fact, it's all men. Australia is a bit that way. The lunch is fabulous—shrimp as big as small bananas, Greek salad, grilled steaks, cheesecake. If you have to do a power plant orientation meeting, this isn't a bad way to go.

We fly on to Melbourne, arriving later than planned (8:00), and head off to bed.

### Day Eight, Monday: Australia

The next morning we visit first our plant in the city itself, a 500 MW plant called AES Yarra. It used to be called Newport, but after we bought it from the local utility in a privatization, the guys at the plant decided it was time to change the name in recognition of the new status. The plant sits on the Yarra River, hence the name. We have a wonderful time, first with a brief tour, and then with a two-hour session with almost all thirty-two of the plant people. Interesting note: when the state government owned the plant, it had a staff of 145 including seven gardeners and fourteen security guards. "What were they securing?" we ask. "Did they think that somebody was going to drive up in a pickup truck and steal the plant?" Dennis makes a convincing talk on the difficulty of being an AES business person and gets good levels of participation. And to commemorate our visit, we both receive authentic Australian hats so we can look like Paul Hogan. Dennis comes closer than I do. I, however, keep a careful watch out for crocodiles.

A helicopter has been arranged to take us to the other plant, AES Jeeralang, in the Latrobe Valley about 150 km north of Melbourne. The valley is a big coal mining site and major industrial and energy center. We fly over a gently rolling landscape of small green farms and rural homes, none large but all neatly laid out. Many of the pastures are edged with trees or hedgerows and speckled with the black and brown dots of cattle. Without much transition, we come upon a really big power plant, four cooling towers each emitting voluminous clouds of steam. We're there. It is impressive in a very different way. The valley is home to at least four major coal fired plants within 30 km of each other. Each plant sits on the edge of a very large open pit coal mine. These mines, too, are neatly laid out with descending tiers of excavation that look from the air like giant black steps. One of the plants has eight stacks, all running, all with little or no emission control, pushing out brownish yellow plumes in the early afternoon sunlight. We are happy that we don't own that particular plant.

AES Jeeralang runs on gas and was constructed to provide peak power, thus it's a different technology—gas turbines—and can be up and running in ten minutes. It can also stop running in ten minutes, and that is how it is now used in the new world of competitive electricity generation. The plant was on for two hours that morning, helping meet the winter heating peak that occurs when people get up in the morning, turn on the kettle and the lights, take showers, etc. It can actually be started remotely from Melbourne, which probably gives the folks at the plant a bit of a start themselves when it happens. These are big machines, and we have six of them. Dennis gives the same talk, with the same degree of enthusiasm as this morning and gets excellent participation. I'm struck by what hard work this is, and I'm just being part of the appreciative audience. We fly back to Melbourne, have dinner with several of the plant leaders, and Dennis takes off to fly—overnight again—back to Washington. Me, I gratefully have elected to actually sleep two nights in the same bed before embarking on this same long flight back.

Love,
Bob

# nineteen

# how to bring christmas with you to rajasthan

January 2000

Dear Aunt Janet,

**PART ONE: INDIA**

I find this a bit hard to believe myself, but I am sitting in the middle of a rectangle of tents on the edge of the Thar Desert in Rajasthan state, India. It is about 9:30 at night, and it is not as dark as you might think, given that any human habitation is probably fifty kilometers from where we are. The reason is a full moon over my left shoulder shining through the clouds in a shrouded fashion. The people here tell us that it is the nearest the moon has been to the earth in 130 years, which accounts for its size and brightness. Because I have had tourist guides before, I am skeptical of explanations of this sort. Does, in fact, the moon maintain a 130-year cycle of closeness to/distance from the earth? If so, does this influence the tides, and if not, why not? Never mind, it's pretty bright. Everyone else in our party of thirty-eight has gone to sleep, or at least they are quietly in their tents like good persons rather than being out here carousing (which would also be OK).

Nope, it's nobody but me sitting here in this uncomfortable camp chair typing on my computer, which is running on its paltry batteries that are due to expire in slightly more than an hour. John Huetter and I have just spent the last two hours discussing life and philosophy—the unending questions of why are we here, is there a God, and why can't John find a decent girlfriend. Others on the planet were no doubt discussing the same things at the same time—well maybe not about John's girlfriend, but you get the picture. This discussion was aided by the presence of several glasses of whiskey and water, not our favorite drink, but when one is in India and working at being a sahib (yes, even after all these years, the spirit is still alive) drinking whiskey and water seems somehow appropriate. I should also note for the record that it is a bit chilly in the Thar Desert, and my fingers are less facile than usual due to the fact that they are cold. The rest of me is wearing a jacket and other warm clothing, but it's hard to type in gloves. Besides, I don't have any with me. This is India; you're not supposed to need mittens.

We are in the third day of our millennium trip. Let me briefly recount the details:

There are thirty-eight total participants in the group:

Hemphill family (14): Me and my dad; my sister Gia's family (5); my brother David's family (4); and Elika and Rich and Leo, my two-year-old grandson.

Powers family (13): Linda and her mom and dad; her older brother Philip's family(5); and her younger brother Brad's family (4).

The Hersons (4), and John Huetter and his two daughters.

Also along: Jay Brodmerkel (he's the expedition photographer) and his wife, Deena; and Chris and Gayle, two administrative facilitators from TCS, the upscale travel agency that helped Linda arrange all this.

2. Itinerary, brief form: Depart US on 18 Dec, overnight in London on the 19th; fly on 20th to Jaipur in state of Rajasthan, India, staying at Rajvilas hotel. Do stuff, details to follow. 27 Dec fly to Kathmandu, Nepal; 30 Dec go to Cambodia for New Year's at Angkor Wat; 3 Jan to Bangkok,

Thailand for three days—home on 6 Jan.

Linda has planned all this out over countless hours with the travel service in Seattle that has never seen someone with the attention to detail she possesses. As a result it is the best and most interesting itinerary we can possibly devise. And so far, all expectations have been not only met, but substantially exceeded.

But let me begin at the beginning.

We took the 9:00 flight from Dulles on Saturday evening, December 18, flying overnight and arriving in London on Sunday morning. Because we are going to places where they don't generally think Christmas is a particularly big deal—India is 80% Hindu, 12% Muslim, and most of the rest Sikh and animist, and not much Christian—and because we have a bunch of young children and teenagers who have never been outside the US for Xmas before, we are bringing with us as much of a US standard, general issue, "you'd feel right at home if you stumbled into our living room" Christmas as we can. This involves, as it turns out, about twenty-one large size cardboard boxes, purchased at U-Haul and filled up with the following:

—Christmas decorations: balls, wreaths, plastic garlands, angels, tinsel, ornament hangers (lots of people forget these), strings of lights with voltage converters (lots of people forget these also when they are going to 220 volt/50 cycle countries, but we are energy professionals), hanging dangly things, hanging shiny things—you name it, we got it in the decorations arena. Plus pushpins and sixteen rolls (I am not making this up) of duct tape to stick things up with if all else fails.

—Traditional Xmas food, i.e., containers of cranberry sauce, bags of Pepperidge Farm stuffing—OK, we know that Nebraskans still make their own stuffing out of dried crusts of bread, but no one else on the planet does—bottles of green olives, one bottle of watermelon rind pickles for old times' sake, boxes of instant mashed potatoes (an item I myself would not have included), cans of pumpkin pie mix, and a source of great discomfort to me: six bottles of bottled turkey gravy. I have personally promised to go into the kitchen of the hotel and show the chef how to make good old-fashioned midwestern turkey gravy thickened with flour, and I have been allowed to exercise this conceit; but we also, at Linda's insistence, have to have with us bottles of bottled gravy. I almost can't write down these words, it upsets me so. She is such a nice girl in all other respects. Anyway, checking in at Dulles was something of a production, as was just getting all those boxes from our house to the airport. We had to rent four sedans, so when we pulled up to the airport we either looked like the entourage of the president of a small country or a Mafia funeral, I couldn't decide which. But off we went to London. After an uneventful and sleepy Sunday in Knightsbridge, we get up early early on Monday, December 20, crowd onto our two big buses, and go to Heathrow to catch our flight to India.

This highly ambitious attempt to transport an American Christmas to Jaipur has been largely successful, at least so far, in that all the twenty-one boxes and five suitcases have arrived here and even gotten through Indian customs with no more than average hassles. Here is the picture: It is 3:00 in the morning and thirty-eight people who have been flying since 9:00 the previous morning, after flying all night the night before, are standing around the Bombay airport customs hall. As are many Indians. Note for the record—there are a lot of Indians in India, and there is a lot of make-work to keep all the lot of Indians employed, and this results in the highest ratio of people standing around to people actually working of almost any country I have visited. China does come close, for obvious reasons, but the Chinese seem to have mastered the skill of standing around purposefully. Sort of like when I was in the Army and they told you that the secret for never getting put on detail was to walk around the area carrying a clipboard and marking on it every so often. Didn't matter what marks.

Anyway these bleary-eyed Americans have all their own personal luggage—which is not a small amount given that we expect to be in Asia for close to three weeks—piled high on metal trolleys. On top of this we have twenty-one somewhat dented cardboard boxes, all of which say "U-Haul Large" on the sides. We look like *The Grapes of Wrath* took a misstep upon leaving Oklahoma and somehow ended up in Gujarat. We are trying to convince the customs authorities that each box is worth no more than $153, and since we have thirty-eight people and since the customs allowance upon entering the country is $200 per person, well then ...we don't feel it is prudent to say "You do the math" since probably at this hour we ourselves can't do the math, but it does seem pretty clear that we should be OK. The first offer from the first customs person we encounter or who encounters us is $600. In hard currency. Not based on any math that we can determine or that he can explain. Linda persists, finds another customs guy with the same white uniform and black shoulder boards but more little silver things on his shoulder boards than the first customs guy, which we assume means more rank, but one never knows.

While these negotiations were going on, of course, there was a very large amount of standing around by most of the people, or to be more precise, leaning around on our respective luggage carts. At one point David came back to the assembled multitude and stage-whispered, "Here's the problem—bottled gravy is an embargoed substance." Made sense to me.

Linda explains it all again to customs guy #2; she brandishes the list of the contents of each box (all boxes carefully numbered, although there are some numbered "five a" and "six a" along with the number five and six boxes—I assume this is a ruse to throw off pursuers); she waves the copies of the passports of all thirty-eight people; she explains that we have come to their wonderful country to spend Christmas and in general acts formidable. Her position is strengthened by the fact that all thirty-eight of us have strategically grouped our carts together in a massive floating island in the middle of the customs hall, which actually isn't all that enormous, so what with all our luggage, and all our boxes, and children playing on the floor and so forth, we ourselves are beginning to look like we might belong in a third world country, and besides we are really gumming up the traffic flow, big time. Customs guy #2 asks to open a box. Fine, picks one out, we open it, sure enough, shiny green plastic Christmas garlands pop out, along with a lot of Styrofoam peanuts, followed by sixteen packages of paper Christmas napkins, followed by four bags of Chex Mix (extra-large size) and forty-eight tuna kits—cans of tuna with some crackers.

At this point had I been a customs guy, I would have been sure that the next layer was diamonds, or heroin, or whatever you don't want in India (F-16s for Pakistan?), but it is all exactly as detailed on the list. Very impressive. Most criminals aren't nearly so well organized. Customs guy #2 either gives up or loses interest, says go ahead. So now we take all our luggage, and boxes, and this caravan of about forty-five very full luggage trolleys moves toward the exit. Next stop—all luggage has to be X-rayed upon leaving. So we manhandle or woman handle all the damn boxes and suitcases off the carts and onto an X-ray machine and back onto the carts, where the luggage seems to have expanded because it now takes up fifty-two carts. I never realized that X-rays had the capability to cause luggage to multiply but now I have proof. We head for the real exit.

Not so fast there, Charlie. Up comes customs guy #3, who is confusing because he is dressed in all dark blue khaki, no name tag, no shoulder boards with metal globs on them, but acting full of authority. Entire dialogue is replayed, including opening a box—and this guy doesn't even have one of those little metal tables for us to set it on. He may have just cruised in off the street to harass the tourists, we can't tell. Lists are waived, ornaments and cranberry sauce are displayed, and even he gives in. The armada pushes forward, our ground agents load people into buses, luggage into trucks for transfer to the domestic flight—no, we're not there yet. We all check into the Leela Kempinski Hotel for a three-hour nap, then onto the plane to Jaipur. The ground agents tell us that we have among us 104 pieces of checked luggage. I estimate approximately the same number of pieces of carry-on luggage. And they say Americans don't know how to have a good time.

Although we had allowed a fair margin, the domestic flight to Jaipur is late so we don't land there and get through the city and into the hotel until 12:00 noon, not the 8:30 a.m. we had expected. Check-in goes smoothly and we all go to our rooms. This Rajvilas is one nice hotel! It's actually a series of villas, many with individual pools or fountains sprinkled about an immaculate garden with flowers everywhere, lots of water features, several peacocks, and staff-to-guest ratio of maybe sixteen to one. It's not a big hotel, and we're probably one-third of the total occupancy, so they are glad to see us. Linda and I are staying in the Royal Villa, which is really a two-bedroom suite with each bedroom detached and a central living room/dining room/kitchen. And courtyard and large pool. It's exceptionally tastefully done and well maintained and overall real impressive. It's even more of a surprise because the drive from the airport is real India—motor scooters and motor bikes and bicycles everywhere; camels pulling carts; cows in the middle of the road; women in colorful saris; men in yellow, orange, and red turbans; folks walking in the street; open market stalls selling vegetables, flower wreathes, food; and everywhere lots and lots of people. Plus lots and lots of small shacks beside the road, dirt and trash everywhere, goats and pigs roaming free beneath Intel billboards— huge contrasts of sophistication and ISO 9000-quality poverty. And then suddenly a quick turn and you're inside this envelope of luxury called the Rajvilas. It either makes you mad—why can't everything in the country be this nice?—or it gives you hope, or both at the same time. India is like that.

But no time for philosophical/geopolitical reflection; we're tourists and we have touristing to be about. After a quick walk about the grounds and a quick lunch, we all pile into our two big white buses, which say—not so discreetly—"Rajasthan Tours" in about eighteen-foot-tall letters on the side (just so no one will mistake this bunch of white folks with cameras for natives) and head for the Amber Fort just outside town. It's a very famous, big stone fortress complex built on a commanding hill outside the valley that Jaipur sits in. Actually the fortification has a bit of a resemblance to the Great Wall and is magnificent both on the outside and the inside where there is very special decoration—tiles, inset small concave mirrors, carved marble panels, etc. What they don't tell you is that you get to ride on top of an elephant to get from where the buses stop at the base of the mountain to where the fort is, logically, at the top of the mountain. You sit on a little uncomfortable square platform stuck on top of the elephant, facing sideways to maximize views (so they say) or seasickness (my opinion), while the elephant bucks and sways up the series of switchbacks with his mahout (little guy in turban, riding just behind elephant's head) beating the crap out of the elephant with his club. Very jouncy and an experience worth having, as Dad notes, <u>once</u>. You can walk up this same small street, and most Indians and some tourists do, demonstrating common sense but only somewhat. Given that this is not an elephant-free zone, in fact quite the contrary, it's laden with elephant poop (birds gotta fly, elephants gotta poop), so walking has hazards. All along the route we are beset with men and boys offering to take our picture, to sell us puppets, to sell us small replicas of elephants, to sell us postcards, to sell us picture books about Jaipur, and to sell us elephant prods so we can beat the crap out of our own elephants back home. This is, as David remarks, "the most unattractive part of India." Well maybe burning up widows is worse, but this isn't great. Although when you think about the merchandise, you wonder about its lack of breadth. Why not film for your camera, why not cold drinks, why not pirated Jackson Browne tapes, why not T-shirts, and baseball caps, and coffee mugs, and key chains all emblazoned with the logo/picture/ representation of the Amber Fort? But no, it's elephants—elephant prods, books, postcards, and pictures. I say they need marketing help. Where is the snow globe with a replica of the Amber Fort inside? I'd buy that.

Fort having been duly visited, we retreat back to the hotel. Linda refers to this as traveling in a cocoon, and she's right. Everyone is totally tired out that evening, so most get dinner and go to bed. We, of course, have twenty-one boxes of presents, food items, decorations, etc., to unpack. Fortunately Elika, Rich, and Leo are troopers and come over and help us unpack. Leo does his part by first jumping up and down on the spilled Styrofoam peanuts, of which there are a lot. I give him credit as they do make a lovely crackling and popping sound when you do this. You should try this in the privacy of your own home, though. Then he decides to eat them. We may have made a tactical mistake by calling them "peanuts." Biodegradable or not, they ain't food. Leo is only reluctantly convinced of this point.

Wednesday morning, 22 December: (I decided to put days of the week with the dates for these entries, not the least because we were confused ourselves for about a week as to what time and day of the week it was) Linda has arranged a visit to a local school which goes very well—our kids talk to their kids, they all exchange e-mail addresses, WHICH ALL THE KIDS, OURS AND THEIRS, HAVE ONE OF AND KNOW HOW TO USE. Yikes! It's impressive. I myself finally figured out how to use e-mail about two weeks ago, making me the second-to-last American in the country to do so. Linda and I now have a game: wherever we go to out-of-the-way third world countries, we look for big signs offering Internet service and e-mail. We have seen them in the darnedest places—places where you can't get running water or flush toilets, you can check your e-mail. Actually I think it's pretty cool.

After the school visit, which some of us slugabeds have skipped, we rendezvous at the Jai Mahal Palace Hotel, a former Maharajah palace (*mahal* means "palace" in Hindi, and everybody uses it indiscriminately—in the UK, everybody is a superstore—in India, everybody's a mahal, and yes, we have noted that calling something the Jai Mahal Palace is a redundancy just for us round eyes and that it translates as "Jai Palace Palace"). On the big green front lawn of the palace, a pathway has been laid out for us, its borders defined in orange marigold petals. Several colorfully costumed Rajasthani dancers and musicians are there, and one of them greets each of us by placing a red dot of kohl on our foreheads and a flower wreath, again of marigolds, around our necks. Hawaii has nothing on Rajasthan when it comes to flowered wreaths. Then comes the best part—half the lawn has been taken up with a playing field about half the size of a football field with goal posts set at either end. Six brilliantly painted elephants wait, all decked out and ready for us to play—elephant polo!

It's just like horse polo, only elephants are bigger so the mallets are longer and thus you can't make those big arcing swings, and the ball is bigger, and the elephants step on it from time to time, and as games of speed go, this isn't one. Not to say that a competitive spirit doesn't quickly develop. After all, we are Americans and we all play team sports, now even the women. The twenty-four of us eventually end up riding around during the four chukkas that we play, but this time we're seated just behind the mahouts, as if we were on a horse. If you think you have to have a certain amount of lower body flexibility to ride a horse, you should try an elephant. Even Linda's mom gets up and plays for a period, and Dad rides around on the referee elephant sitting in a royal seat-type thing called a howdah. The family being what it is, we can't resist asking him, "Howdah like it?" and "Who was the famous Indian elephant puppet star of early TV?" (Howdah Doody).

The afternoon was spent at an allegedly marvelous rug and fabric factory where they weave rugs by hand and do block printing of fabrics, also by hand. They make wonderful stuff, and many of us bought various examples, but as you look at the men sitting in contorted positions working away at rickety wooden looms, rapidly tying 133 knots per square inch, you do tend to think that: first, this really isn't a good job for human beings; and second, how in the world can you ever compete with machines. Maybe it beats herding cows in the desert, but not by much.

That evening everyone gathered in the Royal Villa and we decorated the tree and had a very good Indian dinner. A word about the tree. No, a word about the nature of tour guides everywhere. We have a very wonderful group of people here, part of a local travel company called Ventours. They have been absolutely responsive to all our requests, even the odd and strange ones of which there have been several. For example, we needed a mantel for the kids to hang up their stockings, but because this is tropical/desert India, there aren't fireplaces and thus not so many mantels. Hence Linda asked them to get some wood and arrange a carpenter to build a faux mantel. No problem, they said, and we have one. It's made out of two-by-fours and there's no chimney, but we have explained to the kids that Santa now relies on a GPS system to find all the boys and girls and no longer has to look for chimneys. Mantels remain essential, and naughty vs. nice requirements still apply.

Our other request was for a nine-foot Xmas tree. The Ventours guys tell us that it's illegal to cut a pine tree in India, so they have had to send off to New Delhi for a live one, which they trucked in. Me, I actually find it more than unlikely that it's illegal to cut a pine tree in India. But never mind. The tree is thin, and spruce-like, and tips dangerously to the north. But we love it nonetheless, and besides it's what we've got; and so everybody has Christmas music, and lots of beer and wine, and gin and tonics in honor of the Brits. Linda has packed roughly a hundred thousand Xmas ornaments, including many fragile glass ones, none of which has broken. Unfortunately all the bottles of gravy have survived as well. We decorate the tree, the curtains, the lampshades, the concrete elephants in front of the villa, the thorn tree in the back terrace, the two chandeliers, and most of the vacant wall space. With all our ornament hangers and duct tape, we are rolling! We find that we have several long string/garland type things of colored balls, except that they are all sealed, so in a stroke of genius a really clever person decorates our swimming pool by throwing them in, where they float about like snakes made of colored ping-pong balls. I now firmly believe that if you have a swimming pool you are obligated to decorate it for Christmas.

Leo doesn't try to eat any of the ornaments but does insist on attempting to poke his finger into the light sockets, which at 220 volts vs. the US standard of 110 will knock him into last Tuesday should he succeed. We counsel electrical prudence. Leo finally agrees and reverts to picking up some of the oh-so-cute big, white round stones with which the hotel decorator has lovingly edged the pool and throwing them into the pool. Beats electrocution and makes a design statement. What more could you ask for from a grandchild? Well, admission to Harvard comes later.

Thursday, 23 December: We arise and go off to the home/factory of Mr. Singh, an elderly gentleman who thirty years ago single-handedly revived the art of blue pottery in Jaipur. Yes, he does have a showroom and will sell you stuff, but it's a fun visit because 1) the story is true; 2) he is a class act and not a promoter or hustler, and has trained bunches of people in the craft so that now Jaipur blue pottery is renowned throughout India; and 3) they are still doing it right there—clay, potter's wheel, wood-fired kiln, and all. Best vignette: Mr. Singh turns to my dad (your brother) and says, in Japanese, "Are you Japanese or Chinese?" Turns out he (Mr. Singh) had studied pottery and ceramics in Japan under one of the national treasures for several years and perforce had to pick up pretty good Japanese. And a less than unfailing ability to pick Japanese persons out of a crowd. My father was wearing a pretty strange tweed hat, it must be said, so that added credibility to his disguise. Not to be outdone, Dad answers him back word for word, and a merry old conversation in creaky Japanese is had by both parties. Very remarkable and even touching. He isn't really Japanese, is he? He's your brother so I think you should know.

While we are all sitting in the bus waiting for something or someone (we do a lot of this), one of our guides attempts to explain to us the Indian sense of time, based—he notes—on the widespread belief in reincarnation.

"Time just isn't as important to us as it is to you," he insists. "We Indians think to ourselves: if not this hour, then next hour; if not today, then next day; if not this year, next year; if not in this life, then in next life. . ." Soon, given where we are and how much waiting we do, we begin to quote this phrase to each other routinely.

That afternoon we fly off (after waiting in the airport for an unexplained hour for airplanes we have chartered) into the west, to the Thar Desert and the small town of Jaisalmer. It is quite close to the Pakistan border and thus hard to get to in terms of the airport, which is really an Indian Air Force base and requires special permissions, etc. When you land there, there really is nothing—buses pick you up on the airstrip as elderly Hawker Hunter fighters roar off over your head. Driving to the terminal you pass numerous revetments for the attack jets. And it is all brown, and scrubby, and rocky. "Deserts," I keep reminding myself, "aren't beaches; they do have ups and downs." We pass through Jaisalmer looking out the window at the famous Golden Fort, not stopping because we are bound for the desert for real. After about an hour of driving on a paved but one-lane blacktop road though what looks for all the world like northern New Mexico without Georgia O'Keeffe and the mountains, but with occasional goats and sheep frequently on the middle of the road, we come to the royal tented camp. It's tents! And camels! About a hundred of the darn things, all plopped down on their haunches, all with either young boys or wizened old men, usually with colorful turbans, waiting for us to ride them! (The camels, not the boys or old men). The tents are set up in what looks to me like a regimental square, and the camels are all in a bunch, and it is so picturesque that it almost defies description.

One of Linda's brothers comes up to me and says, "I thought that elephant polo was going to be the high point of the trip, but my God . . ."

Elika says, "This is it, we've become *The English Patient!*"

We stash our stuff in the tents (which have, I hasten to note, indoor plumbing) and all choose a camel, and off we go into the desert. The camels resemble the elephants except: they are cranky, making a sort of croaking, mooing noise in irritation about having to get up (or sit down, or go forward, or stop, doesn't matter); they have bad teeth; some would argue that they don't smell great although I didn't notice; and they have been known to spit at people. This amuses almost all of us except the spittee. Almost everyone rides one, including your brother, although he does note that this too is an experience that one should do once in a lifetime. Good thing we got him in time. We end up at the top of a sand dune overlooking the tented camp just as the sun is setting. A Rajasthani banquet has been set up for us, complete with dancers in incredibly colorful costumes. Some of the food is good, some of it is mutton. Personally, whenever anyone says "mutton" to me, I move rapidly in the other direction. One young woman dancer does a backbend and picks up golden rings with her eyes. Others dance around smacking sticks at each other. Libations are poured, and there is a lovely red-pink sunset. We sit on pillows with bolsters as backrests. It is wonderful, and exotic, and elegant, and highly strange, and terrific. Leo thinks it is great because he has never seen such a big sandbox. Even David finally says, "I give up, you win, this is as exotic as it gets." He's right.

East meets West, episode one: "It's hard to drive a camel." All of us who are lucky enough to have gotten astride these beasts—and that is just about everybody because we are not lacking in good sports— immediately, as Americans, begin to want to either a) relate to the camel driver or b) figure out how to make the camel go where we want, either directly or through the uncertain medium of the camel driver. You get on an elephant, you say to yourself, "OK, whatever." You get on a camel, you think that since it's not as big as an elephant there is some way to make it do what you want.

Vicki Siegel, Michael Herson's smart and game wife, says to her driver who is seated behind her, "How do I make him speed up?"

The camel driver, who has seen perhaps two Americans in his life up close, counting Vicky as one, and who lives in the Thar Desert and makes his living herding goats in a pretty tough place without CNN, responds, reasonably, *"Nam."*

"OK," says Vicki, and turns to the camel and says, *"Nam, Nam!"* The camel goes, erratically, as camels are wont to do. During the entire trip up the sand dune Vicki spurs on the camel by saying, *"Nam, Nam!"* When the camel ride is over, Vicki courteously thanks the driver and walks off. Later we find out that *nam* is Hindi for "gift" or "tip." The camel driver she abandons is deeply sorrowful that, despite all those promises she made while riding up the sand dune, he will not now be able to afford to send his son to Stanford.

East meets West, episode two: "For want of a shoe . . ." Just to make sure we knew we were still in India, during the banquet in this wonderfully exotic location atop a sand dune, a bar was set up along with the buffet. Duly attended by two elegantly uniformed Rajasthani, it was tricked out with good quality basics—vodka, whisky, gin, scotch, soft drinks, beer, and some decent red wine. Except that after the first bottle of red wine had been opened and drunk by other folk than yours truly, both the corkscrews provided by the management broke in the attempt to open wine bottle number two. Astonishing coincidence, but in India karma is important. Fortunately at least two of the Westerners present were armed with Swiss Army knives with corkscrews, and calamity was averted. Now you see why we are so keen on technology.

That evening in the tents some of us freeze our tushes off, because it gets extremely cold in the desert and few of us have brought enough warm clothes. Others are natural polar bears and think it's all just like home. Yet others (yes, me, but don't tell) don't realize that we have small heaters inside the tent whose output we can turn up, and somehow we get skipped on the hot water bottles. Because they have hot oatmeal, and hot tea, and hot coffee in the mess tent first thing in the morning, no one hesitates to get up bright and early. Besides you can hear everything through the tent walls, and the sun is starting to warm things up.

We drive back to Jaisalmer and the Golden Fort, stopping first to admire a reservoir and listen to a vendor saying over and over, "Finest postcards of Jaisalmer and fine picture book of Jaisalmer, no thank you." The town is sort of analogous to a small Tuscany hill town, transplanted to India and then outfitted with a bunch more people in far less fashionable clothing, and cows, camels, pigs, and goats, all wandering the narrow streets. The fort is large and spread out, obviously constructed for defense, and still in good shape. It has crenellated towers, constricted entrances, small windows from which to shoot people, battlements from which to throw stones down upon your opponents, the works. The town that has grown up around the fort resembles Italy or Greece in that all of the buildings are one or two story, flat roofed, interconnected, but since they are all built of the native sandstone, they are golden brown rather than white. We wander through the streets and marvel at the intricacy of the carvings of the balconies that line each side. These are the *havelis*, the residences of the merchants, and they are lovely and exceptionally well preserved. Because it is so hard to get to, Jaisalmer has only about 50% of the tourist accouterments of Jaipur, and its state of preservation—probably the dry desert setting has helped—is wondrous. We are all delighted that we came, despite the obstacle course in the streets that is made up of cows, kids persistently trying to sell you things, the odd open sewer, and cow dung.

We fly back to Jaipur for our fancy Christmas Eve dinner—black tie no less. We have had the hotel chef fly in turkey, and he has used our imported ingredients more or less as requested, so in the middle of this wondrous setting we have a traditional Christmas dinner and a formal photo in black tie and fancy dresses. It was Linda's idea and it works very well.

Christmas night, 25 December: I am sitting here in the living room of the Royal Villa wearing what might appear to a less global, less culturally sensitive person to be a pair of muslin pajama bottoms that are exceptionally poorly designed, or hugely the wrong size, or both, in that the legs are what you might call pipe- stem size, and fit me very snugly on circumference (although eight or nine inches too long on length); and the top where your bottom, and waist, and other stuff goes is appropriate for Paul Bunyan or maybe even Babe the Blue Ox. It does have a drawstring so when you put it on and tie the drawstring waist, two things happen: 1) the legs crinkle up and down around your ankles in fetching wrinkled rows, and 2) the waist, all cinched up, creates the effect of jodhpurs times three around your behind. The clever Rajahstanis, however, have figured out that this is not a flattering look and wear over these faux pantaloons an anorak sort-of shirt that comes down to your knees and covers up your floppy thighs but not your seriously wrinkled ankles. Sounds worse than it is, especially when you add the wool vest in sedately dark colors/fabric and the turban in bright colors. Yes, turban. No, I'm not wearing it now, but for the last four or five hours we have been at the Rambagh Palace for a complete and thorough-going Indian/Rajasthani cultural experience. Again, colored elephants, camels pulling carts and salivating noticeably, fireworks, two arcades of craftsmen selling gewgaws, a magician, a palm reader, dancing girls doing unlikely but family-rated things (feats of skill?), a buffet of Indian and some allegedly continental dishes (but not the one dish of plain roasted chicken and steamed vegetables we had asked for as a safety net), and fortunately a bunch of braziers around the tented dining area, so we could all stand around and warm our hands.

What, you may ask, does this have to do with my pajamas? Well for a reason now lost in the dark mists of prehistory, we planned this event as a costume ball, except that the costumes were that all the women would wear saris and look beautiful and the men would wear *kuta* (pajamas and other stuff, see above) and look faintly ridiculous—Ringo Starr seeking enlightenment. We got measured for our outfits two days ago, and then had a sari assembling woman show up at about 5:00 and a turban-tying guy arrive slightly later. This is not simple clothing. Here is the truly miraculous part: everybody played ball, including the two, three, five, and six year olds, and your brother. To have a big fancy buffet with elephants, fireworks et al., on the front lawn of the Rambagh Palace, it is not, in fact, necessary for all the white folk to dress up like Indians. But it does do interesting things to the ambience. The rest of the guests at the hotel came out and took our pictures as we processed onto the grounds. And I convinced Linda's dad and two brothers to have the henna artist do temporary henna tattoos on our arms. And they hadn't had that much to drink. The bracelets of henna we have drawn on our skin, we decide, have the American version of the five elements of life: earth, air, fire, water, and television. David and John Huetter were feeling pretty much under the weather, as was my wife, but they all got dressed up, rallied, and seemed to enjoy the whole thing. We're talking seriously colorful. India may lack a lot of things, but colorful entertainments ain't one of them.

Back to the real world, at least momentarily: the Rambagh Palace is owned by the current Maharajah, and we had to get special permission to have this dinner/event on his front lawn with the palace outlined in lights in the background. He eventually acquiesced, and so we thought it would be a nice gesture to invite him and his wife, the Maharani (patroness of the school we had visited earlier), to come to dinner with us. Besides if he wouldn't eat the food it might be an important clue to us. He had initially accepted, and then a couple of days ago notified us that he had to go to Delhi instead. He called us at the hotel and was extremely gracious in apologizing, which was nice, but my goodness, we don't even know the guy. At the end of the conversation, he said, apropos of nothing, that he was sorry not to meet us because he had an idea for a power plant in Rajasthan that he had been anxious to discuss with us. Well the electricity at the hotel does go off about once a day for a brief period before the hotel's backup generator kicks in, but how did he know about that dark chapter of my history? I was very amused and said that nothing would please me more than to have him send me the details of his proposal and that I could assure him that AES would be quite responsive. It's nice to be on the board of directors of a big company—people assume you have a lot of authority, which of course is not the case—you get to make general and vague high-level promises, and you don't actually have to do any of the real work.

What else did we do Christmas Day besides get dressed up in our "Last Days of the Raj" outfits? Kids opened their stockings at 9:00 a.m.; big Christmas breakfast complete with very spicy Indian pancakes at 10:00; an optional tour of the City Palace and Observatory at 11:00 mandatory gift wrapping for some of us at the same time; lunch and gift exchange/forced trade from 2:00 to 4:30. With thirty-eight people, this takes a while, and we included our three Ventours guys who have been such good troopers with us—Chris (I can't believe that this is in fact his Indian name), Tarun, and Vivien. Once we explained the rules to them, they got it right away. When Vivien traded in his sports trivia calendar for the Elvis sunglasses, we knew they had it all figured out.

Our tour guide told me these unlikely things, but I believe them, about this India locale:

The natives in the Thar Desert build their houses out of cow dung because it is fatal to insects.

The fort was built entirely of sandstone blocks without any mortar. But now because of global warming, when the limestone absorbs water, they flake off, and that is why the World Monuments Fund is restoring it. (What?)

All these cows are owned by someone who comes to collect them at the end of the day.

Indians actually invented the zero and the Arabs stole it from them.

―――

Sobering notes: last night as I was tapping away at this letter to you, accompanied by miscellaneous parents filling up Xmas stockings for kids, Brad, Linda's brother, came in and mentioned, with what I thought was remarkable aplomb and cool, that the state department had updated its terrorist warning and that some guys had hijacked an Air India airbus which had taken off from Kathmandu—our next destination. Well horse-feathers. The highjackers had onboard an AK-47, another automatic weapon, and several hand grenades. OK children, can you say "airport security"? I know something about AK-47s, and what I know about them, among other things, is that they won't go through that X-ray machine, and you really can't just put one in the little plastic dish and slide it past the metal detector. People will notice. Since we have arranged an Air India charter into Nepal, we are ambivalently perturbed: "Will we get on an Air India plane and be kidnapped and shot/blown up?" and, inversely: "Damn, I bet Air India is now going to tell us that they don't have enough airplanes so they're canceling our charter to Nepal." David's take on all this: it actually ought to be a lot safer now to fly into or out of Nepal due to better airport security. We sagely decide to "wait and see" since we have no other choice. Important to be a sophisticated global traveler.

Sunday, 26 December: We're up at reasonable hour and off to the airport for the normal unexplained delay, then charter flight to Agra for a day trip to the Taj Mahal. Upon arrival we are bused to a beautiful meadow on top of a hill with a spectacular view overlooking the Taj Mahal—so perfect it seems to have come out of Hollywood or Disneyland—and hard to believe that it's real. Tables and tents have been set up there for our buffet lunch overlooking the monument—very nice, and it also includes the obligatory snake dancers. No elephants, though, but it *is* only lunch. Leo contributes by trying to tear down all the marigold garlands to the alarm of his minders but the muted reaction of the restaurant staff. Then off to the actual site. It is at the end of a lovely park on a bluff overlooking the Yamuna River. The full view is obscured by walls and a large red sandstone formal entry building. Once you get through that, the building itself is revealed. It is marvelous and impressive, everybody's right. And so is the love story that goes with it, about Shah Jahan and Mumtaz Mahal. Actually this wasn't her real name but was her pillow talk nickname. It means "The Precious One of the Palace," which does sound a lot better than "Mumtaz." Linda decides that she herself should now be called "Mumtaz" but doesn't add "Mahal" because she doesn't just want to be limited to the palace. And then just as the Shah was getting old, his oldest son imprisoned him for eight years until he died and took over the empire. Being a Mughal emperor had definite risks to offset the benefits. Linda's dad and both brothers are builders, and they are especially impressed with the quality of workmanship, all done without any machines. Linda points out that this monument was being built about the same time that our US ancestors were building forts with sticks.

The crisis of the Air India highjacking from Nepal has caused the airline to halt all of its flights into and out of Nepal for the foreseeable future. And this is inconvenient since that includes the charter we were to go on. We are delayed a day, and everyone breathes a sigh of relief. Gee, we actually get to hang around this lovely hotel and use the spa and enjoy the grounds? What a concept!

We pay for this indolence the next morning by hitting the airport at 8:30 and then having all our flights delayed, and delayed, and delayed. We become quite familiar with the Jaipur airport, which doesn't take long and yields few exportable design ideas for public buildings. Also no place really to get anything to eat, or drink, or buy a newspaper, and certainly no place to make a phone call. Linda and I are charmed by the very big sign outside the airport that announces in large letters and unequivocal terms: "We are

Y2K free."

In response to the down time, the Hemphill family is unable to restrain themselves and starts making up Indian jokes, starting with the food items. Every Indian meal always includes a lentil stew/soup dish, frequently eaten with rice, called dhal. Hence we get:

Jacqueline Susann's first book set in India: *Valley of the Dhal*

Famous Indian Broadway musical: *Guys and Dhals*

Another famous Indian Broadway musical: *Hello Dhal-ly*

Three failed Indian/American presidential candidates: Walter Mon-dhal, Bob Dhal, and Libby Dhal

But nothing can make this group think within the box, so we branch out into other Indian food items and then Indian stuff in general:

Two Indian Beatles songs: "Lentil Be" and "Paperback Raita"

Famous '40s Indo-American travel song: "Gonna Take a Senti-lentil Journey"

Indo-American movie about teaching in east Los Angeles: *Rajasthan and Deliver*

What Indians put on their postcards: Vishnu were here

The admonishment Indian mothers give to their kids to correct behavior: Stick to the straight and Nehru

Tagline from Indo-American football movie set in Rajasthan: Win one for the Jaipur

Indo-American cowboy hero: Roy Rajah

Linda expresses fear that we have not heard the last of these. She is prescient.

Favorite surreal moment number one: On the drive from the Taj Mahal back to the Agra airport we pass a small storefront offering long distance telephone calls and, according to a small signboard standing in front of the store, "Internet and e-mail." A large whitish-brown cow, sacred type, horns, and hump, and all, is grazing the garbage in the street right beside the sign.

PART TWO: NEPAL

11:35 p.m. Wednesday, December 29: this time I find myself in the three-story presidential suite of the Dwarika Hotel in Katmandu. Not too many hotel rooms in which I have stayed, presidential suite or no, are in fact three stories tall, but this one is. The hotel is a labor of love begun fifteen years ago by a Nepali businessman who was walking down the street in K-du (as the freaks call it) and saw some carpenters taking an elaborately carved beam and sawing off the carved part, then throwing the carvings into the fire.

"What are you doing?" he asked, reasonably.

"Just getting down to the good wood," they replied.

He immediately bought all the remaining carved beams and brought them home. He began buying more and more architectural remnants—windows, doors, balconies—all elaborately carved and almost all made of the local teak-like wood, which lasts a very long time. Finally his wife (who told us this story as an introduction to dinner last night) said to him, "You can't but any more," so they decided to use some of the stuff and build guest rooms which incorporated it. The result fifteen years later is a hotel that is a series of three- and four-story buildings and incorporates at every door, and window, and lintel antique Nepali carvings. It's something of a cross between a hotel and a museum, except you don't have to leave at 5:00 p.m. They maintain a workshop out back where they restore badly damaged carvings, and all the modern furnishings inside the rooms are also made in Nepal, as are the fabrics.

This is a country of only 22 million people, 39% literacy rate, infant mortality of 8%, and per capita income of $250. The people who run this hotel have done a marvelous job of blending the needs of tourist/commercial travelers, the local artisans, the need to preserve Nepali culture, creating jobs for women, etc. Unfortunately the founder is deceased now, but we asked his wife, who is running the hotel, what help she had received—USAID, World Bank (which of course has a prominent office in another hotel in town), Asian Development Bank? She snorted, a surprising gesture from a very lovely and gentle woman. "They all said that our project was too small or not worthwhile," she said, "so we did it on our own." Another potential foreign aid home run becomes instead a missed opportunity.

After the ordeal of yesterday—four hours in the Jaipur airport for a fifty-minute flight to Delhi, etc.—we are delighted to be here but saddened that our stay is to be cut even shorter than planned. This morning we all gathered in our buses and took off to the historic city of Bhaktapur, one of the three original cities found in the Kathmandu Valley (the others are Kathmandu—no surprise there—and Patan, not named after the WWII tank commander). Brief history note: Nepal was only unified as a country two hundred years ago by the Gurkhas (one of the then-existing twenty-two small principalities in the area) and then, due to a combination of circumstances that I won't bore you with, was kept isolated, really isolated as in NO ONE CAN COME HERE, until 1950. When the country was opened they had no cars, no paved roads, no schools, no modern medical facilities, etc. Not much air pollution, though. No McDonald's. They have come a long way since then, but one of the benefits of this enforced isolation is that much of the architecture and design of their cities remains as it was hundreds of years ago.

Bhaktapur is a particularly good example of this, which the Nepalis have recognized and have preserved since then. This isn't to say that it doesn't have kids on the streets trying to sell you embroidered purses, and Gurkha knives, and elephants carved out of yak bones or maybe plastic, or that it doesn't have its share of small storefronts selling bronze Buddha images, and reasonably strange Hindu/Buddhist paintings (the one of the two soles of Buddha's feet being my particular favorite), and postcards, and clunky jewelry, and brightly embroidered baseball caps that say "Kathmandu" on them—another favorite among our group. It has all that, but after all it is still a city and I personally am not sure that I'd like to walk down a street, even in the most impressive, and best preserved, and most historically significant urban site in the world (Rome? Washington, D.C.? London? Jerusalem? Marrakech?) and not see commercial life. The temples, called *stupas* here and in Thailand, and the palaces were truly excellent and remarkable, but one of the very nice parts was that the city was also alive with people, most of whom don't survive off the occasional tourist. It was fun.

On to the mountains—after all, Nepal has eight of the fourteen peaks in the world that are higher than 8,000 meters (26,000 feet), including of course Mount Everest, first surveyed by the British surveying team in 1848, led by none other than Sir George Everest. Yep, there's a connection. We drove up to a place called Dhulikhel, pronounced pretty much as spelled, and sat out on the patio of an elegantly landscaped small restaurant/hotel and had a wonderful lunch, mostly recognizable food—no curry, and Tuborg beer, for some reason widely available here. We were high enough up that we had views of the Himalayas to our west, although through a slight haze. On the drive up we were mesmerized by the sight of all the terraces glowing emerald green with three weeks growth of winter wheat. Nepal is a confusing country. At the restaurant there was an enormous cardinal red bougainvillea that had been trained up into a tree and was a cloud of red flowers. The walkway into the restaurant was lined with giant poinsettia bushes that towered over us, all in full red flower. When Dad lived in Hawaii we had poinsettia bushes, but my gosh, we're in the Himalayas. Well sort of. Nepal is actually at the same latitude as Florida, and if it weren't for the altitude would be a pretty tropical place, and it's in the valley floors. But it does take some mental adjustment to see hibiscus in a mountaineer's paradise.

Favorite surreal moment number two: Our Ventours guys have arranged for the Gurkha army band to be up at the mountain restaurant, in full white and red uniform, with brass, and drums, and bagpipes, to play for us during lunch. They start with several rousing military marches, do a couple of British numbers from WWI, and then, to our surprise, launch into a spirited rendition of the theme song from *Dallas*.

Nepal jokes start out to be much harder than India jokes, but we are undeterred:

What is the favorite Nepali Beach Boys song? "Sherpa-ing Safari"

What Nepali comic book hero flies around wearing a red cape? Stupa-man

What is the Nepali military's favorite Irish song? "How Are Things in Gurkha-mora?"

PART THREE: CAMBODIA

4:00 p.m. Friday, 31 December 1999: I am sitting beside the large and opulent pool at the Grand Hotel d'Angkor. As David noted gladly, "We've entered into the Franco-Chinese belt, and that means decent food!" He's right—after flying all day yesterday from Nepal, using 50% of the entire aircraft capability of Bhutan's only airline, oddly named Druk Air but magnificently piloted, we arrived just before dusk at the not very big airfield of Siem Reap, the small town where the Angkor Wat temples are located. You have to land before dusk because they don't have any lights on the airfield. And, we assume, that means no sophisticated, radar-controlled, land-any-time set of instruments and flight controllers and all that. In fact, as far as one can see, there's no control tower at all. Oh very well. We all went, in miscellaneous groups, to the buffet in the hotel café, and it was terrific. No curry, but standing round of roast beef. And pasta with red sauce. And crème brûlée. Well, mango crème brûlée, but even that was fine with us. The group was more than ready for a break from the food of the land. And getting here was pretty interesting.

Erin (Brad and Kelley's three-year-old daughter) goes to the airport: after hanging around the lobby in Nepal for two hours beginning at 6:15 a.m., and getting on the bus to go to the airport (after being promised that the plane was really there; but we're international travelers, we've heard that before), when we actually get to the airport, still suspiciously shrouded in fog, Erin decides that she's had it, and she's staying on the bus.

"Mom," she says in something between a whine and a rhetorical question, "why do we have to get off the bus?"

Kelley, her mother, sotto voce: "So we can sit some more in the airport."

Going through Nepal airport security they did want to open every bag. I had volunteered to carry one of Linda's, like a good person. I cheerfully put the briefcase through the X-ray machine, went through the metal detector, and reclaimed the item. Surly Nepali security person, in an Army olive drab wool uniform (may account for some of his lack of charm—it's hot for wool this time of year) demanded in poor to no English that I open the briefcase. Fine, no problem. I did so. He found, to his and my surprise, that it was filled with plastic wrapped bags of fresh celery (eight) and radishes (twelve). On our advance trip Linda had carefully refused to eat any raw vegetables, as all the books caution, but had become ravenous for same, so this time she simply decided to bring them with her from the US. I have been vaguely aware of this but now become specifically aware.

*Why not check the damn things,* I wonder peevishly as the security person stares morosely at a briefcase full of celery and radishes. He looks up at me, suspiciously, and I wonder if I know anything about the regulations regarding the export of food products from Nepal. Maybe radishes are holy? Maybe celery is an aphrodisiac? I personally have never found it to be such, but this is a different culture. He pauses, seeming confused ("Can this be a weapon? Is it contraband? Explosives?") He says to me, "Fruit?" using what I suspect is one of his very few words of English, although why he knows this rather than, "Hi how are you?" or "Give me money," is not clear to me. Looking him in the eye, deferentially but without caviling, I reply, "Vegetable," feeling like someone in a poorly written spy book. It's the correct password and he lets me go. I pass into the waiting room where I ask Linda cordially just exactly why it was she decided that I should be the celery mule. She is noncommittal.

When we finally left Nepal, we first had to fly to Bhutan. The flight only takes an hour, and you fly parallel to the Himalayas, and since you're up high enough (about as high as the mountains, come to think of it, i.e., 25,000–30,000 feet) you can see five of the world's highest mountains, including Everest. Very beautiful and impressive. Then they announce that we are landing in Paro, the capital of Bhutan, a country with two hundred thousand people. You look down and you see a river meandering between two particularly steep hills/mountains and a little, teeny, tiny concrete strip. This, of course, can't be it. Then the flight steward helpfully passes around a Xerox copy, somewhat worn, of an article downloaded from the Internet describing the landing at this airport as "the most exciting in the world." It is said to be far more interesting than landing at Kai Tak in Hong Kong where you have to briefly turn the plane vertical to miss the large apartment buildings on each side of the runway. In this case you have to turn vertical to keep from hitting the trees and monasteries on the mountainside, actually on the two mountainsides that border this runway. We wonder idly if the reason that Druk Air has only two airplanes, of which we have been able on forty-eight hours' notice to charter one, is because they keep bashing them into the mountains? No suspense here; since you're getting this letter, we made it. Much applause in the airplane. We refuel, head on to Bangkok, refuel again, and make it to Siem Reap late in the afternoon.

Naturally, we couldn't resist a few Bhutan jokes, stimulated in part by the hysterical relief of a safe landing:

Where do they grow flowers in this mountainous, landlocked, small country? A Bhutan-ical garden

And what do they use the flowers for, once grown? Bhutan-nieres

Someone afraid to fly into the capital city is said to be suffering from: Paro-noia

———

Today, our first full day in Cambodia, was devoted to visiting two of the best sites at Angkor—Angkor Thom, which is really a bunch of temples, and palaces, and monuments within a larger enclosure; and of course Angkor Wat itself, the largest individual temple. When Linda and I visited here on our advance-planning trip, we saw essentially no one at these sites. Not so today. The government of Cambodia has put together a big program called "Festival 2000" to celebrate the millennium, and they expect 150,000 persons to show up. They haven't all gotten here yet, but a lot have. And 95% of them are Cambodian, not Westerners or Japanese. Interesting. It was crowded, and it was hot, and it was noisy and dusty with the din of many motorbikes, and there weren't a lot of places to go to the bathroom, and when you did find a place, the toilet didn't flush, and the guides weren't particularly informative, and they spoke so softly that you couldn't hear everything, and there was no signage whatsoever, and there were little kids trying to sell you T-shirts, and postcards, and booklets, and wooden replicas of one of the temples, and bracelets, and all other sorts of stuff. But it was still magnificent.

It's an achievement like the pyramids of the Mexican city of Teotihuacán. And as far as you can tell, every last bit of the sandstone that forms the covering and much of the supporting framework (lintels, etc.) for these buildings is elaborately carved. Because these were royal, and religious, and ceremonial facilities, the carvings represent Hindu deities, or scenes from Buddha's life, or wondrous bas-relief tributes to Suryavarman II or Jayavarman VII's excellent conquest of the (fill in the blanks: Thais, Chams, Chinese, other Cambodians, Vietnamese, Indonesians, etc.). I could have spent hours and hours climbing the steep stairs to the next level of the particular temple and deciphering the carvings. None of it is crude, none of it is poorly done, all the proportions are beautiful. These would be fascinating buildings if there weren't decorated at all. But when you add the carvings—causeways bordered by fifty-four twice life-size gods on one side and fifty-four twice life-size demons on the other (although now that I think about it, what size of god is life-size?); massive railings carved as one hundred-meter-long snakes, cobras with five, or seven, or nine heads; bas-reliefs with battle scenes, and boats, and crocodiles eating the warriors who fall off the boat—it is very, very impressive. I was talking to someone once about the Grand Canyon, which I have never seen, and in describing it the other fellow said, "Despite the tourist hype, there are some places that do not disappoint." The same clearly applies to Angkor Wat.

More unlikely things my tour guide told me, but I believe them, Cambodia version:

Here in front of the elephant terrace they had games where the elephants tried to run around and grab other animals like water buffalo with their trunks and throw them up into the air. When they did they won the game.

They strung a high wire between these temples and acrobats walked across it.

If you climb to the top of this hill at dusk, you can see the sun set on Angkor Wat. (Of course the hill is *west* of Angkor Wat, and even in Cambodia the sun sets in the west.)

———

Vicki Siegel, as part of our preparations for the trip, had volunteered to have her boss, Senator Specter of Pennsylvania, write to the embassy of each country we visited, calling attention to our visit and asking the embassy to respond to any requests we might have. At the pool here today a blond American woman approached us who turned out to be from the embassy. She noted that the consular staff had, in fact, been alerted to look out for "a group of large Americans." Given all we've had to eat, we concluded maybe this was the right way to describe us.

Only two Cambodia jokes so far: 1) What is the favorite Cambodian-American Civil War novel? *Angkor Thom's Cabin* 2) Favorite Cambodian-American WWII movie? *From Khmer to Eternity*

---

10:20 a.m. Saturday, 1 January 2000: Happy New Year! Yesterday evening TCS arranged for the former US Ambassador here, James Rosenthal, to give all the interested persons (about nine of us turned out) an hour's briefing on Cambodia. It was well worthwhile—he was knowledgeable and emphasized both Cambodia's remarkable past as the Khmer empire when it dominated all of Southeast Asia, including most of what is today Thailand, Laos, and Vietnam, and the continual warfare and shrinkage of empire that occurred from the fourteenth century onward. He suggested, in fact, that given the geopolitics and relative national strengths at the time, had the French not stepped in and made Cambodia a colony in the middle eighteenth century, there might be no Cambodia today. His two major points: the Cambodians have perfectly good reasons to fear their historical enemies, the Thais and the Vietnamese; and despite its terrible poverty and truly atrocious recent history, the country is rich agriculturally and can (and does) feed itself. The Cambodians are placing a lot of emphasis on tourism as testified to by all the hotels under construction in Siem Reap, and probably it's not a bad bet. Angkor Wat is a remarkable site.

The hotel put on a big and well done party, a lavish outdoor buffet including fresh Maine lobster (how'd they do that?) and dancing at poolside to Lady Valerie's Big Band From The Philippines, and we all got dressed up again in our black tie outfits and sweated a bit. There were modest fireworks at midnight, a slightly off-key version of "Auld Lang Syne" was played, and the new millennium was declared official. Our objective of being in about as exotic/millennial a venue as you can find has been fully carried out.

The remainder of today was taken up with a visit to two more temples: Ta Prohm and Preah Kahn. Names won't mean much to you, and they certainly didn't to us. Ta Prohm, however, is the temple that has been left with all the jungle trees growing on top of and through it. And these trees, mostly kapok, are striking indeed. Large snakelike roots descend from roofs, cross walls, and drift and drool down stairs until they penetrate the ground. It's not too good for the temples, but it's great for atmosphere and for photographs. If you have ever seen any pictures of Angkor Wat, the first one you see will be Angkor Wat itself, and the second will be a shot of one of these trees draping itself over the ruins of Ta Prohm.

At the second site Linda had cleverly arranged on the spur of the moment for a man named John Sanday, the World Monuments Fund field representative, to give us all a briefing on the temple and the organization's work there to preserve it. This is a US organization headquartered in New York that raises money and organizes programs to preserve threatened monuments around the world. Preah Kahn is their real showpiece, and with Mr. Sanday, a personable and highly knowledgeable British preservation architect to lead us through it, we could tell why. Key Khmer nonachievements in temple building: first, they used no mortar to join the stones together in the structures; they instead had to cut and polish the joints so they fit tightly together naturally. One technique for doing this was to grind together two stones with sand in between. Once they had this done, then they just stacked them up. Kind of like a kid building with a wooden block set. As a building style, this is not unheard of in other cultures— some monuments in Peru use this same technique and endure to this day. Key differences: in Peru, the blocks are much larger. Here, each individual block is approximately the size of a standard US cinder block. In Peru, they are eight to twelve times as large. Equally important, the Peruvian sites are generally arid high desert with much less chance of hydraulic or biological intervention. This lack of mortar in Cambodia meant that water, and tree roots, and even termites can and have gotten into the cracks and crevices between the blocks, eventually forcing them apart. Walls lean, roofs collapse, stone facings fall off their laterite base. Not good.

Second nonachievement: they never discovered the keystone or rounded arch and so used only the corbel arch, a much less effective design which uses stones that stick out over the next lower one until they get to a level where they meet. You can span only much smaller breadths using this technique compared to a keystone arch. Thus no Parthenons, no Notre Dames, etc. The result is no grand internal spaces, but lots of narrow passageways. And here, too, the stones simply sit atop each other with no other support. Things tip outward, lintels crack, walls fall over. We spent over two hours with Sanday listening raptly as he explained not only the historical and cultural and artistic significance of the temple but also the Khmer engineering that went into its design and construction and the current efforts to save and preserve it. I could have spent several days just walking around the site with him.

Sunday, 2 January 2000: One last temple to visit. We had an internal betting pool as to how many of our colleagues would show up for this one, the last on our Cambodia itinerary. Most of us bet low, but in fact all but three people appeared for the buses at 9:30 a.m. Off we went to Banteay Srei, usually represented as the "temple of women" because of the numerous carvings of goddesses and other female figures adorning the wall panels, rather than the usual soldiers, gods, and other male-type personages. Good things: it is about twenty kilometers from the main body of Angkor temples and was built at the start of the Angkor era—tenth century. You get to drive through the countryside to see it. The temple is made of pink sandstone rather than the gray that characterizes the rest of Angkor. It is deeply carved rather than a bas-relief—I believe the term is "haut-relief." It is, in fact, neither a big site nor a tall set of temples. When the French found it in 1910 it had all fallen down, and they carefully restored it, which meant first re-leveling the foundations and then figuring out which set of blocks went on top of which other set of blocks. They did quite a nice job, finishing by 1924. It has stood unmolested since then, other than for the occasional looting of the heads of the images.

Architecturally it is nice but not the Empire State Building. However, it is the temple with the most wonderful and detailed carving we have seen, and all of it to the depth of one to one and a half inches. How it has survived all these years is a wonder. Every lintel panel has a different story, different Hindu gods in different incarnations in different episodes of their stories. And our guide, Tek, is great in that he goes through the imagery in great detail. At least I think that this is great. Others in the party begin to wilt after the fourth of Vishnu's ten incarnations. It is about ninety-five degrees out, very humid, and we have driven forty minutes in the heat through the Cambodian countryside—rice fields, and houses on stilts, and water buffaloes, and all—to get here, and it is our fifth temple in two and a half days, and it doesn't soar like the others, so there is some temple fatigue setting in. When the final incarnation of Vishnu has been explained there is a general rush for the buses. It is interesting to note that some guide-books dissuade tourists from visiting this temple due to concerns about land mines or "bandits" on the road to the temple. We had checked with the hotel beforehand and been soundly reassured, but there was still some uneasiness among our group. As Brad, Linda's brother, remarked, "We're a large, American, and slow-moving target." But we had no problem.

At the outskirts of the village next to the temple, we stop to photograph a sign, actually a billboard, with the image of a large bottle of Coke on one side and four panels on the other depicting a peasant woman walking in the field, finding a mine (or piece of unexploded ordinance), calling for help, etc. We uncharitably speculate that this billboard says: "Find a mine? Have a Coke, then call for help." It is an unlikely juxtaposition, but if Coke is helping pay for such education, then good for them. We're doing our part. Nobody has had a Pepsi since December 17, but we have had a *lot* of Cokes.

Worst joke of the trip (or best, depending on your perspective, which for us at least is beginning to erode): as noted above we are in the Cambodian province of Siem Reap, which means "victory over the Thais" in Cambodian, the Thais being historical enemies whom the Cambodians beat at least once. The fact that the Thais beat them several more times than this is not material or not mentioned. The next province to the west is named Battambang and is on the border with Thailand. The name of the province, we are informed, means in Cambodian "Thais drop all their weapons as they run for the border after being defeated by the glorious

Khmer army." Personally, I am skeptical of this translation, but never mind. Carol Powers comes up with the following:

Q: What is Cambodian for flatulence?

A: Bottom-bang. We may have seen one temple too many after all.

## PART FOUR: THAILAND

11:00 p.m., 5 January 2000: we have just completed our final farewell dinner here at the Mandarin Oriental Hotel. Excellent food—a mixture Thai and Western dishes—including corn on the cob for certain of our midwestern folks and pad Thai (stir-fried noodles) and larb gai (spicy chicken salad) for the more international members of the group (which may only be me and Linda, but we liked it fine). The Mandarin Oriental is one of the grande dames of Bangkok hotels and some say one of the top five hotels in the world. Tonight's cocktail party and dinner in the Authors' Lounge—they have suites named after famous authors who stayed here and wrote a bit in residence, including Somerset Maugham, Graham Greene, and Noël Coward—was fabulous, despite being a set dinner for forty. They had even arranged for six gigantic ice carvings of elephants set around the central fountain. The elephant is the national symbol of Thailand, although not yet of our party, but we are debating it. Your brother read an excellent millennium poem written for the occasion, and David made a nice set of remarks, paying respect to our mom who would have really enjoyed this trip, but, as he noted, would have asked every one of our guides, "What are your sources?" And been disappointed, no doubt. Scholarship is not a high priority here in Southeast Asia, at least not in the ranks of those who carry tourists around. And (dare we say?) maybe not in great demand from those selfsame tourists.

As proof of the preceding assertion, consider the following. Our last scheduled group out-of-hotel activity of the trip began this morning at 7:30. If you have been reading carefully, or if you are the normal human being that I know you to be, you will have an adverse reaction to this early hour—nothing else on the trip other than mandatory airplane flights has started this early, nor should it. Anyway we had scheduled a trip to the "floating market." This used to be held along the Chao Phraya River in

Bangkok and was very popular, but eventually got shut down. No explanations are given, but my take on this is that the riverside real estate got too valuable and needed to be used for condominiums and such, and so the property owners got the city government to close down this unattractive tourist mess so the upscale residents could play tennis or watch the sun rise without such a cacophony in their front yard or front river. The tourist people said, "Hey, this was a good thing," and so were given some space along a narrow set of canals one hundred km to the south, which in industrious fashion they renamed "floating market" and redirected tourists to same. Aha.

So now you get on a bus and ride for two hours, much of it spent getting out of Bangkok. You do get to see something of the countryside, which in this direction at least turns out to be salt flats with Don Quixote-style windmills to pump the seawater into the evaporating beds. Also some banana fields and coconut plantations, and many car dealerships, and several steel factories. After the first hour we stop at the "Orchid Fram" [sic], along with thirty-five other tourist buses which have disgorged hundreds of Eurotrash tourists in shoes with incredibly fat soles which make them all two inches taller than they would otherwise be, black T-shirts, nose rings, and hair the color of one of those crayons in the pack of forty-five that you never used, maybe "carmine."

"Why are they here?" you ask yourself. Is it an abiding interest in Thai culture, a fascination with the minutiae of Thai daily life, or maybe they really like buses? Anyway here you are at the Orchid Farm (spelling corrected), and there are in fact some orchids, although none for sale. Curiouser and curiouser. In terms of square feet it's three to one tourist merchandise—fake Gucci, and Fendi, and Vuitton handbags, garish Thai silk shirts, and robes, and dresses, and scarves, and sarongs, and anything else in the world that you can make out of fabric, and cheap gold jewelry, and coconut wood salad serving sets. Oh, I forgot to mention that this is, in fact, both an orchid farm and coconut sugar-refining factory. No, these two particular activities don't go especially well together, but never mind that. The sugar is made from the buds of the coconut flower. A careful observer will then ask, since the coconut is the fruit, if you use the flowers for sugar, doesn't that lower the output of coconuts? But that's not the point. The only actual reason we have stopped here is that an hour on a bus is a long time, and our guide, who probably gets a kickback from this establishment whenever he brings tourists here, has, in fact, noted that They Have Bathrooms. He's right—as soon as we get out of the bus we see the telltale walls and tiles and, even better, a sign that says "Toilet Man." David quickly notes that this is one of his superhero disguises, and goes in. Could this be like Bruce Wayne and the Bat Cave? We applaud his honesty and his boldness.

Reembussed, we go on to the floating market, but stop well short of it because this is an especially sculptured tourist moment. If you are a round eye, you must ride to the floating market in a narrow boat powered by a disused Chevy engine mounted on a long shaft which angles down into the water where the propeller is found. The boatman sits in front of the engine, ignoring its madly spinning fan inches from his arm and steers by swinging the entire engine and shaft this way and that. It's hard to exactly describe this, but the engine is entirely untethered, fixed only to the shaft, and the shaft is attached on a single gimbal at the back of the boat, so the whole assembly is free to move—propeller, shaft, and all—any which way. How in the world these boat guys (of course no women) keep from getting their arms sliced up in the fan blades I don't know, but it is dramatic—George Lucas and the pod racers in Southeast Asia, only slower, louder, and in the water. Other puzzling thing is that the boats are long, and narrow, and brightly painted (mostly yellows with blue/red/green highlights) but very narrow and have no keels that we can tell, and why they don't just roll over is a mystery. They do have a certain jaunty air to them, however, and very noisy engines. So we board and off we go.

We finally get to the floating market and we do get to see Thailand of the olden times, because it is just exactly, precisely the same as Thailand was—the day before yesterday. I think about Internet jargon: "B-to-C" (business-to-consumers) and "B-to-B" (business-to-business). What we had *expected* at the floating market was "T-to-T," a bunch of Thais floating around and picturesquely selling native goods to other Thais floating around. In boats, probably. What we *got* was a very small canal, like a "T" intersection, and two big warehouse buildings at the arms of the "T" filled with tourist crap. Along the water were, in fact, boats of Thais trying to sell the thirty-five tour buses Westerners' hats, and postcards, and carvings of pregnant elephants, and all manner of equally useful things. It was surreal but not quite what we had bargained for. As John said to me, "Is the floating part of this the fact that we had to get in a boat to get here?" Good question, especially since the bus that had dropped us off at the boat landing was now waiting for us in the parking lot directly outside the tourist market. No real need to take a boat to get here—we just did it because we are sheep and it is what everybody does if they are stupid Westerners. Sadly, we qualify.

One neat thing about the place is that at the far end of one of the warehouse structures housing all this tourist paraphernalia is a real economic activity: big stacks of large pink mesh bags filled with heads of garlic, each bag probably weighing fifty pounds. Also many same size bags of shallots. Some people (real people, not tourists) are preparing the garlic heads to go into the bags, others are loading them into trucks. I think that it's pretty interesting, but probably "Non-Floating Garlic and Onion Market" was not considered to be as much of a draw.

On the way back to Bangkok we stop at Nakhon Pathom, the largest temple or stupa in all of Thailand. It looks a little like a brown upside down ice cream cone, but it is big, I'll give it that. Several of our diminished party decides to stay in the bus judging sensibly that they have perhaps seen enough temples on this trip. We decide that this condition is known as being "stupa-fied."

Other interesting stuff we did in Bangkok: the first day we were here we took a boat ride up the river and through a series of the canals called klongs which interlace the city. Sure enough, people do live along them as advertised. What was not advertised is how many pots of flowers—bougainvillea, and geraniums, and crown of thorns, and gardenias, and orchids, and yellow mandevilla, and on and on—decorate the dwellings along the klongs, even the humblest ones. We then stopped at Wat Arun, the most important temple in Thailand outside of the royal complex. It is big and totally, completely, colorfully decorated, mostly with pieces of porcelain set into the walls. I mean, *really* decorated, hardly an inch left of plain old white plaster. Many of the porcelain pieces look like small, round, high-edged saucers, which seems curious. The whole thing reminds me, on a much grander scale, of the Watts Towers or some equivalent piece of peculiar American folk art, fabricated in a basement over thirty years by a slightly crazed postal worker. I don't really think that this is the temple of the ashtrays, but could Simon Rodia have made a side trip to Thailand?

The next day we go to see the obligatory Bangkok sights: the Golden Buddha, the Emerald Buddha, the Reclining Buddha, and the Grand Palace. The Reclining Buddha is big, actually quite big and, sure enough, reclining. This is the traditional position used when entering Nirvana. He is lying on his side and one notices that, upon entering Nirvana, several things happen: 1) your ankle bones disappear so you can put your feet on top of each other comfortably; 2) your butt and hips disappear; 3) gravity no longer affects your garments, since they stay conformed to the outline of your body even though you are lying on your side. Artistic license?

We visit the Grand Palace and Temple of the Emerald Buddha complex, which is again a symphony of gilt and color and epitomizes the "no square inch is too small to decorate" school of Thai temple and palace design, which I rather like—I mean, if you're the king, why not go for it? As we are about to get on our buses, we see that among the street vendors is a guy wearing a python and holding a sign that says, in hand-lettering, "100 baht" which is about $2.50. I'm confused—seems too cheap to be selling a snake, but it turns out this has to do with photographs. What this guy is proposing is that, if you pay him, he'll put the snake around *your neck* so pictures can be taken, documenting your insanity. I suggest to David that the real economic return comes when he charges 300 baht to take it off. Several in our party take leave of their senses and comply, only to find that the snake is interested in really wrapping itself around their necks. Well there's a surprise. I consider this to be an intelligence test: Would *you* pay someone to drape a very large snake around your neck? Would you let him do it if *he* paid *you*? What is the right answer to this question?

All parties, human and snake, survive, and the humans move on to the next activity which is shopping for souvenirs. I finally find a snow globe and a pen with a floating item in its clear plastic top (in this case an image of the Royal Barge floating down the river), but I am totally defeated in my quest for a "Thailand the Beautiful" coffee mug.

As noted above, Linda has organized a lovely final dinner for the whole group in the old section of the hotel. Every one cooperates by showing up, dressing nicely, and not saying "yuck" when the menu includes some Thai food. After dinner someone tells the teenagers that the trip is over, and they all break down and cry. Well, not Sam Powers, oldest son of Philip and Carol, who has taken to hanging around with the Hemphill side of the family, not because we're so attractive but so he doesn't have to be seen with his parents. We all know how embarrassing that can be! We are now referring to him as "the Teenager Formerly Known as Powers." Nobody makes any more bad jokes, a clear sign that it is time to go home. We get up at 4:00 the next morning, suffer a serious bout of luggage and check-in disorganization at the Bangkok airport, and finally board our (actually United's) 747 to fly back. Crossing the Pacific takes only 43½ days.

Love and kisses,
Bob

# twenty

# entrepreneurs say the darndest things, most of which are not true

August 2000

Dear Dad,

You asked about how things were going in the land of venture capital since last we talked. The short answer is "Well, but strangely." The long answer, as you might have expected, follows. You have only yourself to blame for asking.

Let's begin at the middle. What exactly is venture capital? Could it be: 1) an interesting way to while away those pesky work hours when you can't find anything gripping on the Internet and all your e-mail is either dull or else consists of messages suggesting you can make a million dollars in your spare time at home with no work at all, or refinance your house with a no-interest loan, or travel everywhere for free, or meet young ladies with interesting talents which they have been saving since birth just for *you*; 2) a good way to lose a lot of money; 3) a good way to become rich almost instantaneously as your Internet start-up goes public at sixteen and has its stock soar to three hundred even though it has no revenues and certainly no earnings, and is hemorrhaging money like Mrs. Marcos in the Neiman

Marcus shoe department; 4) a respectable form of investing small amounts of money in very young businesses that are just starting in hopes you have stumbled across Bill Gates and/or the next Yahoo; 5) a place where crazy people come up with business ideas so weird that it defies description, then press you to fund them. Well, yes, it is all of the above; I hope you didn't read ahead for the answer.

It used to be a small subset of the general realm of finance but sadly has become quite trendy in the last several years, due largely to number three above. All sorts of parvenus have venued into the business, including of course yours truly, without knowing the rules. Fortunately the rules turn out to be quite easy to learn, even if somewhat harder to apply. "Buy low, sell high." Here are the rules as best we can determine them:

**Rule One: Ten and five**. Any VC (standard abbreviation for venture capital—bet you could have figured that out—but for us old infantry officers of the Vietnam generation, the initials every so often elicit a bit of a twinge in the shoulder blades) investment should have a good chance of returning ten times your money in five years. And all business plans come with a set of projections about how well they plan to do, which prove just that. So, it's pretty easy except that . . .

**Rule Two: All business plans lie**. The entrepreneurs don't try to lie, it's just that everybody knows the rules, and besides they're making statements about the future, a devilishly difficult area in which to exercise the science of prediction. Predicting the past is much easier, although not entirely foolproof. Honesty compels me to point out that when we wrote the business plan for AES and ran around trying to get people to fund us, our plan was to build cogeneration plants using small efficient gas turbine technology, burning natural gas, selling mostly steam and a very small amount of electricity, and have these projects cost about $30 million each. Our first project used big, not-so-efficient down-fired boilers, burned dirty black petroleum coke not clean nifty natural gas, sold mostly electricity and very little steam, and cost $273 million. In fact, I don't think we ever, in the company's history, did a project that has come anywhere close to what we set out in the business plan. We did, however, *sell something to someone*. This is an important business principle, and one that not enough of the Internet businesses seem to have grasped.

**Rule Three: Bet on "A" people with "B" ideas, rather than "B" people with "A" ideas**. Said differently, it's the entrepreneur who makes the difference; don't fall in love with the technology. This rule immediately raises several questions: What happened to the "A" people with the "A" ideas? They probably go to big-time venture capitalists in Silicon Valley. All of us who don't live there and don't have offices on Sand Hill Road, the most famous VC location, feel a little jealous and inadequate, despite the fact that those guys are now opening up offices in northern Virginia, after all, and we have AOL and they don't.

This rule is also troublesome because frequently the technology is far more attractive than the entrepreneur and much easier to fall in love with. Academic studies confirm, in addition, that almost every start-up that grows to become a big and successful business has replaced/displaced one or two of its original founders in this process, the very people you were supposed to be betting on. Besides it's pretty easy to get a handle on the technology; it's not nearly so simple to figure out whether the human being sitting across from you at the meeting will be terrific once he or she has the money and it's six months later. This is another version of "But will you respect me in the morning?" We have at least been smart enough to add to our own subset of aphorisms, my favorite being the following: "This is the nicest they will ever be to you." This means that if the entrepreneur during the evaluation/negotiation period (read: "courtship") isn't respectful (fawning is even OK), doesn't promptly return your phone calls, fails to agree that your suggestions and insights into his business are brilliant, laughs only tepidly at your jokes, and never complements you on your hairstyle, then he or she darn sure won't after the funds have flowed. Or flown.

**Rule Four: Fashion rules**. Hard to admit, but like most realms of human endeavor, the herd determines much of what is done. The VC world is small, and clubby, and its members are remarkably prone to copy each other. The turnover in what is fashionable is, however, incredibly swift. Here's a recent chronology of what was/is hot, with the caveat that by the time you receive this letter something else will have moved into the top hot spot:

» Twelve months ago: online communities, where persons with a common interest (say, retired Air Force officers) would come together and do, uh, something, and thus you could make money by, uh, figuring out something to sell them or, uh, some way to charge them for, uh, something. Really, that was the business model, such as it was. Everyone Wanted To Be: 1) The Street.com, a financial web site for young New York swingers dressed largely in black, even though on the Internet no one knows you're wearing black. Stock currently (twelve long internet months later) at 5% of its fifty-two-week high. 2) iKimbo, a local firm whose idea was to host friends and relatives on a site through which they all could communicate with each other, just announced that it is instead now going to sell software to large businesses, calling this "an exciting new strategy." You may note that our family doesn't seem to have any trouble communicating via e-mail without the aid of a third-party website and thus wonder why any VC would have ever given these iKimbo guys money in the first place.

» Eleven months ago: "portals," how you would enter the Internet, as in the first site you would go to check your e-mail, read the news, be subjected to ads, etc. Everyone Wanted To Be: the next Yahoo. Few have been.

» Ten months ago: auction sites. Everyone Wanted To Be: the next eBay. With good reason. I have to interject this story from early last year. My friend John Hulka has a late teenage son named Evan. No, that sounded wrong; he's not dead, he's just an old teenager. Of course, if he's a teenager he's not really that old. Oh, forget it. Anyway, Evan is a smart and basically nice kid, although when he was eleven he and a friend hacked into the FBI computer system, which led the FBI to come visit John, expecting a major crime syndicate. They were surprised to find only an eleven year old but nevertheless received assurances that such activities would not reoccur. Recently John had set up a checking account for Evan, you know, to teach the kid a little about managing money, and he was reconciling the statement one evening when he noticed that Evan hadn't asked for his allowance for five months and was still running a four-figure balance in his account. Hmm.

About the same time his wife, Judy, comes back from the post office. She had gone to drop off a package, and during the process the clerk looked at her name and said, "Say, do you know Evan Hulka?"

"Well yes," says Judy, "he's my son."

"Gosh," says the PO worker, "he's one of our biggest customers; he's always in here shipping out something, or receiving a shipment." Armed with this pool of disconcerting information, with visions of "My Son the Drug Dealer" dancing in their heads, they confronted their seventeen year old. It turns out that what Evan is doing is this: he has found out that there is a big market for the old plastic LP albums of '70s-era rock bands. Every so often he goes over on the subway to Berkeley where there are lots of stores that have these, buys them at an average cost of $15, and then sells them on the Internet at eBay for an average of $30, net of shipping. He has customers as far away as Finland and Japan. His folks are much relieved to find this out, and quite surprised. When asked why he didn't tell them what he was doing, Evan replies that they were real busy and he didn't want to bother them. John tells me this story over a beer, we both laugh heartily, and then I say to him, "What's eBay?" Now I know.

» Eight months ago: consumer-facing Internet sites pursuing e-commerce, also known as B-to-C (business-to- consumer). Everyone Wanted To Be: the next Amazon. Many are now bankrupt, and Amazon has yet to actually turn a profit. Several start-ups talked about being "the Walmart of the Internet," and then Walmart heard about it and got mad and set up their own Internet site, proclaiming that Walmart was, in fact, going to be "the Walmart of the Internet." No one I know of has claimed that they want to be the Kmart of the Internet.

» Six months ago: B-to-B (business-to-business), mostly described as "vertical marketplaces" for businesses like the one set up by the three automakers to do all their purchasing and procurement online. Someone realized that, of all the transactions done in the economy, consumers do a couple of hundred billion, while businesses do three trillion. Everyone Wanted To Be: the next Chemdex, a site set up for buyers and sellers of research chemicals. Last year's revenues: about $76 million, losses $120 million, market value about $5.6 billion. Don't ask why, there is no answer.

» Four months ago: Back-end software to handle all the B-to-B sites being set up. At least that follows. Everyone Wanted To Be: Ariba or Commerce One or MicroStrategy. One such competitor, Cysive, just had to admit that it was losing $5 million in annual revenues from a client who ordered the services but couldn't pay, and as a result had its market value diminish from $4 billion to $2.7 billion. No, I didn't confuse the "m" key and the "b" key. Billion. MicroStrategy (a local company) rented out the Redskins stadium in late January for a Super Bowl party for its employees and guests, and then about a month later had to "restate revenues and earnings" for previous years, since it had become confused about just what counted as a "sale" of its software products. Confused in the direction of going ahead and counting things that really hadn't been sold. You shouldn't do this. One would, in fact, think that "sold" and "not sold" are sort of bimodal and hard to confuse. Its stock lost 95% of its value as it went in two months from $333 to $17.31.

» Two months ago: bioinformatics, the process of using clever computer programs to try and get something useful out of all the data that has come and is coming out of the human genome project. Everyone Wanted To Be: Compugen, a very smart bunch of Israelis who do this using mathematical algorithms (okay, that's redundant; I don't think there are any other kind of algorithms, but that's what everybody calls them). We actually tried to invest in them two years ago (Linda is good at this), but they wouldn't take our money. Much of the VC/entrepreneur dance does really resemble a courtship, and from both sides.

» Last month: optical networking. Somebody has to carry all these ones and zeroes around, and fiber does it better than anything else, so you need lots more fiber, and then you need switches to send those little photons to the right place so they can be converted back to ones and zeroes in your computer and finally into the confirmation of your order for a denim work shirt from L.L.Bean, a process you diligently pursued using the glories of e-commerce even though simply looking in the catalog and calling them up would have been about ten times quicker and one hundred times less aggravating. Plus the pictures are better and they "come right up" when you turn the page. Imagine that!

Statistical interjection: according to recent studies, 75% of the people who put things in their shopping cart when visiting an Internet site **never check out**. Try and imagine running a supermarket where that happened! Back to optical networking. Everyone Wanted To Be: Corvis or Yurie Systems.

» Today: Peer-to-peer computing, a confusing process that lets people share information that is on their hard drives without going through a central clearing server, the usual way that information is stored and made available on the Internet. Said to be more fault and hack resistant, but may have nefarious implications as well. At least I think that's what it is; us hicks on the East Coast only find out about this stuff by reading *Wired* and *Red Herring*, and *The Industry Standard*, tech magazines put out, of course, from San Francisco. Everyone Wanted To Be: Napster or Scour except not being sued by the record industry or the movie industry.

**Rule 5: Despite all your best efforts, seven out of ten of your investments will fail completely**. You will lose all your money and it will never make a collect call once in a while to say hello; it will just go away to wherever that land is that lost money goes to, and lie on the beach drinking fancy rum drinks garnished with little parasols and pieces of tropical fruit stuck on plastic toothpicks shaped like pirate swords. Thus the other three surviving investments have to do really well, or your overall returns will be no good and you will have to get an honest job. So far, we haven't experienced this, but we have had to sue one company, threaten to sue another, and resign in disgust from the board of a third. And the Honesty in Scorekeeping Act compels me to note that we have only made eight investments. On the other hand, we have had "exits" from two of those eight, and in both cases we made decent returns, in one case, extraordinary.

OK, that's it, now just add money and you too can be a venture capitalist!

Well, no maybe not just yet. You have to learn a few key words and phrases. All businesses have specialized language or jargon, and this one is no different. Fortunately it has fewer acronyms. The words that matter most or are most frequently thrown about are:

"Business plan." Simple enough, it's the key document every entrepreneur is supposed to prepare and that they use to convince people like us that we should give them our money. A good business plan has just about what you'd expect in it: an executive summary, and then some reasonably straightforward sections explaining things like just what you're going to do/make/provide, how big the market is for the idea/thing/service, how you will get people to buy it from you. This is known as "marketing" and as far as we can tell is the major weakness in almost all tech business plans. *Field of Dreams* thinking prevails: if you build it they will come. Not necessarily, it turns out. Killer phrase: "The product will sell itself."

The plan should also, at least in passing, touch on the competition. Way too often we see phrases like "there is no real competition for our [idea/thing/service]," and then we have to throw up. It makes you want to grab the author of these words by the lapels and scream dementedly at him or her: "Do you really think you're the only smart guy in the world, and that you and only you have recognized that there is an ENORMOUS unmet need for your idea/thing/service, and people will pay lots of money for this, and it's simple enough to make/build/create that you can do it, and it will make you and all your investors fabulously wealthy virtually overnight, and yet 'there is no real competition'?"

Dennis and I had a saying at AES that we were never more than two weeks ahead of anybody, and it was important to remember that and to act like that. Actually when we signed our contract for the Shady Point project in Oklahoma, the Oklahoma Gas and Electric guys remarked to us, "You all were the first folks to visit us and propose a cogeneration power plant, so we went with you, but right after your first visit some other guys showed up with the same idea."

"How soon after?" we asked.

"About ten days," was the response.

"Have to revise our internal guidelines," I said to Dennis. "It's not two weeks anymore."

But back to the business plan. At the back you have to have financial projections, and these projections have to show that, after a couple of years of building your business and spending and losing the money kindly provided to you by your investors, your revenues and earnings take off like a rocket. This logarithmic curve is known in the trade as the "hockey stick projection." Entrepreneurs spend a lot of time on these economic models, and VCs spend very little. We all do look at them to make sure that the supplicant knows he is supposed to have them, and that he can actually use Excel to do a spreadsheet, and that he knows there are such things as revenues, costs of doing business, and profits, but more than that we don't care. It's sort of a test, but passing it isn't dependent on the answer; it's a matter of showing that you understand the process.

One final comment: having a "business plan" is sort of like when we were financing movies; everybody had a screenplay. Now everyone you meet has a business plan, or has a friend who has a business plan, or is working on a business plan. This is very good for the paper industry. We receive probably fifty or sixty a month without even trying. We've made six investments in eighteen months. You can figure out the odds of us giving you money without even using Excel.

More jargon: "valuation." Is this even a word? Reminds me of my wholly unsuccessful crusade in the US Army to get people to stop "orientating" their maps and to simply "orient" them. It's not clear that as a second lieutenant in training I was ideally positioned to get twenty-five-year veteran highly decorated and generally grizzled master sergeants to understand the nicety of English usage herein envisaged, but I tried. For a while. My success rate was zero, and to this day anyone who has been in the military "orientates" his map when he tries to line it up in accordance with compass points. Drove me crazy. Same thing here. It actually means "value" but is used as "What is your pre-money valuation?" asked by VC of entrepreneur. It's an important question, of course, since the VC is basically being asked to buy some portion of the company that the entrepreneur has created and, as the creator, currently owns 100% of. It's really one of the oldest business questions in the world: Who puts in what, and who gets what? If you give the company $4 million, how much of the company do you own? If the answer is 50%, then the "pre-money" valuation was $4 million, and the "post-money" valuation was $8 million. Yes, I realize that it isn't logical that the company suddenly doubled in value overnight, but we're talking jargon and language here, not logic.

"Exit strategy." Another concept to drive one crazy. Required in all business plans, on the theory that no one is building a business that they want to keep or that they expect to be around for very long. Correct plan entry: "Our exit strategy is to do an IPO within three years or be purchased by a strategic investor." I have made my little speech so often that Linda now no longer lets me make it, but it goes like this: The worst thing the VC industry ever did for entrepreneurs is to invent exit strategy. If you focus on building a good business that delivers value to customers and to owners, you won't have to worry about an exit strategy. Just work on the building part, it's hard enough; forget about the leaving part.

Now that you are fully schooled, why would you want to be a venture capitalist? Actually the best part of it is you get to deal with a wealth of interesting new ideas, and you get to meet, on a routine basis, some very smart and creative people, and some who should be institutionalized. In either mental institutions or prisons. What other business gives one such opportunities and such happiness?

Here are some of our favorite stories from this interesting and slightly off-kilter land:

» A friend of ours runs a fund for Lazard Frères, the snooty Wall Street investment bank most famous for having had Felix Rohatyn as a partner. The fund focuses on computer technology, Internet stuff, software, and the like, much the same as we do, and as just about everyone in the VC business does today. They picked him because he came up with the idea; he actually used to run a software company that he had sold for an interesting amount of money, and he was willing to put in some of his own money into the fund. Why he picked them is less clear. His irreverent daughter insists on referring to them as the Lizard Brothers, so you can see that she is not as awed by white-shoe investment bankers as she should be and probably gets this irreverence from her father. He says that despite their fancy pedigree, they have yet to bring the fund a single investable deal.

He was in New York for the weekly fund meeting, and the LF guys were all excited; one of their clients from another part of the firm, real estate development it turns out, had a surefire computer guy with the Next Great Idea. So they all gather in this lovely thirty-seventh-floor conference room on Wall Street, views out over the water including the Statue of Liberty or maybe the Brooklyn Bridge, and they listen to "the pitch." First the real estate developers, two middle-aged big-waisted white guys from Atlanta named Jake and Gus, explain how they've been doing real estate for thirty years in the south but it's hard; you actually have to buy land, and come up with construction plans, and apply for and get permits, and come up with financing, and then actually build the buildings, and make sure they have tenants, and make sure the tenants pay the rent, and make sure nothing in the building breaks, and all this takes lots of time and energy. So they got to thinking and they decided that software was a much better idea: write it once, sell it a million times, and look at Bill Gates anyway, he didn't even finish Harvard. Neither had Jake or Gus, so they had a lot in common. They looked around and found a wonderful guy, a wonderful software opportunity, and here he was!

Attention shifts to the third guy in the room from Georgia, who is actually either a nerd by his very nature, or has carefully studied and mastered the stereotype. He is, in fact, wearing a short-sleeved white shirt, has a flat top but not the trendy kind, no mousse, and black glasses, but no pocket protector, and a not very good but not very expensive brown plaid sport coat and a poorly tied cheap tie.

"We found ol' Jerry here," Gus says. "He's a software expert, and what he's done, you all are gonna find just as amazin' as we did, and we're sure you're gonna agree with us that this is the software idea of the decade! We been backing him with our own money, but now he's ready for the big time, which was why we decided to come to New York. Go on, just tell 'em, Jerry."

So Jerry blinks twice, looks around owlishly, and begins in a high monotone. "In 1994 I was sitting at my computer and I said to myself, 'Microsoft Office sucks!' so I rewrote it. In seventy lines of code."

Pause, the guys from Atlanta look at the guys from the Lizard Brothers, muttering, "How 'bout that!" and nodding.

Jerry continues: "In 1996 I was sitting working at my computer and

I said to myself, 'Windows sucks!' so I rewrote it. In one hundred lines of code."

Editorial pause: Windows 95 isn't nearly as good as it should be; everybody on earth except Bill Gates and three other people at Microsoft agrees with that. It also, as a program, requires about forty floppy disks to back up and thus one presumes is somewhere in the 10 to 20 million, yes, *million* lines of code in size.

After this second proclamation by Jerry the software genius, the Lizard Brothers guys sit silent and unmoving, waiting, like all investment bankers, to take their lead from someone who actually knows something. The two real estate guys, mistaking silence for approbation, say happily, "Well how about that? Isn't that something? We thought you guys would be impressed and want to invest with us in this new company Jerry is talking about forming. We're real excited . . ."

Our friend is dumbfounded, as it occurs to him that he is the only person in the room, including all the successful real estate talent from Atlanta and the expensively dressed bankers from New York, who has actually ever written a line of code, knows what a line of code is (How long is one line, you ask? Is there some standard? Is it so many characters? Beats me.), or possibly has ever read any even semi-technical magazine about the computer software business. He is also obviously the only person in the room who knows that programmers routinely write programs with hundreds of thousands of lines of code in them, and that large and complex programs like Windows and Microsoft Office are made up of lots and lots and lots of lines of code. He turns to the Atlantans and thinks about saying, "This guy is either a fraud or severely delusional or both" but doesn't. Instead he says, softly, something like, "It's a remarkable accomplishment, but it doesn't sound like it meets the profile of investments that we're looking for."

And the best part is that after the real estate people leave, the LF guys want to know just how he could be so sure that there wasn't something interesting and even worth pursuing here. "Maybe we should have asked for a demo," suggests one.

Our friend says that what he really thought was that one of his partners at the fund had hired these guys as a joke, and that they were actors or something. Marvelously, they were not. Ah, the fun never ends. And you thought that only novelists, and short story writers, and schizophrenics had interesting and creative ideas. Our friend now refuses to go to any meetings the Lizards set up. With reason.

» Another friend is a typical but skilled Washington person who makes a nice living getting government grants and contracts for small and deserving and undeserving clients, most of whom have some sort of new or different technology to offer. These aren't exactly the Lockheeds or the General Dynamics of the world. He referred one to us, because he knew we were interested in the telecom area.

His client had a system for using the electric lines to carry telephone signals, an idea that is not in itself either foolish or contrary to the principles of physics. In fact, a number of people have tried various ways to accomplish this, but it's tough to do in practice, because the electric signal is strong, it can't be interfered with, and when the voltage is changed to a higher or lower level as the power goes through a transformer, as it does frequently in all electric systems, the telephone signals riding along on the same wire get wiped out. These guys, however, claimed to be using the magnetic field surrounding the electric lines for their phone signals.

Equally interesting, they had recruited Henry Kissinger and Bob Livingston (former Congressman from Louisiana who was Speaker of the House for about thirty minutes until he joined the ranks of the "undone by an undone zipper" politicians) to serve on their board of directors. But after that it kept getting weirder and weirder.

Item: They were located in Dallas and it was difficult for us to schedule a trip there because they were so busy; they explained that they were working hard filling out the Nobel Prize application for their chief scientist, Luke Smith. Your irreverent son soon came to refer to this guy as Luke Skywalker. Now if you've ever been nominated for or won the Nobel Prize, or have lived in the last half of the twentieth century and ever read a newspaper, you probably know that, in fact, the Nobel committee doesn't really need help in finding prizewinners, and there is not a nomination process, and there is no such a thing as an application. You can't call them up and have them send you one. You can't get one off their website.

Item: They needed $14 million to demonstrate the technology and couldn't demonstrate it in the lab—it had to be a full-scale demonstration on an electric utility system, and they were negotiating with several, including one in Great Britain. Why just exactly $14 million, you may ask? And why in the world couldn't you demonstrate this in the lab? That's what good old Alexander Graham Bell did with the first phone system. We could never get a straight answer to these questions, just more invitations to come to Dallas, after the Nobel Prize nomination form was completed.

Item: When asked about distance limitations on this technology, such as whether you would have to amplify the signal after a certain distance (a characteristic of almost all telephone technologies, for obvious reasons: signals weaken over distance due to resistance in the carrying medium, even light moving through glass), they said no. When pressed, they had only gibberish as an explanation, something about magnetic fields not weakening over distance. If this were true, no iron filing would be safe.

Item: we asked about overseas transmissions. There are no undersea electric cables from here to Europe, for example, or to the Far East, only undersea telephone cables, so their system was clearly only applicable domestically. They suggested that their system was so good that it didn't even really need the electric cables and the associated magnetic field to send the telephone signals. "Goodness," I said, "so you could communicate with Japan right now if your system were perfected, and you wouldn't need wires of any sort?" Yes, they said. When further questioned, they said something about the earth's magnetic field.

Item: They were selling "units" of ownership to anybody who wanted to give them money. Given that they are not a public company, such sales are supposed to be limited to what the SEC defines as "qualified investors," usually high net worth individuals who might be expected to know better. But never mind those pesky securities laws, they're just standing in the way of us pioneering technologists.

The planets didn't seem to be aligned just right on this one, but we sent off our smartest technologist and a telecom consultant to meet with Luke Skywalker and get the firsthand explanation. Before they went, Linda and

I sat our guys down in our conference room and presented them with nice little beanies we had fashioned out of aluminum foil, with pieces of coat hanger sticking out of the top. These are two pretty straight guys, one of whom is even German, and they looked a bit baffled. "Take these with you," we said, "and if this whole thing is a unuseful as we fear, when you get to the meeting with Luke and Han Solo, put them on. When they ask what you're doing, just explain that you wanted to be able to have your colleagues in Washington participate in the meeting via brain waves . . ."

Sadly, I don't think that they actually did this, but they did report back that the whole thing was scientifically nonsensical. I take a bit of solace in the fact I found out later—from someone at a telecom conference—is that Cisco Systems, the world leader in network communication and the most valuable company in the world—passed Microsoft a couple of months ago—had also sent someone to Dallas to talk with these guys and had also concluded (whew!) that they were chowderheads and frauds. What happens to Dr. Kissinger and former Speaker Livingston when this whole thing blows up, I know not. Maybe they should be more careful about what boards they join.

We didn't need a scientist to help us turn these down:

» A Hungarian scientist, and we use the second term loosely (he probably was Hungarian), had set up in his bedroom a special fast battery charger, but during the discussion thereof explained that he couldn't explain to us how it worked because it was a new principle of physics he had discovered, and principles of physics can't be patented, and so he was afraid we would steal his idea, even though we volunteered to sign a nondisclosure, noncompetition agreement valid in six languages and immediately at the World Court at the Hague. Instead of trying to understand it all, he was clear that we should just give him the money. It was when he next divulged that he could make electricity flow using only one wire (i.e., not a complete circuit) that I told him we had to see a man about a dog and besides I thought I heard my mother calling.

» An entrepreneur with a company called Tecore who had just secured the franchise to sell prepaid phone cards in Sierra Leone. Presumably he would sell them to UN peacekeeping forces about to be taken hostage by one of the many and wonderfully named militias or gangs of thugs in that country, like "West Side Boys"—did they get that from Leonard Bernstein and Steven Sondheim? It was not clear from whom this franchise had been secured, nor by what phone network these calls would be carried, Sierra Leone being a country now where nothing at all works and didn't work really well before all the recent disintegration. Of course, if someone bought the card but then couldn't find a phone to use it on, the entrepreneur still got to keep the money. Seemed unlikely there would be much repeat business, however. Eventually the UN guys will stop being taken hostage.

» A Chinese proposal for growing lawn on the walls of houses, buildings, and apartments. The inside walls. I am not making this up; we have an Internet site that claims we have venture capital available, and we get stuff from everywhere. The beauty and the terror of the Internet. Helpful excerpts from the business plan follow:

Self-recommendation of project: As you can imagine, how does it profit you if you find the well-trimmed lawn wall designed by grass and flowers in your scriptorium, office, or in the drawing room of your apartment?

I myself have always wanted a scriptorium. There comes later a discussion of the economics of this idea:

*Going on the market potential of enterprise is big, and period is short: Based on the product in enterprise is very unique, and the market resources to the huge market of the whole world own being that monopolizes and long-term, and the product profit is clear and definite, and the so huge market needs a large number of fund. I would like to melt money in order to go on the market to give up even more share."*

We were unable to fund this unique idea because we already had more than enough US entrepreneurs who had huge markets that needed a "large number of fund," and who were undoubtedly going to melt money once they got it. They just weren't as honest about it.

» Kids say the darndest things, and so do entrepreneurs looking for funding. We were in discussions with a guy who seemed to have an interesting idea for speeding up the Internet, so we asked him for a list of references for him and his colleagues. This is a routine request, as you can understand. We don't usually know these people from Adam, so we try and find out whether they will at least make a good faith effort while they're losing all the money. The reference list came back, and for the CEO the list included, in this order, a lawyer, an accountant, a banker, and a fourth entry that read: "William Jefferson Clinton, President of the United States—he is a big fan of [the CEO's] work and writings. He can be contacted at the White House, Washington, D.C." We thought about it, then decided that maybe this management team had egos that were too big for our modest investment to satisfy.

But it's not all work. Last week as I was perusing the *Montgomery County Gazette*, source of much inspiration, I noticed a story on the upcoming County Agricultural (is there any other kind?) Fair, wherein, among the sheep shearings and pie judgings and the like, our local electric utility, Pepco, was sponsoring an Amateur Cheese Carving Contest. It was noted that a Professional Cheese Carver would be there as well. How could one resist this? Is there really a cheese carving profession? Electric utilities and cheese—always a winning combination! Maybe they were using electric knives. So off I went.

Now the fair is, in fact, held at a fairground with barns, and big exhibition buildings, and even a track where that evening a demolition derby was to be held. At one time I'm sure this was out in the middle of open land, but now as Montgomery County is the tenth richest county in the nation, the real estate has developed somewhat. The fairground has as its neighbors an interstate highway, a Borders bookstore, a Hilton hotel, and a CompUSA computer store. Ah, modern commercial America! I went to the cheese carving undeterred by this evidence of encroaching civilization. Many people were at the fair, most of them wearing jeans, dragging their children around, and talking on cell phones. At the cheese carving the contestants were well underway. But they were working with not very big pieces of cheese, like about the size of two of those blocks of cheddar you'd buy at the Safeway. Pepco, this deregulation stuff has made you too cheap! The contestants carved the following items:

» A milk carton (this contestant had white cheddar, which no doubt inspired him, since everyone else had orange). The square chunky thing had "Milk" carved into its side so you could be sure of what it was.

» A horse, except made of all right angles—maybe a miniature replica of the Trojan horse, except I don't remember cheese playing much of a part in the story.

» A tree or maybe a squarish lollipop, colored orange.

» A house, with a bent paper clip coming out of the middle of the chimney and meant to be, despite this technically inaccurate placement, a TV antenna rather than a wisp of smoke. It seemed unfair to be able to add adornments to the cheese.

» An owl. Squarish. Or perhaps a hawk or a very sick orangutan with no arms.

» A lighthouse, off-center and blocky. Or else a bowling pin. Or maybe a replica of a Coke bottle. Hard to tell. Didn't win a prize.

The prizewinner: a bag of feed, looking very much like a bar of soap but with "FEED" carved diagonally down its front. Not quite as square as everything else. And besides it was an agricultural fair. I wandered off to have a corn dog, but not a cheeseburger, and call the office on my cell phone.

You can tell that the Internet has conquered when you hear your first country music song about it. Yes, there is one; it's called "American Offline" by a singer named Tony Stampley, brother of Joe Stampley, a medium-successful country singer. Lyrics are something about how the singer is NOT in fact interconnected, online, doesn't have a computer, or a pager, or a cell phone, or at least doesn't take it to the county fair. It's a terrific song. I just bought a copy of the album at Amazon.com. Couldn't find it anywhere except on the Internet.

Love and kisses,
Bob

# twenty-one

# in my next life i plan to be the schnitzel king

September 2000

Dear Dad,

"Once every ten years they put on the Passion Play at Oberammergau," she said, "and this is the year, so I think we better go. I'm working on tickets, even though we're really, really too late but we have this new travel agent named Rudi who's supposed to be terrific according to *Condé Nast Traveler* magazine, and he says we can pull it off, and also we should at the same time, well no, not exactly at the same time, obviously, go to Oktoberfest, which as everyone knows actually is in September. And it's in Munich, so it's quite close to ole bare amber cow, only we'll be staying in garnish parting curtain so we can go to the Disneyland castle. Only it's the original one. Of course you have to go to tee ball easy at the same time, but you can probably just fly down there and fly back and not miss much, maybe just the ride up the zoog spits."

"Are you speaking English?" he asked idly.

"Yes, of course, pay attention."

"OK, I am. Really. Um, this play thing, it's in German right?"

"Of course it's in German, it's in Germany. They speak German there."

"And how long is it?"

"Eight hours."

"OK, so we're going to somewhere in Germany?"

"We're going to Bavaria in southern Germany."

"So, on the spur of the moment, we're going to somewhere in southern Germany for a week to watch an eight-hour play in German, which blessedly is only put on once every ten years? Even though at the moment we are trying to sell one company, sell the stock we got from selling another company, sell two houses, design and build one house in Utah on an accelerated insane timetable, start our own telephone company in Utah, hire two new administrative assistants, complete the lease for new office space, design it, get it constructed, and move into it, publish a book of our war letters, and redesign and reconstruct the front and back of our house in Potomac. Oh, and finish our taxes for this year." He paused, thoughtfully.

"That's right," she said, "but we're always trying to hire an administrative assistant. Anyway, we'll be taking five adults and three kids under seven along with us—my parents, Brad and Kelley and their two kids, Erin and Colin, and Rich and Elika and Leo," she added helpfully.

"And the reason we want to do this . . ." he faded away.

"Easy," she said, "three words: beer, sausages, and Wiener schnitzel."

"I'm there," he said. He knew Wiener schnitzel was probably two words, but it hardly seemed politic to point it out.

———

There'll always be a France (whether we like it or not). Item one: On Friday night, the 11th, we flew Air France over from Dulles—me, Linda, Elika, and Leo. Flight left at 7:00, so Elika showed up really early like they threaten you to: "Please be sure to arrive at the airport two days and seventeen hours in advance of your flight time because due to additional security measures, surly airport check-in agents, obscenely crowded airports, a complete lack of parking, bad weather up and down the East Coast of every continent including Antarctica, no luggage carts complimented by no red caps, security machines set off by the credit cards in your wallet although not by folding stock AK-47s, a two-bag carry-on limitation imposed on you but not on any of the other passengers, the mandatory use or the prohibition of e-tickets—whichever is less convenient—and a general crisis of confidence in the industry, check-in and boarding procedures may take longer than usual."

Once Elika and the kid got checked in there wasn't a lot to keep a pleasant but spectacularly energetic almost-three-year-old occupied except feed him. Airport cuisine being what it is—and what it is, is standard US fast-food-type cuisine (there are not so many Michelin one-star restaurants at airports). I find this is so probably because that guy all made out of tires can't get through security to test the food, because he's wearing nothing but steel-belted radials, but at least, unlike Firestones, your tires don't fly apart while you're driving down the road in your Ford Explorer, making you flip over several times and thus also causing the Concorde to crash on the road into Paris.

So they had a couple of cheeseburgers. Immediately upon boarding the plane they were given fancy menus, mostly in French but with a grudging English translation. After an hour the steward came around to serve dinner, but Elika suggested politely that they weren't hungry. Actually she made the tactical error of admitting that they had had cheeseburgers at the airport. Said of course in that charming open-faced American midwestern way, not exactly apologizing but rather sympathetically explaining. Bad plan: the French flight stewards were all quite exercised. "But Madame, did you not know that we would be serving *Air France cuisine* on the flight [emphasis not added by me]?" Think about that question for a moment. We were expecting maybe Delta, or Alitalia, or Dragonair cuisine? Maybe the caterers got confused? Like the stuff is any different? Shucks, next time I'm on that Southwest flight from Baltimore to Cleveland I'll just order me up a little Air France cuisine instead of that nice little bag of peanuts they give me to go along with my one third of a can of Diet Coke.

There'll always be a France, unfortunately, item two: when you are flying all night to Paris from D.C. on an airplane, a very active little boy is more than a handful, and when he finally gives up and goes to sleep, so can you. When they turn all the cabin lights on suddenly, to full bright, a mere forty-five minutes later although we are still two and a half hours from landing, just so they can bring around breakfast, it's a bit off-putting. Elika explained that she really wanted the kid to sleep, but the various French stewards came by and asked her at least three times, noisily, if she didn't want breakfast for Leo. At the third decline, the chief steward came over and, in the spirit of French cultural superiority, said, "But Madame, it is a *croissant* [emphasis again not added]." True story.

TABA France, no matter if we don't think it makes sense, item three: Although we were going to Germany, a country where all the words are too long, not just the place names, we were on Air France because the only nonstop flights to Munich are on United, and they have been having their share of French-like behavior on the part of their pilots. But this meant that we had to change in Pairs. Ah, Paree, the Eiffel Tower, the Champs-Élysées, the charming accents, the air of harsh unfiltered tobacco . . .try instead Charles de Gaulle terminal number two, which I personally believe is the great man's revenge on all persons non-French (and thus by definition subhuman). Never mind landing at terminal one (the original doughnut-shaped number, quite an architectural statement in its day but a tad seedy now) and trying to get over to number two—this feat is technically impossible. You have to go into Paris first. Instead remember that a) terminal two is in two parts, distinct and separate (no, I don't know why they didn't call it number 2 and number 3 like the Brits did at Heathrow— may has something to do with cultural honesty); and b) no one will tell you this beforehand. Furthermore, it is illegal under the Code Napoléon for any flight that comes from anywhere outside of France (including by definition former French colonies still garrisoned by French troops) to connect to a flight in the same terminal. Sorry, if we make an exception for you, we have to make one for everyone. Remember also that you check in (*enregistrement*) at a desk with a *number*, eight in our case, but you then board at a gate with a *different number*. Emphasis added. And the check-in desk numbers appear to bear no relation as to geographic placement compared to the gate numbers. Maybe this is Cartesian logic, no one knows except Jean-Paul Sartre, and he took the secret with him to his grave.

Most important, you must always keep firmly in mind that some group of essential workers is always on strike in France for some irrational reason whenever you want to go there, and the group, no matter what it is, always manages to screw up 1) air transportation, and 2) Parisian taxis. Doesn't matter who's on strike—beet farmers, casino dealers, Marseilles dockworkers, fish gutters on the Loire, hairdressers from Lyon, lycée students—the planes and taxis are screwed up. In our case, after finding terminal 2D, having landed at 2C (Hah! You think they are close just because the numbers so indicate! Foolish American!), and checking in at the aforementioned desk eight, and going to the requisite Gate #55, located somewhat near check-in Desk eight for no knowable reason, we then found that: a) the flight was delayed, no time given for estimated departure, and no explanation available as to cause of delay; b) suddenly it was not delayed but we had to immediately and very quickly board onto some buses sitting on the tarmac (this is the largest, newest, and most modern airport in France); c) once we were all crammed on the buses we sat or rather stood there sweltering for, no kidding, thirty minutes while the bus moved not at all. I began to have visions of the cattle cars taking prisoners to the camps. Only they moved faster. And d) Once the buses finally moved, they drove us around for a while and then let us off at some stairs which took us *back up* to the midpoint of a walkway that connected with both the plane and the terminal. The careful reader will note that it does not seem essential to take a bus to such an interim destination, that one could, in fact, walk from the terminal across the walkway and into the plane, as happens in most Western and many non-Western countries. Hmm, yes. To make up for this annoying and peculiar behavior, when we all landed in Munich we discovered that four of our fifteen bags had not made it on the delayed flight. It was explained that this was due to the fuel strike. Since the bags weren't carrying fuel, this seemed unlikely.

OK, we're here in Garmisch-Partenkirchen (garnish parting curtain was close) and it's quite lovely and mountainous with valleys, and green pastures, and white houses with brown roofs, and flower boxes everywhere with cascades of red and pink geraniums flowing from them. It looks exactly like it is supposed to look! And men walking around in lederhosen (as you probably know, strange inflexible leather shorts—why one would choose this as a clothing item for any purpose, let alone strenuous hiking, cannot be determined), and some of the women in dirndls—very nice indeed. Add to this lovely bright early fall weather, low 70s and no humidity, and you can certainly see why you would want to sit on uncomfortable chairs inside an auditorium for eight hours with nothing to eat or drink.

What can one say about the Oberammergau passion play?

1) It is, in fact, in German, but they have little books you can buy that give you the English text, so you can try to read and watch the play at the same time. Sort of reminded me of when we first went to Japan and you decided for acculturation purposes that we needed to attend a performance of the Kabuki opera—six hours, all in Japanese, with a short confusing synopsis of the action so you could "follow" what was happening: "Prince Nishita sends his two faithful retainers to the castle of Lord Kurito to recover the bride of his sister. During their journey they stop to drink wine and are accosted by Ronin and imprisoned in a secret cave, where the ground spirits are summoned to aid their escape. Many years later the shogun's mother cries mournfully over the castle wall as cherry blossoms decorate." Except during the Kabuki performance it was okay to get up and get things to eat, chat politely with your neighbors, drop peanut shells on the floor, etc. Not so here—pretty serious. Also no pictures allowed and aisle patrols for enforcement. Vaguely reminiscent of detention in high school.

2) It's held in a large auditorium that resembles a giant Quonset hut, but the stage is open to the air and you can see the mountains in the background above it. The building is quite nice and large but doesn't have enough bathrooms. Especially, as usual, women's bathrooms.

3) The play actually only takes six and a half hours, and is split by a three-hour lunch break. Lunch breaks are good.

4) Some parts of it are very theatrical—sheep and goats and horses on stage as well as the occasional pigeon but no cows, and tons of people. The cast numbers over five hundred humans, livestock not listed separately. To be eligible to perform there are strict rules: you must either have been born in OAG (the German town, not the airline guide) or have been a resident for at least twenty years. The qualifications for the sheep and goats were

not discussed.

5) The audience is predominantly very elderly, and two people have to be carried out during the performance, perhaps to heaven.

6) The tickets cost $75 and you have to get them several years ahead of time unless you have our terrific agent.

7) There are no surprising plot twists. Our Jesus does look like Dennis Miller and is pretty mad all the time, or maybe that's just how German regularly sounds.

We actually have two day's worth of tickets, but after it's over everyone decides that seeing it again the next day is probably not activity choice number one. We did get to have beer and sausages for dinner though— Erin got a frankfurter platter that had four foot-long hot dogs on it. There are some very good things about Germany.

Monday is angel and other religious figure wood carving viewing and buying day, a craft for which the town is noted and an activity for which the tourists are noted. You have to do something in between plays. In the various small shops you can actually get: two different passion play coffee mugs, three different passion play T-shirts including one where the image of Jesus looks like the Shroud of Turin, a passion play key chain, a passion play baseball cap, and a passion play small plastic TV slide viewer sort of thing. Most important, I am happy to report, you can acquire a passion play snow globe complete with cross being dragged up Golgotha.

The more serious members of the group were focusing on the wood carvings, which was full-time work. One may purchase, conservatively, five billion wooden carved religious figures in OAG, and they will ship. Alternatively, you can just look at each one. Which we did. My personal favorite was the cherub wearing a Tyrolean hat and carrying a rifle. And you thought cherubs were universally cute and cuddly—not this kid. Linda liked a large and elaborate nativity scene, one among many hundreds that we saw. This one was exquisitely carved and beautifully displayed in a shop window; the tableau included three shepherds, four or five sheep, a cow, the holy family, a donkey hanging over the manger (looked to me like he was trying to lick the baby Jesus but I was scolded for this observation), the three wise men, a camel, and an elephant (third wise man probably took a cab), and standing in the back corner of the manger scene a guy playing the bagpipes. "Amazing Grace" or maybe "Silent Night," you couldn't tell from the carving. After a while all the crèches began to affect my mind, and Elika's as well, and so:

What is the favorite breakfast food of nativity carvers in OAG? Crèche-sants

What is their favorite soft drink? Orange crèche

Which tool do they use most often for making home repairs? Crèche-sent wrench

What is their favorite five-and-ten cent store? Crèche-ge's

Favorite alternative rock group? Crèche Test Dummies

Favorite throat lozenge? Su-crèches

Favorite church supper dish? Tuna crèche-erole

———

Linda finally made us shut up by taking us out to dinner and plying us with beer and Wiener schnitzel. But still our minds churned:

Favorite fried cutlet of post WWI Germany? Weimar schnitzel

Favorite fried cutlet of Olympic champion, 1936 games? Winner schnitzel

FFC of disqualified-on-a-technicality Olympic games competitor, 1936 games? Whiner schnitzel

FFC of disqualified-on-a-technicality Australian competitor, 1936 Olympic games? Whinger schnitzel

FFC of Weight Watchers program? Leaner schnitzel

Yuppie FFC? Beamer schnitzel

FFC of movie star, former wife of senator from Nebraska? Debra Winger schnitzel

My personal favorite: FFC of Steve Case, chairman of AOL? Time-Warner schnitzel

Perhaps there's a twelve-step program for this.

Because I had already committed to my AES board colleagues to be their representative, on Tuesday I flew from Munich to Tbilisi (which is not really pronounced *tee-ball-easy*, but close) in Georgia (the country not the state) via Vienna (the city in Austria not the sausages in small cans) to attend an AES conference, this one a gathering of representatives of all our electric distribution systems from around the world—of which there are, at last count, one in the US, four in Brazil, one in Venezuela, three in Argentina, two in El Salvador, one in the Dominican Republic, one in Tbilisi (our host), one in India, and two in Kazakhstan. This probably represents 40 million people depending on us for electricity, and a somewhat smaller number who actually pay for it. Ah, the challenges of third world businesses!

Getting to Tbilisi, should you be so inclined, ain't easy. There could be a whole talking blues song here, the name is so great—"Airline that you fly (take your pick, Air Georgia or Air Ukraine—some choice), gonna make you queasy, flyin' on down to Tbilisi. Food they serve, kinda greasy, down home in Tbilisi. Police boys check your passport, make you uneasy, come on in, meetin's in Tbilisi, etc." Or maybe: "Gonna look aroun', see if I can be a VC, lots of good start up high-tech businesses here in Tbilisi"—no wait, I've gone too far. Some other candidate rhymes would be more of a stretch but have possibilities. Candidates include: strip-teze (long "e"), Sneezy and Wheezy (two of the Seven Dwarfs), and Lumbeze (river in Africa—very hard to make logical connection). Oh, to be musically inclined.

Flights in Europe were screwed up ("thunderstorms all up and down the east coast of Europe have resulted in substantial delays to airline service—no, wait, Europe doesn't have an east coast, that's Russia over there . . .") and flights to what probably isn't called "The Small Easy" are limited—one or two days a week. Details aren't interesting. Geography lesson—Georgia (the country not the state) is the next country north of Turkey, has Russia directly to its north (Chechnya, actually, what a terrific neighbor) and Azerbaijan directly to the east. West is the Black Sea. We never had to study this geography in school because it was all just the USSR. Different now and better politically, but getting better economically only slowly.

I got here in time to go out for the welcoming dinner, a Georgian tradition called a supra. You may remember that I had already been through this ritual before, so I should have been prepared. But I couldn't figure out how to get out of it. This one had mixed food, not so very good wine; name tags hadn't yet been handed out and no one there really knew the other folks so conversation was stilted, but since there was a four-piece singing group whose principal characteristic was earsplitting volume, it probably didn't matter anyway. At one point they sang a "native Georgian" song that had a refrain something like, "The moon is glorious over the river tonight, my love, but sadly I must leave you to increase production of pig iron at the steel plant." This was a Khrushchev-era song—he had an extremely big steel plant built right outside of town, employed fifty thousand people, for which he also had built an entire new town of those awful apartment blocks. I drove past both on the way to see one of our plants—makes Pittsburgh look like the minors, it's incredible. Steel mill is now entirely shut down, although most folks still show up for "work" but don't get paid anything except about $4/month. More evidence, if any were needed, that the Soviet system didn't really work that well. But I digress.

Next song was Russian, and since a bilingual Kazakh woman was sitting next to me, as well as one of our guys who speaks Russian, I believe I was receiving an accurate translation. The song went: "My love, you are as beautiful as a totally uninhabited desert island. Many ships have sunk trying to get to you. Therefore I want you, my darling." There's just no explaining, guys. The singing group followed up with a rousing and high-volume rendition of "Volare." Is nowhere safe? At least they didn't do "My Way."

Most of the conference was unremarkable, although interesting if you're interested in this sort of thing. Thursday morning we had some free time so I went out to visit our new plant, recently acquired from the government of Georgia (the country, etc.) for $10 million. It's an 860 MW two unit, gas-fired plant in the usual horrible state of repair, coupled with unbelievable overstaffing, and they threw in 120 MW of hydro plants just to sweeten the deal. Just to help you calibrate, to build a new power plant costs about $400/kW (gas plants) or $1,500-2,500/kW for hydro plants. Thus the replacement cost of these two plants would be about $584 million, fifty-eight times what we paid. We were the high bidder.

The plant is a mess, as would any sophisticated electrical/mechanical system be that, while running full out, had had no money for spare parts or maintenance for ten years, a screwed up way to manage people, inadequate training, and crummy or more recently, no salaries. Roof leaks, water-treating system was shot. For three months they ran raw river water through the boilers and turbines, because they had no money for water-treating chemicals. This is the equivalent of trying to run raw crude oil mixed with drilling mud and water through a gasoline engine. It's amazing that it ran at all, but this is pretty sturdy Russian equipment. Now that we are in charge, things are getting fixed, painted, cleaned up, trash and junk thrown away, etc., but it's going to be a long process. I talked to one of our guys who works at a plant in Indiana and volunteered to come over here and help for three months. A good, solid midwestern guy, maintenance background, never been outside the US before.

"I learned more, and I grew up more in the last three weeks here than I did in the first forty-five years of my life back in the US," he said. It's amazing and reassuring what some of our folks can do, and even more amazing what they're willing to attempt. And not just the Americans. There are guys at the plant helping out from AES facilities in Hungary, Northern Ireland, and Kazakhstan—anywhere we've had plants long enough for the culture to take hold. It's pretty neat. And incredibly hard work.

The conference ended on Friday and I flew back to Munich on Austrian Airlines, once again through Vienna. To give credit where due, on both the trip down and the trip back, due to delayed takeoffs, I had no more than twenty-five to thirty-five minutes to connect, and both times the airline managed to get the luggage on the proper plane. Actually I wasn't sure in either case that I was going to get *me* on the proper plane, and as they only fly to/from Tbilisi twice a week, fixing lost luggage would have been hard. Those Austrians are good at schnitzel and baggage handling. These national skills are not fully acknowledged—well the schnitzel is, but not the luggage. Probably has something to do with walking around in leather pants and yodeling all the time.

Saturday was the start of Oktoberfest in Munich, which opens at noon with the mayor hitting an unoffending beer keg with a hammer and uttering the poetic "O'zapft is!" which means, "It's open." Closest analogy

in terms of US poesy is at the racetrack—"they're off." How can you dupli-
cate the experience of going to an Oktoberfest beer tent in your own home,
you ask? Easily. First select a room with no air circulation, sized to hold six
persons. Close all the doors, board up the windows if any, set up a boom
box playing tuba music in German (including that old Teutonic favorite,
"Country Roads"—John Denver, if you only knew!), turn the volume up
REALLY LOUD, cram two picnic tables inside placed so closely together
that none of the benches are movable and anyone sitting on one is poking
the person behind him with his elbows, and heat the room to eighty-five
degrees even though it's cold and raining outside. Invite twenty-three
friends, tightly squeeze them into the room, have each of them smoke
eleven cigarettes in fourteen minutes while drinking a lot of beer and
hoarsely singing along with the stereo, and give yourself a triple dose of a
powerful laxative. There! You've got it! OK, I'm kidding about the laxative,
that was just a thoughtful extra touch I brought along for myself, courtesy
of something in Tbilisi but I was too selfish to share with my companions.

It is, as they say, an "experience." The doors open to the tent at 12:00
on the first Saturday. We were at the tent by 12:20, early by our standards,
by which time the 16,000 persons inside the 12,000 capacity structure
("tent" is a bit misleading—the Denver airport is also a "tent") looked like
they had been there drinking, and smoking, and perspiring, and singing
for months. They do have really good roast chicken, though, the natives
are friendly, the beer comes only in really big heavy glass steins, the waitresses are dressed up in traditional costumes, and they really do bull their
way through the crowds carrying as many as eight full steins in each hand.
Probably it's obvious why no one wants to mess with them. All this stuff
about women not having upper body strength is clearly wrong. I could
barely lift one, with both hands. Beer stein, not waitress. Oh, one more
authentic touch—make sure there's a long line to your bathroom so most
of your guests can go outside and pee on the trees in your yard.

After we did this for a while, we all decided to go back outside so we
could breathe. I took my Tbilisi parameciums back to the hotel for a rest—
they were so excited to be in Germany, but I didn't want them to be over-
tired—and everybody else went off to various museums and art galleries.

Sunday morning we went off to the parade, another of the seminal events of Oktoberfest. Fortunately it was again cold and raining, and thus not crowded. We sat in bleachers, outside (OK, very hard to have a good parade inside) as a really lot of people in various costumes walked/danced/marched down the route for three hours. Also, about every fifth group was either a beer wagon pulled by big, beautiful horses (Budweiser did not invent this, it turns out) or a wagon demonstrating peat cutting. Not clear what the latter has to do with beer, but there must be some connection. The parade sections were all tidily numbered and described in detail in the program, very organized. And the marchers all seemed to be in the correct order. This is Germany. Much leather was being worn, clarifying for me where all the stuff that goes inside sausages comes from—sausage as lederhosen by-product—and there were many, many, many "traditional Bavarian brass bands," yes, there were. No one played "Country Roads," although one band did play "The Washington Post March." As the paramecia, encouraged by strong drugs, had decided to take the day off, I felt better. It was indeed a colorful display of the incredible differentiation of dress that takes place when a country is put together out of a very large number of small political units. Some of the women, for example, had a row of flowers stretched across their bosoms, and others had strings of silver coins. We found the symbolism obscure. People apply to get into this parade, and the waiting list is as long as twelve years; some units have been marching in it for fifty and sixty years, and it's all just for the honor. Quite impressive to us history-challenged Americans.

That evening Linda and I went back to the Oktoberfest and I got a better, less jaundiced—no jaundice wasn't what I had, never mind—view. It's really a combination of a gigantic midway à la the Nebraska State Fair, except on both sides of the large main street there are not only rides, games of chance, food stalls (even one called *Schnitzel König* which means "Schnitzel King"—and here I thought I was the only one), but there are these incredibly large beer tents. We peeked inside a couple—same thing going on as noon of the day before. Maybe same people, hard to tell. We wandered around as Linda took pictures and bought beer mugs, and coffee cups, and T-shirts, and other souvenirs (even a snow globe!), and I tried not to get collided with by those less capable of navigation than I. This was a surprisingly small percentage of the crowd, but probably because it was early and they were all still inside the tents, staying dry and really warm. Easily a third of the people were in some form of traditional costume; the guys tended to favor leather knee-length breaches with long white socks and the women either leather or peasant blouse/skirt sorts of things. Also many Tyrolean hats, both sexes. My favorites were the ones dressed head to ankle in local costume as above, but with colorful running or basketball shoes on their feet. I blame Michael Jordan.

Final note: One of the traditional items of the fest is a large heart-shaped cookie with a clever saying written on it in icing. One wears this suspended around one's neck by a ribbon. I don't think you eat this, but I can't be sure. It is wrapped in plastic to keep out the rain. A lot of people really were wearing them. The icing probably says clever things like "hi there, hot stuff," or "ready for love," or "ready for beer," or "ready for a cigarette," but you can't tell, they're in German. At least I can't tell. At the entrance to the fair several people were handing out commercially inspired cookies, or replicas, which lots of people took, put around their necks, and wore. On one side they said in German "E-mail me" and on the other, in English, "Do you Yahoo?" Linda noted that the German word was a made-up one, and that "e-mail" is not a verb. I suggested that as far as I could remember, neither is Yahoo. The language dies but the technology marches on. Of course, although this letter is written mostly in English, I am e-mailing it to you.

And I did in fact miss the ride up the Zugspitze.

Love and kisses,
Bob

# twenty-two

# tour rural china in the dark!

July 2001

Dear Dad,

**DAY ZERO, London and the air over Europe**: well, guilty I suppose. I *am* flying in business class. In my defense I must ask while sitting in the middle section, where there are four seats abreast—yes, two middle seats, not one—in a narrow seat with packaged food, no pillow, no blanket, and no cute little courtesy package of tiny tooth brush, facial aerator, socks without heels, and not even a handle on my plastic coffee cup (it's just some round thing looks kind of like the bottom of a shell casing): isn't business class for *successful* business persons? It's more a Willy Loman, *Death of a Salesman*-sort of business class. I am flying on a *German* airline and we all know how much the Germans have pursued global business ambitions since the war, usually pretty successfully. And I am flying to Kiev to look over our recent acquisitions of privatized electric distribution systems. I am traveling with Dennis Bakke on another round-the-world tour of AES projects and opportunities. We have so much stuff that I doubt any of us really knows exactly how much or exactly where. Hence it's a good idea for the CEO to do this occasionally. Our now-remarkably multinational AES corporation has businesses in forty countries, as we proudly proclaim in our fact sheet, and offices in others, and potential business in every doubtful location except possibly North Korea, and Azerbaijan, and the Congo (the Country Formerly Known as Zaire/Kinshasa/Congo K/Belgian Congo), although these are all probably next. I fear that all this evidence makes me a real potential target of demonstrations. And you thought your oldest son would never amount to anything!

As evidence, I point to an article I am mulling over in the *Herald Tribune*, where the upcoming meeting in Genoa of the G-7 plus Russia is discussed. Quick, now, who are they? I think I can name five, US, UK, Germany, France, Japan, probably Italy since we're meeting there, but as to number seven, maybe Canada? Australia? Saudi Arabia? Beats me. This aforementioned meeting will bring forth protests by one hundred thousand demonstrators, it is said, including the dreaded White Overalls. Their spokesman, when asked what was the protest focus, said, "Neoliberal globalization and the empire the G-8 represents." He further elaborated that this empire "runs the rules for social life around the planet," which may explain why my friend John Huetter is having a hard time getting a date, and is "highly violent, as we saw with the thirty-nine pharmaceutical companies in South Africa." Hmm, pharma companies have cops now? "You better take this pill or we'll beat you silly!"

You know, I never figured myself for an agent of Neoliberal Globalization, but now I are one. I would have thought of it as "conservative globalization," but I am out of the loop on protest vocabulary. I must point out, though, that calling yourselves the White Overalls doesn't have quite the same ring as being known as the Black Panthers. Darn, I almost miss Stokely Carmichael. "Neoliberal" indeed. And how come we're an empire and not a conspiracy? Some pretty fuzzy thinking is going on here. Oh, and as final proof of my NLGZN credentials, I am carrying with me my new Nextel cell phone, alleged to work in "eighty countries worldwide." Why these words are juxtaposed is not clear, since one could testily suggest that it either works in eighty countries or it works worldwide. Ah well.

I flew over on Friday evening, two days early, so I could meet with some developers who have an interest in buying our house in Hampstead and turning it into flats. I believe they are also part of the Neoliberal Globalization Empire, since their name is Regime Properties Ltd. I mean "Regime" really can't be more certain than that. How can I have been so blind to all these obvious signs? Anyway I stayed at the Sheraton Park Tower Hotel in Knightsbridge, which has the advantage of being the ugliest hotel in London and thus easy to find, and close to Harrods. I note for the record that Harrods was having its annual sale and thus was open until (gasp!) 7:00 on Saturday and even (double gasp!) 12:00 to 5:00 on Sunday! Maybe the Brits are finally giving in and adopting twentieth century marketing practices. Like being open when your customers aren't working and thus can actually go shopping. Harrods, as you no doubt remember, is owned by someone from the Middle East who the UK refuses to let become a citizen. I am unclear whether this is or is not an example of the NLGZN Empire at work. What is clear is that the food in the UK hasn't gotten any better, and they still insist on serving their beer warm. There will always be an England.

**DAY ONE AND TWO, Ukraine**: We landed at Kiev in the early afternoon, and dropped our bags at the Hotel Ukrainia. We were in Kiev for Dennis to talk to the people at our recently acquired facilities about what it means to be an AES business person, a talk that he gives extremely well. We have only owned these two electric distribution businesses, purchased in a privatization, for a month and a half and have yet to really make all the changes that are necessary, so in some senses our visit was a little early. We had a bit of unscheduled time, so we asked to go out to the offices of the nearest of the two distribution companies, Kievoblenergo. It is now known, much more euphoniously, and as a result of a contest to pick a new name, as "AES Kievoblenergo." Marketing may not be our strong suit. Since we had nothing scheduled we wandered around the office building, and maintenance shops, and warehouses, sticking our heads into places and introducing ourselves. Interesting results/observations:

» In one shop, we were chatting productively with two of the working folks when their boss appeared. Conversation diminished to zero, boss took over. Nothing useful followed.

» Another person we talked to said, when asked what changes it would be a good idea to make, "I have worked here for twenty-four years, and I have always heard the language of change, and I have never seen any changes."

» In the mill shop, we talked to a gray-haired, gray-mustached person who warmed up to us.

"What do we need to do to change this place for the better?" Dennis asked.

The response as the interpreter translated, "Get rid of the managers." The millwright interrupted her, and she retranslated, "Get rid of the Communists." He continued, matter-of-factly. "My grandfather was a priest and my grandmother sang in the church. They were both exiled and killed when I was very young. My father was in the army, and he was killed in the purges in 1939. I have been followed by the secret police since I was nineteen." He was earnest and quiet and low-key, and it was chilling.

» The place is pretty dumpy. It needs painting and new signage, it needs to have its lawns mowed and the lightbulbs in the corridors fixed, it needs people to take more pride in the place they work. This is pretty common in newly acquired facilities. It will change.

» The vehicle yard was a sort of a disorderly mess with lots of variously sized trucks around—trucks with buckets to lift people to the top of poles, trucks with big drills to dig holes for new poles, medium-sized trucks to carry stuff around, vans, small trucks, etc. Two-thirds of the trucks were painted a very military shade of olive drab, which was a tad disconcerting; the remainder were either light blue, red, cream, or dark blue, and none had logos or identifying information painted on their sides; very surprising—I have never seen this before. When AES trucks are out blocking traffic we always want you to know that it's us. As I thought about this later, I realized that we probably saw more than half a million dollars of automotive assets in the yard, unemployed, in the middle of the workday. Not being maintained, not being loaded up to go somewhere, not being washed, just sitting there. Kind of makes you wonder if maybe we don't have a few too many trucks.

Other cogent and/or miscellaneous facts from later discussions with our transition team at the company:

» The two companies combined have 6,000 people and probably need only 2,000 or maybe 2,200. Under the terms of the purchase agreement we are not allowed to terminate anyone for a year, but we are preparing a voluntary severance package and a reorganization to implement very quickly. Average age of the folks in the business is more than forty.

» As you might expect, there are many layers of supervision, combined with no delegation of authority. The head of the utility signs off on purchase orders for amounts as low as $5. Now there's a good use of time. And there are 400 "managers" at the company. Probably busy approving the $2 procurements.

» All but 91 of the people are in the union, including most of the managers.

» None of the purchasing that anyone can find has been done through competitive bidding; all of it is sole source. I repeat: all of it. Could be some opportunity for kickbacks there, hard to be sure.

» Bill Prebil, the AES person now in charge of AES Kievoblenergo, may have discovered a remarkable shortcut for getting everyone to take responsibility for all aspects of the business. Losses are a very big problem here, again as usual. Because we did even worse than usual in June in collecting the bills, he delayed the July paycheck, rather than call Arlington and get some money advanced. Dennis and I agreed that this was a brilliant strategy and just needed to be explained to all the people there. Attention to the basics of the business, like "it is important to collect the money," is bound to pick up.

We had dinner last night with the key AES people at a country restaurant, complete with a sound system playing Adeste Fideles as we walked in. I learned several things, including that it actually wasn't Christmas in Kiev. First, if you order *golubtsis* or maybe *golubtsy* on the assurance that it is a very good, unique Ukraine specialty, you will be disappointed to find that it is good, but it's just stuffed cabbage.

Second, the real national food passion of Ukraine is something called *salo*, which is, plain and simply, uncooked pork fat. They eat it on bread and elsewhere; some say everywhere. I put some on my bread (monkey see, monkey do), and it tasted better before I learned what it was.

Third, they make pretty neat dumplings, very similar to Chinese dumplings except only steamed and not panfried, but the most authentic kind is stuffed, not with meat or mushrooms (these are available, but are Russian, so not as authentic) but rather mashed potatoes. Yes, dumplings stuffed with mashed potatoes. I suggested that these might be Bolshevik dumplings, but everyone said they really were Ukrainian.

Fourth, the alphabet is Cyrillic but when written in script makes you think you can read it. Hah! Actually it was explained to us that it is the same alphabet as Russian (no help there) except it is missing two letters that Russian has, and has one that Russian doesn't. This encapsulates the traditional Ukrainian experience with Russia. Anyway, the local beer served at the restaurant is called, or rather spelled, "Crabymuy," which I thought was then actually pronounced "Slavutich," but then it was explained to me that the latter is the name of the brewery, and no one orders crabymuy because it is unpronounceable. Slavutich is also the short name for the Dnieper River that runs through Kiev. It means "the glorious and pretty great river" which is okay although kind of long for a nickname. At the bottom of the beer glass they have written the words for "another one please" which you can see shimmering through the golden fluid. Pretty clever. These words are spelled "*Buunu we*," and of course pronounced "Vwee pwee share." This may be a difficult language to master.

Things about Kiev you might not otherwise know:

» It is quite a pretty city, wide streets with tree-lined centers, lots of poplars, not too much traffic, decent scale buildings no taller than five or six stories, many of them restored, not any skyscrapers and not any big monumental plazas or castles—sort of a little of residential Paris, a little of Munich, and a touch of the Mediterranean. Gary Levesley, our division director for the CIS, says it's the most attractive of any of the CIS capitals.

» No air-conditioning anywhere that we could see, except in our nice and new hotel where naturally it was too cold. This means that all the men go around in short-sleeve shirts and no ties, and the women the equivalent. Quite casual but nice. It was ninety degrees so the question was not so academic.

» Ukraine has 50 million people and is a country the size of Germany and France combined. It has been around for a long time, but usually conquered by someone else—Austro-Hungarian Empire, Poland, even Bulgaria had a piece at one point. It was an independent country in 1917 for about three months, during which time the president, who was a poet and historian, disbanded the army because he believed one was not necessary for a peaceable state. Then, seventeen minutes later, the Bolsheviks took over and it remained a part of Russia until the smash up of the Soviet Union. OK, this is not exactly a Kiev fact, more a Ukraine fact.

» Mr. Kuchma, the President, used to be head of a missile factory, and at one point in his tenure had constructed a very large and monumental shiny aluminum alloy statue of a stylized woman holding up what looks like a large pepper mill and wearing a peasant outfit. One is disappointed to find that this is not some great Ukrainian legendary figure or the Goddess of Dumplings, but a Soviet mother of ten sons, all of whom perished in the Great Patriotic War. People in Kiev suspect that there is a rocket engine in the bottom of it, and it does look a little spaceship-like in a Buck Rogers sort of way. It sits on a big hill overlooking the river and you can't miss it. It may be the shiniest big monument I have ever seen. No explanation given for the pepper mill. I don't think she was a waitress in a trendy restaurant.

» My cell phone works here, tra la. Also worked in London and Frankfurt, but that's not much of a test.

» They have chicken Kiev here. Looks like a fried softball wearing a pom-pom, but they do have it. Thank goodness.

**DAY THREE, Kazakhstan:** We flew all night from Kiev to Astana, capital of Kazakhstan, changed planes but not clothes, and flew on to our Ekibastuz plant, one of the largest coal-fired power plants in the world in one of the world's most deserted places. I had visited two years before with Dennis, and the plant is now in much better shape, selling more power, no longer having to sell electricity for barter (salted fish, anyone?), staff level more appropriate, etc. In fact this year for the first time ever since we purchased it, the plant sent back a $2 million dividend to Arlington. This is real cause for celebration, albeit qualified. We purchased the plant for an official price of Not Much: $3 million for 4,800 megawatts, I seem to recall. This is the lowest price ever paid for an existing power plant as calculated on a dollars per kilowatt basis—62.5 cents. A new gas-fired plant costs $350 to $500 per kilowatt and the Worlds' Stupidest Power Plant, Three Gorges in China, will cost about $8,000 per kilowatt, so 63 cents would seem a pretty good deal if the plant worked, which it didn't hardly at all. We have now invested a further $92 million, so the cost is still a pretty good bargain and getting $2 million is very much better than the previous dividend rate of squat, and took a lot of hard work by a lot of people at the plant, but it is not quite competitive with savings bonds. Yes, we management geniuses here at AES are always working for you, the shareholders. But better days are clearly ahead.

On the flight in we did get to see the coal mine whence cometh our coal. It is "The World's Largest Coal Mine," not easily confused with the World's Largest Outdoor Buddha in Hong Kong. It also has associated with it what must be the World's Largest Slag Heap. Remember, north central Kazakhstan is flat, you could play billiards on it without a table; really, it makes Nebraska, your home state, look positively roller coaster-like. Just beside the town of Ekibastuz sits the coal mine named, creatively, Ekibastuz, and its own six-mile long, several hundred feet high mesa, name unknown, although I suppose one could guess. The mesa is made out of coal mine waste. And gently smoking, since the waste coal in the tailings tends to combust after a while when exposed to air. These are normally called slag heaps, but that hardly does this one justice. You could be in New Mexico looking at a mesa and wondering if Georgia O'Keeffe had painted it, except the smoke here smells like coal, not piñon. And you can't get decent salsa. The mine itself is a really extremely big, long, deep hole in the ground, looking exactly like the Grand Canyon would look if it were black, and didn't have a river at the bottom, and was not quite so deep, and had big trucks driving up and down its sides. Soviet central planning may have had its flaws, but they did dream big dreams! Big, stupid, geographically misplaced and remarkably poorly executed dreams. But my cell phone works here, which is pretty surprising.

Dennis talked to all the plant folks, and then we flew on to our other energy facilities in east Kazakhstan, again all named for the towns wherein they reside, or maybe the towns were named for them, it's not clear. We toured one of our dams. It's fifty years old and still running fine, except since it's all Russian equipment from a supplier long since departed to central planning heaven, we now have to make by hand all our spare parts. Consequently the guys at the plant have become quite skilled machinists. Then to our very large combined heat and power plant at Ust-Kamenogorsk, another Very Large Facility that supplies electricity and heat to the town of Bakersfield—no, just kidding, to Ust-Kamenogorsk. Again there is much to celebrate: these facilities have sent $4 million to headquarters this year, another first ever. K'stan remains a very remote and difficult place in which to do business, but there is clearly progress in the five years we have been there, both in the economic performance and in the outlook and perfor-mance of the people. I feel my attitude toward these plants getting even more positive, especially since, after Dennis's excellent speech to all the AES people there, they fed us some terrific barbecued pork with onions. Wonderful! No cabbage. Tomorrow we head to the Land Where Nothing Gets Done, But It Does Get Discussed A Lot.

**DAY FOUR, Delhi**: We successfully avoided flying into any of the impressive Himalayan mountains, although we did fly right over K-2, which is one big mountain, and we didn't get shot down in Afghanistan since we flew around it, and we weren't mistaken by the Indians as a Pakistani fighter nor by the Pakistanis as an Indian attack jet, and thus didn't get attacked over Kashmir, since we flew around it, too. Dangerous place, South Asia. As a result we were an hour late, despite leaving at 5:30 a.m. (never, by the way, my favorite time of day). The India team met us at the hotel and we proceeded to switch from Missionary Mode to Attack Mode.

We have two businesses in India and neither is satisfactory. Both are in Orissa, a relatively poor state on the east coast. We have been working or attempting to work in Orissa since about 1991 when Paul Hanrahan first came here on the train from Calcutta (that is real devotion). Orissa is allegedly leading the way for all of India in privatizing its electric system, which prior to this was owned and run by the state government. Initially we won the right to build a new power plant in Orissa at Ib Valley. This was one of India's ten top priorities and was given "fast track" status. It has never been built, nor, I believe, have eight of the other ten. Three years ago we purchased 49% of an existing two-unit generating plant, also in Ib Valley, with the clear understanding that we would shortly be allowed to purchase 2% more, and we would run the plant in the meantime. Neither of these things has happened. Two years ago we were asked to purchase one of Orissa's four distribution systems, CESCO, after an auction to sell it held by the Orissa government failed to attract any bidders. And we did, with assurances of support, fair regulatory treatment, etc. The bottom line on all this is that all our folks have finally come to the point of being ready to force change, at least in CESCO, or to leave. The brief particulars:

» Rates have been set so low by the Orissa regulatory structure that we cannot recover our full electricity costs (we buy from a central Orissa grid, that in turn buys from generators such as our generating plant), let alone pay operating and maintenance costs. Never mind any return on capital or any upgrades of a system that is in desperate need of same.

» We can't even collect the bills that we send out now, at the rates that are too low, because we cannot get police protection and there is no law and no prosecution system to deter theft of electricity. We cut them off, and they just reconnect themselves. One of our offices has been burned down by our customers, and many of our collectors have been physically intimidated.

» We inherited 8,500 people that we cannot fire, even for incompetence, sloth, corruption, or total lack of technical qualifications. We could run the system effectively with 2,000 people, maybe even 1,500.

» The government of Orissa doesn't even pay its own electric bills; they owe CESCO $12 million of back payments and show no inclination of ever paying.

» We have been ordered by the regulator to put all the money we collect into an escrow account to pay our electricity bill. This will leave no money to pay salaries. Probably someone among the 8,500 so-called employees will notice. Perhaps they will riot and burn down the offices. I doubt they will write their congressman. Nice added touch: if we do not follow this reasonably silly regulatory prescription, our person running the system, a very good guy from Brazil named Charles Lenzi, will be subject to criminal prosecution and three months in jail in Orissa. That is not a prospect that would make me comfortable.

It's not just us. The World Bank has put together a $350 million loan package for the Orissa electric system, disbursed a small portion of it, then suspended the loan and written the clearest letter I have ever seen coming out of the bank, saying just the same things I listed above. It's rare when you see the bank get this tough, but delightful.

We consult, and discuss, and strategize, and finally write up a paper listing the problems. We have decided to sequester the money, not pay the people, and be willing to walk away from this investment if the government doesn't solve the short-term problems immediately and commit to move on the long-term problems expeditiously. It will be too bad to have to write off the investment of $10 million in buying the system, but this is silliness and a waste of very capable and dedicated AES people. To this end, we use the afternoon to go see the World Bank and let them know what we are going to do the following day in Orissa, then give the same briefing to the central government Energy Minister and staff. Finally we hold a press conference and make the same announcement and argument. At least they'll know we're coming.

Enron also has a project in India, one that Linda financed when she worked there, called Dabhol. It, too, is now in trouble, as the Indian state government of Maharashtra (west coast this time) has reneged on its agreements to buy the power and is probably bankrupt as well, probably for the same reason: the rates are too low, and you can't collect the bills anyway. The Energy Ministry staff has been hinting that we should take over the Enron project, as the whole mess is an embarrassment at many levels and quite well reported in the international press. So when we asked to see the Minister, he was delighted, thinking we were probably coming to bail out/

offer on Dabhol. Instead he gets yet another energy crisis with a foreign investor. He didn't seem pleased.

We had a reasonable discussion of our problems, they were concerned, and he and his staff offered to be helpful by calling Orissa. We did emphasize that this wasn't a "We hate India" response, and, in fact, we would be interested in other assets in the country under the right conditions. They seemed to appreciate this.

The Minister then told us that he had worked up some very real solutions to India's electricity problems. No more policy studies, he said, no more talk of reform, we've had enough of that, we need concrete action. He pulled out a three-inch stack of spiral-bound workbooks with printed paper covers. "We are going to send these to every distribution company in India," he said, "and demand that they follow these procedures! I can make sure you get a set!" We looked at the stack. The top workbook was "Maintenance Procedures for Medium Voltage Transformers in Rural Areas"; the rest were similar. A short pause followed while we swallowed our tongues. "Very nice," said Dennis diplomatically. We exited. Without the workbooks.

**DAY FIVE, Bhubaneswar:** As we fly in, we can confirm from the air that there is serious flooding, again, in the state. This is the same area where two years ago the "super cyclone" caused enormous flooding, loss of life, and property damage. We had just purchased CESCO, only to have about 50% of the distribution system wiped out. Not a good start. And now they have almost the same thing all over again. This may not be a lucky place to do business. On the other hand, it's tropical, and warm, and less jammed and hectic than Delhi and Bombay, and I've always liked it better.

We meet with various levels of officials, delivering our message, including the State Energy Minister and the Chief Minister, the equivalent of a state governor in the US. India has a very federal system. It is suggested that we be patient. It is suggested that the threats of criminal prosecution are just misunderstandings. It is said that all the bills can be quickly paid. We can work together to get this all sorted out in six months; we are already working on everything you suggest; don't be in such a hurry to cause this crisis. Dennis is polite but clear. These are the same answers we always get when we come here; these are the same responses we have received for years. What is so infuriating is that the senior people are all smart and well educated, and always agree with the problems, and are always working on them. Finally the Minister says they will examine our proposals and give us a response. It is the same old song. At least he doesn't offer us workbooks.

We go off to a dinner with the AES people we have recruited to work here. Dennis makes a brief talk about our discussions with the government and then asks them what they think. These are young men and women who weren't part of the original CESCO system, who we have brought in to help us clean it up and make it an AES business. All of them are from the subcontinent, most are Indian, and only a few have worked in other AES businesses. Only a very few of them have ever met us before. Many may well lose their jobs if AES leaves. But they are unanimous in their views, unafraid to speak candidly, and articulate beyond expectation. "We do not have the tools to do what clearly needs to be done. This is not a place where we can feel good about our jobs. The system is broken. We cannot work here in accordance with our values. We must have the changes suggested or we should leave."

**DAY SIX, Bangladesh**: Wow, traffic! Traffic! Traffic! Traffic! No, not the Steven Soderbergh movie about cocaine. THERE IS A LOT OF TRAFFIC HERE. It appears to be made up of probably 60% buses, 20% trucks, 10% bicycle rickshaws, 20% motorcycle taxis, 10% bicycles (with one to four people on them), only 25% cars and 60% buses again. And it's the weekend, Saturday afternoon, for gosh sakes, why aren't these people home watching television? Or shopping at the mall? Or watching their kids play soccer? Every big city I have ever visited likes to boast about how bad its traffic is—Houston, LA, Bangkok, Beijing, London, Paris, you name it. They're wrong. Dhaka wins. Takes home the gold, retires the trophy, has its jersey hung up in the rafters of the field house. We are driving to our plant sites from the airport after flying overnight (natch) to get here. It's only about twenty miles straight line to the plants, and it takes an hour and a half. Scott Kicker, our head guy for Bangladesh, is in the car with us and points out that Bangladesh is the most densely populated nation on earth. I am willing to concede this, but what I don't understand is why they have all decided to come with us to visit some power plants. By the way, did I mention the traffic?

Both the plants are in great shape. Hyundai is building both, doing a good job, and they have great names: Haripur and Meghnaghat. I believe that Rudyard Kipling was consulted on these names. Also they have a terrific logo, a tiger in the center (after all this is Bengal, although if there's any tigers around they're probably in a bus somewhere stuck in traffic). The first of these, Haripur, is in simple cycle operation. We leave the main road to visit it and find ourselves in a densely populated village, on a narrow dirt road only wide enough for one vehicle, but filled with people, bicycles, the occasional chicken, motor bikes, lots of palm trees, etc. Actually the palm trees are beside the road. *This is stupid*, I think to myself, *the driver must have misunderstood and thought we wanted to take a quick tour of a typical village.* Suddenly we turn a corner and BAM! run right into the gate for a large, beige, seven-story power plant building with stacks, machinery, small wisps of steam coming out of the places steam is supposed to come out of, and so on. The visual impact is remarkable. As is the plant. Let us note for the record that Bangladesh is *not* widely known in the world as a country that gets things done or that has an incorruptible bureaucracy, an enlightened political system, etc. Plus it really is a very poor country. Yet we only started working here four years ago, and we have one plant in operation and a second more than half complete.

It is said that when you compare Pakistan, India, and Bangladesh on electricity reform, you get the three "p's." Pakistan offered a 6 cents/kWh contract to all takers, so it got *power*. Bangladesh opted for competitive bidding, reasonably transparent, and got *price*. India got *process*.

My favorite sign at the plant, put up by the Koreans who are building it, at our insistence says: "No smoking at inside of project area. If anybody disobey this order, he must be dismissal."

That evening, as is customary, the AES folks gather for a dinner and a chance to talk with Dennis. They have given him a local costume to wear, so he does. This is the definition of a good sport. He is decked out in the traditional cream-colored, long, silk, embroidered overshirt that comes down to your knees, and the cotton pantaloons that are tight around your calves and ankles and all wrinkled, plus sandals. He seems to have forgotten to have someone draw henna designs on his feet, and he doesn't have the little white hat, but it's otherwise perfect. Everyone else, of course, is wearing slacks and golf shirts. Dennis looks like the reincarnation of Mohammed Ali Jinnah.

**DAY SEVEN, Beijing**: we leave Dhaka at midnight (traffic still the same) and fly overnight to Singapore, getting in about 6:00 a.m. Our evil plot to bankrupt all hotels in Asia by avoiding staying in any of them during our trip continues. Our flight to Beijing isn't until 9:00 in the morning, so we go to the lounge. I discover that they have noodle soup with shrimp, so I have this for breakfast, topped off with Häagen-Dazs chocolate ice cream. You have to take your opportunities as they arise. We land at Beijing in the late afternoon and find that it has a new airport! They do want the Olympics! We go to the St. Regis Hotel, a very nice five-star place, lots of brass and marble. In true Chinese fashion, sitting right next to the hotel is the Tropicana Disco, a small building whose entire two-story front is a brown stucco tiki head; you walk into the building through his breastbone. At least it's not through his nose. The disco's lovely gray concrete entry area is decorated with tall, green, concrete palm trees, five totem poles (from the tropical part of Alaska, no doubt), and a number of pots of real palm trees, all real dead. I seek meaning in the iconography but come away only puzzled. The fact that immediately next door to the Tropicana is a Kenny Rogers Roasters fast-food place does not add further enlightenment. There are now Starbucks in Beijing, though—more progress.

That night the China team takes us to a special Chinese restaurant called the China Club, where we have—guess what—Chinese food, except they have gotten a fancy German Black Forest chocolate cake for me with birthday greetings on top. I indeed feel very much a part of the Neoliberal Globalization Empire.

**DAY EIGHT, Yang Chung Power Plant, Shanxsi Province, China**:

Dennis goes off to Jiangsu Province to negotiate a power deal, and I fly to Changzhi airport on a small chartered plane to visit our biggest power plant in China. This is one that Paul Hanrahan and I worked on when we were first doing China eight years ago, but I had never visited, partly because it's so darn hard to get to. Example: Changzhi "airport" is not one by most definitions. It is a former military strip with no commercial flights, no electronics, actually with no airport-type people at all. As you land and roll down the runway, you can look out and see sheep placidly grazing on each side of the strip about twenty-five feet away from the plane. So not a lot of animal control. And even here we are still two hours by road from the plant.

Driving through the countryside is pretty interesting. It's rolling hills, and agriculture, and the occasional small roadside town, and brick factory. And lots of small coal mines and the associated trucks rumbling around. Actually almost every building and shop has a small pile of coal outside it. This is coal country, they weren't kidding.

And everywhere there isn't a coal mine, corn is growing, frequently up the hillsides on terraces. I'm from Nebraska, I can tell these things, but I thought that terraces were only for rice. When you stop to think about it, I don't remember eating much corn in Chinese food—every other darn thing in the world that might be conceivably considered edible—but no corn. No corn bread, no corn on the cob, no cornmeal mush, no tortillas, not even those little baby corns you get in American-Chinese food. I ask the guys from the plant what the story is. Animal feed, maybe? Much consulting, and finally the answer is that it's used for producing sucrose, corn sweetener. Perhaps this, too, is progress, I can't tell. Probably it's all shipped to the US so we can make all our food even sweeter.

The visit to the plant is wonderful and encouraging. This is one big power plant, built out in the west here where the coal is, with the power sent to the east coast where the need is. Far better than sending the coal. It is six units, each 350 MW, two already in operation. We are a 25% owner, with five other Chinese partners, but we have had significant influence on the operations. We have a terrific team on-site, and the plant manager, James Fung, is a smart young Chinese man, out of the Chinese power bureaus but with very different ideas. He has only 450 persons at this facility, and most of them are young, just out of technical school. A standard Chinese plant this size would have five or six times as many people. Everybody is in a uniform, including him! This is not standard "management" performance for China.

Naturally I hang around too long and so have to rush back in the car to the airport. Along the way it starts to rain, and night begins to fall, as it frequently does about this time. We finally make it to the plane, only to find that they cannot take off in the rain, and then they cannot take off in the dark. I have no one who speaks English with me and haven't had a chance to get any RMB (Chinese currency). Plus I doubt seriously that there is a Howard Johnson in the vicinity. And Dennis and I are scheduled to go to Mongolia on the morrow at 7:00, where we have meetings scheduled with the Prime Minister. So if I don't show, he will probably have to go without me, much as he treasures my company. And we were actually going to spend a night in a hotel!

A certain amount of conferring takes place among the various Chinese persons present and some not present (thank heaven for cell phones), and then I am handed the phone and informed that the team leader's driver, who has already taken me to the airport, will now drive me to Beijing. "How long will it take?" I ask idly. Nine hours. Given that it is then about 8:30, I will just get to the hotel in time to shower, pack, and catch the plane to Mongolia. Alternatives seem limited, somehow; the plane cannot take off in time to make the morning flight out of Beijing. So away we go. On a whim I try to call Linda on my cell phone and am astounded to find that it works! I wonder what would happen if I dialed 9-1-1?

I do not actually recommend driving for nine hours through the rural Chinese countryside in the dark of night. First, there's not much to see, and not much light, electric or otherwise. There are a very amazing number of gas stations, but not much else. The roads are better than I expected; my experience here six years ago on rural roads was pretty bad, but there has been a major improvement since. The last part of our journey is even on a freeway.

I am initially surprised that my driver, and everyone else, seems to favor driving exactly down the center line of the road, the little white lines splitting the car. Then I note that, first, taillights are at something of a premium on most of the vehicles we pass, as in few or none. That's okay in the day but disconcerting at night; you really cannot see them until you're real close. This is especially true of the trucks. They do have headlights, however, so you can see them coming toward you and swerve at the last moment. Second, there are lots of people and bicycles on the road, and you absolutely cannot see them. No reflectors and a perverse preference for dark-colored clothing. Mostly the bikes and people are at the edges of the road, and the dark trucks halfway in, hence our position in the center. Begins to make sense to me.

Time passes, albeit slowly. It's also a tiny bit frustrating not to be able to read any of the few signs. Finally we see one that says "Beijing 442 km." Aha, information! Funny how much better I feel.

Who else is on the road at that hour, you ask? Well, I answer, I have analyzed this carefully and conducted my own traffic count. During a distance of 115 km, we passed exactly 100 trucks. We passed in this same stretch two buses and were passed by two passenger cars. That's who. It's pretty surprising about the cars, and we already knew that all the buses are in Bangladesh for the summer.

Beijing finally shows up at 5:00 in the morning. Or we show up at Beijing; by this time I'm a little hazy. They're not many folks around; not even the Chinese get up this early. And Mao was wrong; I have seen the sun rise over Tiananmen Square, and the east is not red, it's sort of grayish yellow. So there.

**DAY NINE, Mongolia**: We fly into the airport of the capital, Ulaanbaatar. I tell Dennis that this city is brought to you by the letter "A," but it's been a long time since he's watched *Sesame Street*, so he isn't as amused as I am. The city is small—nine hundred thousand people set in a valley between hills that are sort of fuzzily green—with grass but no trees. It's also sort of scruffy in a classic Soviet/Bolshevik fashion. Big apartment blocks, again. Power plant right on the outskirts of town. Park areas all weedy and unmowed. Very few large buildings, one decent hotel, modest traffic. To my disappointment, leather-armored archers mounted on tough war ponies do not ride up to meet the plane. The country itself has only 2.7 million people, way down from the horde days, and a huge amount of land. The population density is about one person per square kilometer, lowest in the world. And here it sits between Russia and China, neither of whom for some obscure reasons of history, it trusts. Actually not-so-obscure reasons; one or the other neighbor has ruled the place for all but a very few years of Mongolia's existence. Sort of like Ukraine. At least these guys had Genghis Khan, or Chingis Khaan as he is locally called, and for which most things are now named—the hotel, the local beer, etc. It's been somewhat downhill since they ruled the entire known world, however. But we're here to fix that. Oh, did I mention that it's a bit chilly in the middle of July, and that in the winter the temperature goes to minus forty frequently, and never gets above minus ten? That's centigrade but frankly it's still too darn cold. Also it never rains. This is a pretty tough place.

AES people have been coming up here from China for more than three years, and so far we have nothing. No other Westerners have undertaken this level of effort, let alone set up an office. Perhaps they know something that we don't? There are plans and discussions to privatize the distribution system, or one or two of the power plants, and so forth, but the elected governments keep changing. AID consultants are hard at work on recommending how to do a privatization (yikes, more process!) and things are going slowly, if at all. We huddle with all the team and decide that we'll suggest just taking over the distribution system, using a management contract. Don't have a lot to lose, and when they finally privatize it, if we don't win the bid we'll leave. In the meantime, we will invest $10 million in the system. There's more, but that's the essence. Actually it's not a bad scheme. We trot around to our meetings: head of the State Property Commission, the Energy Minister, the Prime Minister. We duly explain our proposal, cold, to folks we have never met before, and everybody buys it. Just like that. Now I've been a government official, and I've been to Government Official School, and the first thing they teach you is never to agree to anything that anyone from the outside proposes, because all knowledge resides in the government. But these folks are thinking quickly and saying yes. Of course, they are getting new investment into their power system, without having to give up ownership, so it's not a bad deal. But to have this approved in one day? Can we ship these folks out to India? Better yet, can we give them some horses and have them conquer India? We are pretty excited and pleased.

**DAY TEN, Tokyo**: We have to wait until 1:15 in the morning to leave Mongolia, not because we are dying to sample the hot spots of Ulaanbaatar (unlikely thought) but because our jet can only get clearance to land at Narita at 6:00. It's a four-hour flight, which is four more hours of sleep than I got in the back seat of the Toyota the previous evening. It is said that the Carthaginians tortured high-level prisoners taken in battle by keeping them awake, and that after being kept awake for four or five days straight, humans actually expire. And here I thought Dennis liked me.

Tokyo is even more built up and cleaner than it was the last time I was here five years ago. Now there are even tall skyscrapers that look down into the Imperial Palace grounds, which I recall as previously being prohibited. On the drive in from the airport we note a power plant with its side sculptured into a sailboat, and one where the entire building is shaped like a fish. Actually they are so elegant that it is hard to be sure they're power plants, but really no other form of industrial activity has the telltale combinations of tall stack and rectangular blockiness, even in a fish disguise. Gosh, we just paint big AES letters on ours.

In the intervals between ogling power plants I try to call Linda on my wonderful worldwide cell phone, which didn't work in Mongolia but worked great all over China—even the rural parts in the middle of the night—and Kazakhstan. Naturally I assume it will work in Japan, the world's second largest economy. I mean, really. But it doesn't. I find that Japan doesn't use the same standard as the rest of the world, so no one's phones work here, even ones that worked in Mongolia. And vice versa. I fail to see that this is A Portent.

We are in town with Mike Nikkel, our energetic business development guy, because Japan is said to be liberalizing its electric power industry. It currently has a traditional integrated monopoly structure—nine big utilities, with Tokyo Electric Power (TEPCO) the largest—and the highest rates of any country in the world. Residential rates are 22 to 25 cents/kWh.

US average is probably 5 to 7 cents/kWh. Unbelievable! It just doesn't cost that much to make electricity. Even if your power plants have to look like fishes. They have just started to experiment, extremely gingerly, with letting a little competition into the sector. The US has been at this for twenty years, the UK for fifteen, even Europe for a while. Perhaps even France, being dragged along kicking and screaming by the EU bureaucrats.

The Industrial Bank of Japan (IBJ), one of our long-time financiers, has arranged a bunch of meetings for us so we can both get a better sense of what is happening and actually talk to a potential partner. Very well, I'm game, although I would have bet that having the Japanese power market open up to outsiders was likely to occur about the same time members of the porcine genera achieve lift-off.

We go through the standard meetings, including a nice chat with Senator Baker, the newly appointed Ambassador. It's funny to be staying in the Okura Hotel, where we used to eat fancy dinners when we lived in Japan in the '50s and to be in the Embassy and see Dr. Reischauer's picture, the American Ambassador you worked for when you were here at the Embassy. Neither building has changed much except that they are now totally surrounded with larger, glassier, modern high-rise office buildings. The most interesting discussion is with and about a company called Electric Power Development Corporation (EPDC).

EPDC is a funny beast, initially a creature of the government, created to focus especially on hydro plants. It's sort of like TVA; started with government money, but in EPDC's case it built plants and sells power from them throughout the country, to the nine utilities; it's not regional. And it has never, unlike TVA, which was weaned from the government dole in 1954, had to become a real person. Maybe a microcosm of the Japanese penchant for mixing government support and direction into activities that should be exclusively private. IBJ says that the EPDC people are very impressed with our record and would like to become like us and participate in some of our projects. Outside of Japan, of course. Dennis suggests that this is hardly an exciting prospect. Nonetheless, we meet with them. Small, hot conference room, and none of the EPDC guys speak English, which is strange for Japan. They talk for a while, Dennis tells the AES story for a while. It's all very polite and somewhat vague. I have heard the AES story before, and although I never tire of Dennis telling it, I amuse myself by looking at the numbers in the EPDC annual report. Then I get very interested. The company is "corporatized" but is owned 67% by the government and one-third by the nine utilities. The government has decided to privatize it. All right so far. This decision was made three years ago and will be carried out, no one is sure in what form, two more years from now. Well, heck, no sense hurrying things. The EPDC leadership thinks they should do an IPO. Here is what a few minutes with a pencil and some long division tells you:

» They have 8,000 MW of hydro and 5,000 MW of thermal (coal) generation. The coal plants run at 65%, the dams run at 15% capacity factor. The coal plant numbers are decent but not particularly good. Most dams, however, when placed correctly run in the 40% to 50% utilization range; ones with decent reservoirs run higher. Fifteen percent is an unheard of low number in any reasonable utility system. It means that a very large amount of capital has gone into building stuff that hardly ever runs. Wow.

» They have $19 billion of debt on their balance sheet, and equity of about 4% of this. That turns out to be $1,200 of debt per kW of capacity. For old, existing plants. New plants anywhere in the world cost $700–$1,000 per kW. Why is there so much debt? Haven't they ever paid any of it off? Of this large mountain of debt, $14 billion is government supported, either guaranteed or from direct borrowings.

» They sell their wholesale power for 8 cents/kWh. This is a wonderful price—our plants probably average 3 or 4 cents. But their operating costs are 7 cents, before any allowance for paying off debt. And that's with a lot of hydro plants where, as you might imagine, the water is free and the operating costs should be nil. This number is almost unfathomable. And operating costs this high mean they have only about $300 million a year to service all that debt and pay any returns to shareholders. And $19 billion of debt, even at a 5% interest rate, takes almost a billion dollars a year just to pay the interest. They can pay interest of about 2% on their debt, with no amortization of principal. At last! I have actually found the legendary 2%, twenty-year Japanese financing! Except they're keeping it all in Japan. Wish we could get financing terms like that.

The EPDC is an unusual nightmare. At a subsequent meeting, we recommend to the electricity reform people at the Ministry of Economics, Trade, and Industry (the old MITI with a slightly new name, METI) that EPDC be chopped into pieces, the government debt forgiven, and the plants auctioned off. This would jump-start competition in the market for sure. The officials we meet with explain to us that the Japanese system requires consensus, and that we must be patient, and they don't want to create another California. I don't know how patient I would be if I were paying 25 cents/kWh to cool my house. When California prices got to 10 cents, it appeared that the world was ending. This system is already roughly two and a half times more expensive than California at its most troubled. It is hard to imagine that any change could make it worse. Actually they would be lucky if they could create another California; it would lower their rates.

Our last meeting of the day is with TEPCO. The President meets wih us, and is quite polite, but gently baffled. We respectfully ask his advice about how to proceed in this market, and he reasonably says the equivalent of "however you want." We ask how rapidly things will change, and he says that consensus is important. We ask about what he thinks the shape of the changes will be, and he says it is still being discussed. Dennis has to leave for the plane. I begin to reconsider dispatching the Mongols and the ponies to Japan first, then sending them to India.

Instead I go back to the Okura to take a nap, and then fly home. This being a scout for the Mongol horde is very hard work. Good thing that the Neoliberal Globalization Empire is worth it.

Love and kisses,
Bob

# Afterword

It's August of 2001. AES stock is trading well above its IPO price. The company is expanding dramatically, now even into Africa. I am on the board, and well regarded. Since I know Roger Sant, the Chairman, and Dennis Bakke, the CEO, so well, I rarely disagree with their plans and proposals. This is how one gets to be "well regarded" as a board member. Our strategy is to buy as many power plants in as many weird places as we can, and we're executing aggressively. We are in the middle of the largest sell-off of utility assets in history, all around the globe, as "privatization" is the order and fashion of the day. We are buying stuff as fast as banks lend us money, and this is very fast indeed. And every time that we decide to buy something, the market cheers us on. One of our guys says, "Let's buy nine power barges from Enron and take them to Nigeria, since we know nothing about either barges or Nigeria except that one of these floats and the other is somewhere in Africa," and so we do. Having done this exotic transaction, we watch our stock go up another $2 per share. It is irresistibly seductive. If no matter what one does one, the market rewards one, then eventually one decides that he or she is in fact a business genius.

George Bush is President, and the major political ruckus of the day is a fight over DNA research funded by the federal government. The Dow is at an all-time high, and the NASDAQ is over 3000, and Internet millionaires are being created on paper at the rate of about one a minute.

What could possibly go wrong?

Find out in the next volume of letters to Dad, tentatively titled *Been Up, Been Down, and Up Is Better*, which will be published in 2015.

# Acknowledgements

Many people have read these letters over the years, and generously encouraged me to continue writing them, and to assemble them into a book, which I have now done. I have listed each of them here, although I am not certain that my records and memory are perfect with regard to this list. In any event, to all of you, listed or not, who have been so encouraging, my special and sincere thanks.

Jonathan Aberman, Veronica Kayne, Abraham, George Abraham, Joel Abramson, Aina Jumabaeva, Aneliya Erdly, Angelina Tutino, Apostolos Kotsaris, Becky Cranna, Michael Cranna, Bonnie Guo, Carter Atlamozoglu, Corinne Oneto, David Amico, David Flory, Denyu Hristov, Ellen Gallup, Enrique Collado, Erik Bue, Federic Marchand, Greg Boryan, Jin Bahk, Julia Velichkova, Kristen Panerali, Lola Namazova, Luis Herrera, Maria Taft, Todd Swanson, Patty Rollin, Tim Montgomery, Juan Antonio Lopez, Claudio Pisi, John Crosson, Kim Rew, Liviu Floriae, Pauline Idogho, Marc Van Patten, Dan Diamond, Fillipo Chiesa, Irene Chiao, Jody Allione, John Motta, Luigi Capussela, Marcelo Lando, Matteo Quatraro, Olga Bukharina, Pascal Thomas, Rossana Altomari, Tony Haramis, Valentina Merola, Mai Nguyen, Carolina Canaveras, Julie Ratcliffe, Maya Enright, Julien Degranges, Rich Watson, Sanjeev Gupta, Ben Parry, Maya Enright, Sam Adams, Megan Adams, Claire Adams, Nathan Egge, Kojo Ako-asare, Sally Aldridge, Ralph Alexander, Michael Allison, David Anson, Hunter Armisted, Mike Garland, Ed Arulanandam, Henry Aszklar, Raj Atluru, Andres-Jacques Auberton-Herve, James Avery, Mike Avon, Ziad Awad, Mike Azeka, Roger Ballentine, Allan Baker, David Barrick, Kumar Barve, Maureen Quinn, Matt Bartley, Adrienne Behmke, Jon Bengston, Paul Bergman, Don Beyer, Megan Beyer, Jack Biddle, Fore Biddle, Stephanie

Biddle, Jean David Bile, Jason Birn, Leah Bissonette, John Blake, Dixie Blake, Guy Blanchard, Julie Blunden, Brian Bolster, Gaetan Borgers, Terry Boston, John Bottomley, Woody Boynton, Joe Brandt, Javier Brito, Britaldo Soares, Tim Broas, David Brooks, Jeremy Brosowsky, James Brown, Jon Brown, Quinlan Brown, Rich Bulger, Hamis Bunn, April Burke, Matt Burkhart, Ellen Burkhard, Tom Burkin, Dane Butswinkas, William Byun, Kara Callahan, Tom Calder, Chad Canfield, John Carrington, Sara Casey, Felipe Ceron, Uri Chang, Judi Rieder, Brian Chatlosh, Bud Cherry, Anessh Chopra, Lindsay Coates, Stephen Coats, Brooke Coburn, Sharon Cohen, Tony Colman, Rich Confalone, Leo Confalone, Nicholas Coons, David Corchia, George Coulter, Tyler Coyle, Martha Coyle, Clark Crawford, John Creasy, Kenneth Crews, Louise Cromwell, Marty Crotty, Genevieve Cullen, Greg Curhan, Scott Darling, Alan Dash, Kathy Davis, Robert Davis, John Davis, Glen Davis, Scott Deghetto, Mark Dennes, Frank DeRosa, Bill Delphos, Brian Detter, Phil Deutch, Jennifer Didlo, Greg Didlo, Bruce Driver, Charlene Dougherty, Robin Duggan, Werner Dumanski, Lounette Dyer, Jeff Eckel, Karen Edson, John Ein, Mark Ein, Dan Elliott, Roger Feldman, Amy Feng, Paul Ferguson, Tom Firth, Chris Johnston, Nancy Gibson, Mark Fitzpatrick, Phil Flynn, Bart Ford, Eric Fornell, Reggie Fowler, Kerri Fox, Peter Fox-Penner, Susan Vitka, Brian Frank, Paul Freedman, Alexandra "Alex" Migoya, Dave Freeman, Jon Fouts, Judith Gardiner, Rajeev Garside, Libby Garvey, Vic Abate, Danielle Merfeld, Matt Guyette, David Gee, Tom Gibian, Todd Giardinelli, Julie Gill, Andy Gilman, Diane Rudo, Peter Giller, Brent Glass, Kelton Glasscock, Andres Gluski, Adriana Gluski, Les Goldman, Sue Goldman, Dan Goldman, Andrew Perleman, Rob Gray, Mark Green, Bill Green, Tristan Grimbert, Einar Gultstad, Elizabeth Hackenson, Ronnie Haggart, Chuck Work, Joan Halbert, Jim Hall, Ned Hall, Annie Hall, Erik Han, Paul Hanrahan, Rodanthe Hanrahan, Andrew Hansen, Victoria Harker, Susie Hart, John Hemphill, Holly Hemphill, David Hemphill, Jennifer Hemphill, Lydia Hemphill, Elizabeth Hemphill, Stu Hemphill, Berit Henriksen, Martin Herman, Tom Buttgenbach, Phillip Herrington, Michael Herson, Vicki Siegel, Jason Hicks, Sharon Hillman, Chip Hoagland, Maurice Hochschild, Michael Hoffman, Tim Howell, John

Huetter, James Hughes, Frieda Hulka, Chris Hunt, Kelly Huntington, Natalie Jackson, Alan James, Bengt Jarlsjo, Mary Dale Jenkins, Vaughn Fritts, Janet Jenkins, Bob Jenkins, Deb Jenkins, Susan Jenkins, Steve Herndon, Jim Jenkins, Kathy Jenkins, Kristina Johnson, Frank Jungers, Julie Jungers, Tim Kaine, Richard Kauffman, Susan Kennedy, Catherine Kerkham, Cheryl Kessler, Scott Kicker, Stacie Kim, Doug Kimmelman, Tom Lane, Peter Labbat, John T. King, Nancy King, Bill Kingsley, Richard Kingsley, Alice Lemon, Frank Kinney, Dave Kipper, Terry Kipper, Drew Kleibrink, Jay Kloosterboer, Marty Klepper, Arlene Klepper, Etta Kolombatovich, Ben Kortlang, John Koskinen, Steve Kossack, Francie Kossack, Tony Kranz, Tom Kunde, Phil Lader, Felicia LaForgia, Martin Lagod, Luis Laguna, Jim Lambright, Ray Lane, Kate Lardeaux, Yoann Lardeaux, Chris Laursen, Alex Lee, Jeff Leonard, Mark Leslie, Xiaodan Li, Don Liddell, Aina Liddell, Mariana Lieu, Michael Lipford, Joanne Olson, Peter Lithigow, Jennifer Lowry, Mary Dell Lucas, Ron Lumbra, Mitzi Lumbra, Kristina Lund, Bill Luraschi, John Lushetsky, Bill Lyons, Laura Macdonald, Fred Malek, Dave Magill, Brad Mantz, Rick McQuain, Leith Mann, Tham Nguyen, Laura Manz, Dorrie Marsh, Fred Martin, Jeff Martin, Keith Martin, Ed Mathias, Vince Mathis, Hilary Maxson, John May, Pat McCullough, John McLaren, Terry McLean, Kathy McLean, Stephanie Meeks, Cathleen Mello, Steve Meyer, Robert Mill, Brian Miller, Harris Miller, John Milliken, Chris Milliken, Francisco Morandi, Rob Morgan, Stan Morris, Drew Murphy, Pat Murphy, Jeff Walsh, Stuart Murray, Ann Murtlow, Fory Musser, Mujinga Mwamufiya, Rog Naill, Venu Nambiar, Prabu Natarajan, Julian Nebrada, Bernie Nelson, Gerrit Nicholas, Chris Nicholson, Rob Nicholson, Pete Norgeot, Bob Nordhaus, Jean Nordhaus, Brad Nordholm, Keith Oberg, Phil Odeen, Tom O'Flynn, Matt O'Connell, Libby O'Connell. Chuck O'Neil, SuLin Ong, Kim Oster, Ahmed Pasha, Robin Pence, Eric Pendergraft, Manuel Perez Dubuc, Nicholas Perrins, Nancy Persechino, Ryan Pfaff, Miguel Picache, Michael Picker, Bryan Poffenberger, Jon Poley, Gil Porter, Linda Powers, Carol Powers, Evelyn Powers, Christine Powers, Sam Powers, Brad Powers, Kelley Powers, Lois Powers, Keith Pronske, Shahzad Qasim, Dick Raines, Nancy Raines, Bob Reisner, Lindsay McAuliffe, Sandra Rennie,

Nick Yost, Olivier Renon, Alan Richardson, Julie Richardson, Gabrielle Riera, Laura Rittenhouse, Marla Rosenthal, Chuck Robb, Art Rolander, Millie Rolander, Ted Roosevelt, Martin Roscheisen, Didier Rotsaert, Judy Rowland, John Ruggirello, Pat Ruggirello, Stu Ryan, Jim Sahagian, Jane Sahagian, Sven Sandstrom, Lex Sant, Vicki Sant, Roger Sant, Rich Santorosky, Ivan Selin, Joan Sellers, Sandip Sen, Ben Seto, Lisa Shaffer, Steve Bartram, C.P. Shankar, Nina Shapiro, Barry Sharp, Chris Shelton, John Zahurancik, Brett Galura, Jonathan Silver, Melissa Moss, Isabel Simmerman, Rob Sims, Phil Singerman, Kathy Roth, Gita Sjahrir, Frank Slattery, Sarah Slusser, Jan Smutney-Jones, Rose Snow, Cecille Walsh, Dawn Knott, Yvonne Mason, Jean Solari, Tim Soncrant, Nancy Conley, Stephen Spurlock, Karin Styrdom, Paul Stinson, Richard Sturges, Mike Sutcliffe, Krista Sweigart, Marius Szkudlinski, Bruce Weintraub, Wil Taft, Ron Talbot, Steve Taylor, Amy Tercek, Mark Tercek, Christi Tezak, Steve Thompson, Bowdy Train, Rita Trehan, Jim Tower, Carla Tully, Tom Unterberg, Ann Unterberg, Margi Vanderhye, Greg Van Dyke, Gene Varanini, Trae Vasallo, Andrew Vesey, David Vieau, Gary Vollen, Chaim Wachsberger, Biddy Walker, Jim Walker, Jeff Walsh, Steve Walsh, Michael Ware, Mark Warner, Lisa Colis, Mark Wasilko, Olivia Wassenaar, Neil Watlington, Bob Watters, Mary Wood, Ken Woodcock, Dottie Woodcock, Mark Woodruff, Jim Woolsey, Sue Woolsey, Jay Worenklein, Kerry Yeager, April Young, Catherine York, Gary Zahakos, Joe Ribando, Erik Korngold, Nan Zhang, Flora Zhao, Haresh Jaisinghani, Alison Zimlich

# About Robert F. Hemphill

Mr. Hemphill for much of his career was employed at AES, a global electric power generating and distribution company, where he served as Executive Vice President and Chief of Staff to the CEO. Hemphill was one of the three executives who began the company in 1981, growing it from a million dollar six person start up. AES owns and operates 38,000 MW of power plants in 21 countries around the globe, is publicly listed on the NYSE, and had approximately $18 billion of revenues in 2013.

Recently, Hemphill was the founder and CEO of AES Solar Power Ltd from its inception until his retirement in December 2013. The company, formed in March 2008, is a joint venture of the AES Corporation and Riverstone LLC, an energy focused private equity fund. AES Solar is a leading developer, owner and operator of utility-scale photovoltaic solar plants connected to the electric power grid. These installations, ranging in size from less than 2 MW to more than 250 MW, consist of large arrays of land-based solar photovoltaic panels that directly convert sunlight to electricity. Under his leadership, the company designed, permitted and constructed fifty-one solar plants (526 MW) in seven countries: Spain, France, Italy, Bulgaria, Greece, India and the US.

He has also been a senior policy official at the Department of Energy and Deputy Manager of Power at the Tennessee Valley Authority.

Mr. Hemphill graduated Magna Cum Laude from Yale University and earned an MA from UCLA and an MBA from George Washington University. He served as an airborne infantry officer in the US Army in Vietnam, and in the Special Forces.

His interests include geraniums, unsuccessful participation in Final Four pools, sporadic exercise, competitive duck cooking and tribal art.